Bowhunting for Whitetails

Bowhunting for Whitetails

Your Best Methods for Taking
North America's Favorite Deer

Dave Bowring

Line Drawings by Brad Long

Stackpole Books

Copyright © 1985 by Stackpole Books

Published by
STACKPOLE BOOKS
Cameron and Kelker Streets
P. O. Box 1831
Harrisburg, PA   17105

Printed in the U.S.A.

Library of Congress Cataloging in Publication Data

Bowring, Dave.
    Bowhunting for whitetails.

    Includes index.
    1. White-tailed deer hunting.   2. Hunting with bow and
arrow.   I. Title.
SK301.B69   1985   799.2'77357   84-16187
ISBN 0-8117-0289-8

To Bud Kissinger, who made that first stave bow with his own hands.

Contents

The Best of It All

Bowhunting for whitetails is the best there is. If you're reading this book, you agree with that. No contest at all. Bass fishing's fun, hunting grouse over a good dog is relaxing, canoeing provides exercise and camping with the family is good recreation. But bucks and bows go together like soap and bubbles, steak and potatoes, beer and conversation.

It's this way with millions of us, judging by the way bowhunting's growing every year, and no wonder. With more and more hunters using less and less open space, it's natural that hunters move up to a primitive weapon such as the bow that allows more hunters on less land. But this doesn't mean we're giving anything away. Far from it. There is simply something special about using a bow and arrow to take your deer. I could talk your ear off trying to explain it (which may be a big part of why I wrote

this book to begin with), but any short explanation comes up short. It's just, well, *special*.

Of course, if all we had to do was hike a quarter-mile off the nearest country road, pick the buck of our choice and stick him at close range with a hunting arrow, it wouldn't be much fun. It wouldn't be hunting, either. It would be gathering, similar to shopping at the supermarket.

As plentiful as is the white-tailed deer, and as widespread as it is (all of the continental United States except the extreme southwestern corner, as far north as the southern Canadian provinces and well down into Mexico and Central America), this animal is no pushover. In fact, many a big-game hunter with everything from polar bears to tigers in his trophy room still has a bare spot on the wall where the whitetail is supposed to go. Many old-time hunters believe the whitetail to be the toughest big-game animal in North America. The deer didn't get that reputation by being easy, and you darned well know it.

The teenage son of an attorney friend of mine was on his first-ever deer hunt when his father spooked a big buck off a ridgetop and it ran down and stopped within 20 yards of the boy, right out in the open. The boy's first shot went high but the buck stayed where he was. The follow-up went into the buck's spine and dropped him on the spot. I suspect the boy went home believing that all the stuff he'd heard about how tough whitetail bucks can be is a lot of bunk. He'll spend the rest of his life finding out just how wrong he is.

The whitetail is a tough trophy wherever he's found. I spent three days hunting the Edwards Plateau of Texas until I saw my first fresh track, and another two days before I saw the animal that made that track. Southeastern Ohio's deer-rich ridge country is where I cut my hunting teeth, and it still took me four seasons before I bloodied my skinning knife. I can remember driving home after all four seasons were over, the little green gremlin of envy eating my guts out every time I passed a car with a deer lashed across the top.

Michigan is said to have a statewide herd of a million whitetails, and Alabama reached that figure some years ago. Even Ohio, with far fewer deer but some of the biggest and best-antlered in the United States (Ohio rates sixth nationally in Pope & Young trophies), has gone from fewer than 10,000 deer only 30 years ago to more than 150,000 today.

Where can you find whitetails? All over the place.

Bowhunting for whitetails is much tougher than hunting with any type of firearm, be it rifle, shotgun or even replica muzzleloaders. It's more of a challenge, and this helps explain why the sport is growing so much. It's similar to the chap who's caught big bass on heavy tackle and plastic worms for years, gets a shade bored with what he's doing, and goes to a flyrod and poppers. It's tougher, sure. But when a big bucketmouth inhales his bug and that longwand comes alive, he's back to enjoying bass fishing again. It isn't the bass or the deer that is important to the sportsman, but the manner of its taking and the skill required to do it.

Bowhunters get into the woods first because most states give us a season that opens well before the gun hunters get their chance. We see the whitetail most often as he should be seen—relaxed, and casually moving through his home range of about 40 acres. What we do as bowhunters doesn't make the deer the frantic and afraid animal that gun hunters must be satisfied with. Because we are there first, and because it is integral to the bowhunter's sport that we become good woodsmen and a part of, and not an intruder in, the wild community, we have the best of it all.

The reddening of poison ivy leaves along rural fencelines is the first sign that another bow season is coming. Soon after the maples turn golden, the oaks turn brown and noisy and the fox squirrels are going nuts with all the abundance of mast to be found and eaten. The deer woods and farm edges call to us then, and the heart beats faster in this Season of the Deer. Hunting's critics claim that we disgrace ourselves as civilized men by hunting for sport, but this

Not every buck can be a record. The author took this small forkhorn long ago in South Carolina.

is only because they do not understand the origin of sport. But I say to these critics that perhaps none of us is quite so civilized, nor quite so neutered, as they like to picture themselves. There is a pulse in us of what we once were and still are, a pulse felt in the throb of a bent bowlimb, the flicker of an arrow through dappled sunlight, the solid *thunk!* of a hunting shaft going home where it belongs. I can't believe that the species of animal that is the white-tailed deer minds our sport very much, or there wouldn't be so many of them around.

See you in the woods come October.

Dave Bowring
St. Louis, Missouri

1

The Deer That Waves Goodbye

America's love affair with the whitetail probably started back when a man either brought meat home for the pot, or he and his family went hungry. He could shoot squirrels and grouse and maybe the odd wild turkey, but no single animal filled the need as did the whitetail. Locally plentiful in the natural woodland openings of the Northeast and Atlantic areas, large enough to provide several meals for even a large family, and offering such extras as buckskin for clothing, lashing material and so on, the whitetail quickly became the most desirable game animal for the settler and pioneer. Think of it from the early hunter's viewpoint: For the small price of a tablespoon of black powder, a square inch of cloth for a patch and a single lead ball of a caliber in the mid-30s or so, a settler hunting for food could feed his family for a week or more, not to mention add to their meager supply of soft-soled shoes, belts, shirts or jackets.

And as the settler cleared more woodland and saw others in the area do the same, the deer increased in number and availability, naturally drawn to the new openings and the succulent plants such "edge" encourages. The availability of deer hides became greater, and so did the trade in these useful skins and the garments made from them; a deer hide was said to be worth $1 in trade, and it was natural for that dollar to become known as a "buck," and this nickname for our currency remains in use today.

As American settlement pushed westward, so did the settlers' dependence on wild meat. Woods buffalo (actually bison), eastern elk and bear joined deer meat on the settler's dinner table;

This sleek whitetail buck carries an average 8-point rack, and his slightly swollen neck shows him to be in the rut. The buck's neck swells partly because of sparring with small trees and bushes. *Ohio DNR*

all of these, plus the meat of deer, are properly known as venison, but a narrowing usage of the word "venison" has caused most people to think of venison as strictly deer meat. Like the term buck, venison has come to mean deer meat.

Once the majority of the continental United States came under settlement, hunters turned to the whitetail for sport as well as food. Highly adaptable and therefore quite able to live virtually in our backyards, the whitetail's numbers have burgeoned over the past half-century, but it wasn't always so. Late in the 19th century, the lack of comprehensive game laws and sufficient enforcement, plus the loss of widespread habitat, brought whitetail numbers to a low ebb in many places. Entire regions that formerly had deer were nearly devoid of them as forests matured and market hunting took its toll. Many states finally realized that action was needed to restore the herds, so deer hunting was either prohibited or the hunting seasons were greatly shortened.

Slowly the deer responded and increased in numbers. By the 1950s, the whitetail had once again reached huntable numbers in many states. Ohio, for instance, went from as few as 10,000 deer to a present-day statewide estimate of 130,000 animals, thanks mainly to the small farms in the state's southeast that went bust, permitting their former cropfields to grow brushy.

Today, many states boast fine deer herds. Alabama claims to contain 1 million deer, and Michigan isn't far off that mark. Pennsylvania has long claimed one of this country's biggest herds, and so do New York State, Georgia and Florida. The list goes on.

The whitetail isn't restricted to only the green and forested East, South and Midwest, either. Many western states have huntable populations of whitetails. While bowhunting mule deer in southeastern Colorado a few years ago, I heard about a real buster of a whitetail buck that hung out in a few small patches of creekbottom cover just off a major state highway. The guide and I did a little poking around in there and located the buck's tracks readily enough, but the only look at the actual buck I managed was the usual goodbye wave of a buck in full retreat. My guide went in one end of a little piece of buckbrush while I waited at the other end, nocked arrow ready. All was silent for maybe 20 minutes and I was able to actually see the guide's progress through the thick brush and trees when the big buck zipped out of my end of the cover less than 20 feet away and went leaping and snorting up the dry creekbed (arroyo) while I stood there, as my father used to say, with my teeth in my mouth. Whitetail hunters know all about such frustrations when it comes to trophy-sized bucks.

A local herd of whitetails will often become so overpopulated that their predation on valuable domestic plantlife becomes a real problem. I used to hunt the Great Swamp National Wildlife Refuge in northern New Jersey every year. The U.S. Fish & Wildlife Service, which administers Great Swamp, welcomed hunters in an attempt to trim the local herd, balancing it with the area's ability to support deer. Now you might recall that New Jersey is this nation's most populous state in terms of humans per square mile; it is also one of the smallest states in the Union. It still contains up to 125,000 whitetails, however.

The hunter who brings down a mature whitetail buck has one of the toughest-to-get trophies in North America, despite the species' abundance. *NJ Fish, Game & Wildlife*

The problem surrounding the Great Swamp herd was the disappearance of valuable evergreen tree species on the refuge's moist lands. At least two species of wildlife, as listed on New Jersey's list of rare and endangered species, could no longer be found within refuge boundaries because the deer had so depleted required tree species through overbrowsing. Anyone who has seen and recognized a browse line in a forest knows what this means: the line extends as far up the edible trees as a deer can reach on its hind legs. Most or all of the edible tree species will be eaten away in this manner. A few acres of land bordering on the Great Swamp NWR in New Jersey are dedicated to conservation, and the powers that be there thought it would be nice if local school children planted several thousand cedar trees to start a grove. After much effort, the task was eventually accomplished. The following spring, exactly

Like the cottontail rabbit, the whitetail does very well in agricultural surroundings, hiding in the small woodlots and feeding on corn, soybeans, wheat and garden crops.

three trees remained of the thousands that were originally planted. All the others went as unintentional deer fodder when the local whitetails pulled nighttime raids on the tree nursery, nibbling away everything within reach. A nurseryman in Ohio annually suffers the same fate and has opened his lands to unlimited public hunting as a result. Deer can and will make pests of themselves.

Odocoileus virginianus is today found from the southern parts of most Canadian provinces south into Central America, and from the North Woods of Maine westward into the Pacific Northwest. The size and weight of individual deer depend on where they are found; the whitetail bucks of southern Ontario are relatively few in number when compared to, say, those in Alabama, yet an Ontario buck may weigh 280 pounds on the hoof while his counterpart from the Heart of Dixie tips the scales at only 140 or so. The tiny Keys deer of Florida, one of a dozen or so subspecies of whitetail in this country and one of the 30 sub-

The tiny Keys white-tailed deer lives in southern Florida and is so timid that it is seldom seen. This buck's rack is still in velvet. The Keys deer is considered threatened in Florida and endangered nationwide. *Fla. Div. of Wildlife*

species on this continent, may weigh only 40 pounds or so and is the size of a German shepherd dog, while the Coues, or Arizona, whitetail usually weighs under 100 pounds and has adapted to arid life in the deserts of our Southwest.

Quite literally, we have deer *all over* the place, and this, as much as anything else, encourages the tremendous popularity of the whitetail as a game animal. Present in every state of the contiguous 48, predictable enough to be huntable but unpredictable enough to be both a challenge and a frustration, the whitetail remains today as our most popular medium-sized game. Moose are much larger; elk bulls develop more massive racks compared to whitetails; bighorn sheep are less accessible; and the bear clan adds a bit of danger to the hunt; yet it is the whitetail that reigns the clear favorite of hunters everywhere.

With longbow or recurve, compound or crossbow, archers will continue to go afield when the October woods turn bright with fall colors and morning air carries a nip that is welcome after the long hot spells of summer. September rains have washed away the dust of summer and the old tracks of deer, so any track or scrape we can locate is brand new and worthy of a few hours in a treestand or hidden in a copse of golden-red maples. Moose and elk and sheep may fall to bowhunters every year, but it is the whitetail buck we all talk about and prepare for and hunt for. Let's take a closer look at this creature with the handsome rack of antler, the autumn-swollen neck and the still-unresearched knack of doing precisely what we said he wouldn't do after three days of careful scouting.

The Whitetail Buck

There are those who refuse to believe it after a fruitless week of bucks-only hunting, but the male of the species outnumbers his female counterpart at birth by about 51 percent to 49 percent. In short, there are more bucks born every spring and summer than does. This seems to be nature's way of allowing for the buck's greater vulnerability when the rigors of the rutting season leave him thin and worn and susceptible to disease and predation. Perhaps over the centuries nature has begun to allow for a fall harvest of bucks and is producing more bucks to assure enough to reproduce the species. Whatever the reason, deer researchers know that more buck fawns are born every year than are doe fawns, and although the advantage is but 2 percent or less, it might do your confidence some good to remember this the next time you have only one hunting day left in the bow season and you've yet to lay eyes on your first set of antlers.

Unlike his sister, who might remain with her mother for up to two full years following birth, the yearling buck normally departs parental company in his first autumn. Bucks courting his mother contribute to this, I believe, as there are few mature rutting bucks that will tolerate the presence of even a half-grown male fawn when the buck comes in response to the mother's estrus scent. Once I was bowhunting on Kentucky's Land Between the Lakes federal recreation area, in the Bacon Creek area, and witnessed a mature buck's intolerance of a yearling buck fawn. The doe was quite willing and ready to accept the buck's advances, but the buck fawn running

The very heavy main beams and tines on this rack show that the buck was getting plenty to eat, plus such naturally-occurring minerals as carbon and phosphorus, both important to antler development.

Year-old female deer usually give birth to twins, but this captive doe in southwestern Ohio gave birth to triplets. Two of the fawns survived to maturity.

with the doe was chased repeatedly by the big 8-pointer. Finally the little fellow seemed content to fade into some nearby brush. I doubt he left the area entirely, probably hoping that his mother would rid herself of the troublesome buck and allow the fawn to return to her company. I happen to know how it turned out because I put an arrow into the buck as he and his newfound love trotted by my treestand, and I'm sure the fawn rejoined his dam shortly thereafter. But when the buck is not removed

from this type of situation, I believe that the buck may remain with a willing doe for two or more days before wandering off, and this alone would seem to encourage the yearling buck to strike out on his own, unwilling though he may be.

And perhaps the buck fawn's forced independence helps explain his rather independent behavior as a mature member of the deer community, as compared to that of a typical mature doe that runs in a small herd with her girlfriends

This spotted fawn, less than three days old, lies hidden where its mother left it. Devoid of scent and motionless, newborn fawns go undetected by most predators. After three days, the fawn can run like an adult to escape danger.

all year, except when she goes off to bear her fawns in early summer. As soon as those fawns are up and running around, however, the doe returns to the herd, following an instinct for company that marks her sex.

If you've ever witnessed buck behavior, you'll know that when all of the does he's been with for the past two days depart a field by a certain route, the buck for unknown reasons chooses to pick his own route from field to woods, perhaps to rejoin the herd later that night or the next morning. What makes the buck display such independent behavior compared to other deer? Conditions are the same for the buck as they are for the does, and surely the lead doe's instincts are just as sharp as those of the buck, so that couldn't be the reason. What causes a buck to lie down in knee-high grass and let hunters pass within feet of him when the does all scamper away in plain sight? And what is there about even an old buck that sometimes causes him to remain in thick brush, less than 10 feet away from approaching humans, unless and until one of the hunters hap-

The buck is usually a bit taller and heavier than the doe, although the two can be difficult to tell apart when the bucks are antlerless.

pens to spot the hidden animal and make eye contact, at which point the buck jumps to his feet snorting and goes leaping out of sight?

I can't answer these questions, and neither can deer biologists who have worked with the animals for decades. But from the hunter's point of view, it's good that the buck is truly tougher to hunt than does, or we'd all hang antlers in our dens come autumn and the sport would be too easy. There are a few spooky things about animal behavior, including that of the whitetail buck, that border on the Twilight Zone.

As I write this, I can look up on the wall of my den and see the mount of the best whitetail buck I've killed to date. The buck carried a 9-point rack with an inside measurement of nearly 23 inches, and he weighed a certified 202 pounds field-dressed, *sans* heart and liver. I arrowed him on the season's opening day after passing up two lesser bucks, a small forkhorn and a decent 8-pointer, in hope I'd come across something better before day's end. It was amazingly simple: I walked out to the point of a wooded ridge, looked down, and saw my buck just getting up from his bed less than 30 feet from me. A slight crosswind kept my small movement sounds from the buck's ears, and when he was broadside to me I raised the bow, drew and released. The arrow punctured both lungs and he ran only 50 yards before collapsing. When I first spotted the buck and drew my bow and fired, I was in plain sight but a little uphill from him. He seemed intent on listening to something on the next ridge some 300 yards away—maybe another deer or perhaps some hunter crashing through dense brush. But I doubt I will ever again have

such a perfect shot at a true trophy whitetail buck—unless the next monster I encounter displays the same inexplicable behavior that 9-pointer did.

For all of their overly cautious and independent behavior, whitetail bucks can and regularly do some really dumb things, or at least dumb in terms of avoiding close contact with hunters. A good friend and hunting buddy of mine was perched in a treestand some seasons back when the call of nature refused to be denied, so he hauled a plastic sandwich bag from a pocket, filled it, tied the top with a string and tossed it over his shoulder. A loud and indignant snort nearly frightened the hunter off his perch, and when he looked he saw a fully antlered buck wearing the now-emptied plastic bag impaled on one brow tine, its contents having splashed right down the buck's forehead. The hunter later reported that he didn't shoot the buck because to do so seemed at the time to add injury to extreme insult.

Or take the experience of Dave Fulmer, an avid bowhunter who hunted Kentucky's Blue Grass Depot annually for whitetails until ill health forced him to stop.

"I'd gone to my favorite stand tree and put up my platform," said Fulmer, "when I noticed a very small buck sniffing along the very route I'd taken to the base of my tree. He kept coming closer and closer, and since he was a smaller buck than I wanted, I just watched. Finally he sniffed his way right to the tree trunk and then lifted his nose against it as if to follow where I'd climbed the trunk, and when his eyes met mine I couldn't resist any longer and leaned down to shout *Boo!* That little fellow just about turned himself inside out getting away from there, and I nearly fell out of the platform because I was laughing so hard."

Yet, as obviously "dumb" as some bucks—especially yearlings and the like—often seem to be, there are more than enough instances of cunning behavior on the part of older, bigger bucks to balance the scales. Many is the bowhunter who's hunted country full of buck sign and failed to spot one buck. Even good hunters get skunked, too. I know a bowhunting husband and wife team who bought 500 acres of hunting woods two years back, and they have yet to take a buck off their own land. "We've scouted that place so well that I can walk it in my sleep, and show you where at least half a dozen bucks leave sign, but I can't seem to get close to them when the season's open," the husband laments. It's the same for many of us.

But bad luck doesn't last forever: it just *seems* to sometimes, so it's worthwhile to be able to judge antler formation when the moment arrives. Just how good is that trophy you see moving slowly through the woods over there?

Whitetail racks can be tough to judge under typical hunting conditions. The buck may be in deep or mottled shadows, and he may well be moving through open or dense woods, a brushy field and so on. So what do you look for, other than a *lot* of antler?

Generally speaking, there are two basic antler formations found on whitetails in this country. The so-called Wisconsin rack is generally taller than it is wide, and the overall impression given by the rack when seen from the front, back or side is one of height. A Wisconsin buck will often appear to have most or all of its antler tines in a vertical or nearly-

vertical position; all the points are of good length and seem to point straight up after departing the main beam, which itself is frequently of excellent thickness. Westervelt Lodge, which is owned by Gulf States Paper and located in northwestern Alabama, boasts mostly Wisconsin racks on the walls of its handsome main living room-lounge. Some of the racks on these walls are perfectly symmetrical, and all feature sweeps of vertical points that are enough to make the most jaded bowhunter slobber all over his camouflage.

The other basic antler type is the Texas rack. Unlike the tall Wisconsin racks, Texas racks feature much greater width than height, with the inside spread often extending far beyond the buck's ears and the individual antler tines only a few inches in length.

It's been my experience that bucks in a given geographical region tend to all feature the same sort of rack, Texas or Wisconsin. This is reasonable, considering that any given region has only a limited gene pool from which future generations of bucks spring; and since genetics are at least one third of what determines antler growth (the others being age and diet), it's no wonder that most or all bucks in an area will sport racks of similar basic type.

The rule of thumb for judging racks in the field is this: If the antlers are wider than the buck's ears, and approximately as tall as the distance from his brisket to his withers, you're looking at a deer well worth a place of honor on your den wall. Some of us can't afford to be quite so choosy when it comes to waiting for a real trophy, and instead take the first decent buck that wanders by. This can be a good thing in the long run, however. By removing the spikes and small forkhorn bucks from your hunting area over a period of seasons, you at the same time remove bucks of probably inferior genetics from the pool of breeding deer, leaving the larger-racked deer to do the breeding and pass on their superior genes to future bucks. Not many bowhunters are entirely willing to hunt just the smaller bucks, given ample opportunity at a trophy, but if things just work out that way (as they all too often do), you can console yourself with the thought that your efforts (intentional or not) are helping to develop bigger and better trophies for the years ahead. At Georgia's Burnt Pine Plantation, east of Atlanta, staff members are given the chance to hunt deer during that state's extended deer season, but they are restricted to

This massively-antlered nontypical buck, discovered dead in northeastern Ohio in 1983, scored 342 3/8 points, replacing a Missouri buck as the new world-record whitetail. *N.A. Whitetail*

taking only spikes and forkhorns, leaving the bigger bucks to breed. Over the years the quality of deer trophies there has improved markedly; this is all the proof I need to believe in the practice of removing small bucks for herd improvement.

Antler tissue is said to be among the fastest-growing tissues in nature. It would almost have to be, considering that a trophy buck sheds his entire rack in late winter and almost immediately begins to grow new headgear from a pair of rather bloody knobs between his ears. If antler growth begins in, say, May, that buck will have developed a heavy, multitined set of antlers by early October. During the growth period, antlers are covered with a soft, fuzzy material called velvet that carries blood to the antlers as they grow. At this time the buck is very aware of his budding rack, taking great care not to damage it against trees or other hard objects. As mid-autumn approaches and the testicles drop from inside the body and become scrotal, the antlers have reached their full growth and the once-protective velvet dries up and begins to itch and irritate the buck. To rid his rack of annoyance, he begins to rub his antlers on small trees and bushes in an attempt to scrape the rack clean of loose tissue. If you've ever seen a buck at this time of year, you know he can look pretty ridiculous, with long strands of dried velvet hanging from his antlers. Soon, however, all of the velvet has been scraped off and the rack is clean. The rubbing determines what color the rack will be; if the trees and bushes the buck scraped against are dark in color, the rack will be dark. A place in western Ohio I hunt every year features bucks with nearly white antlers, indicating the light hues of the foliage they use to clean their antlers of velvet.

This habit of horning bushes and saplings continues right into the annual rut, or breeding season. At this time of year the steady horning of bushes and trees enlarges the buck's neck muscles, giving him the typical swollen neck of a rutting buck. All he wants to do at this time is fight and copulate, sort of like a sailor on shore leave, and this urge is what makes an otherwise wary old buck do dumb things, such as leap through the picture windows of rural houses, chase dogs through fields, or be so intent on following the scent trail left by a ripe doe that he walks into the bowsight of a waiting hunter.

Maybe we can't explain everything a buck does; if he could talk, I suspect he couldn't explain it all, either. But for the hunter using bow and arrow, the whitetail buck is North America's premier game animal, and thank God he is as he is.

The Doe

I personally would rather sit and watch the normal antics of a doe whitetail than those of a buck, simply because the doe is so much more of a character. She displays a far wider range of behavior than the male, is the only one with a voice she uses to much extent, and can be just plain comical now and then.

On those few times when bucks actually fight, they do it with their antlers and a great deal of bluff. Does, on the other hand, really combat each other. One doe will try to steal half an apple core or maybe an ear of corn from her neighbor, and right away both deer put their ears back, rear up facing one an-

When buck and doe are together, the doe usually leads the way with the buck following, especially if fields or other openings will be crossed.

other, and strike out with those sharp forefeet hooves, sometimes leaving one or both badly cut and bleeding.

I've watched a mature doe leading her twin yearling fawns during bow season, and she had a real talent for teaching the youngsters how to get along in the woods. In fact, I think the ability to communicate with other deer is much more developed in the doe than in the buck, simply because does spend so much of their time with other does. Much of it has to do with body language, only a portion of which we can interpret correctly, and some of it is accomplished with the voice. Does can bark, for example, and usually reserve this sound for those times when they are frightened or surprised; it's probably a means of warning other deer in the vicinity. Does and fawns have been known to bleat to one another, especially when separated by brush or some object that prevents them from seeing one another. All whitetails use the snort, of course; this loud, sudden sound is used when danger is seen or scented at close range, and is often immediately followed by the whitetail's famous leaping run, tail flag waving goodbye as the deer disappears among the trees.

Foot stamping is another trait common among does. I've seen this when a doe encountered a hunter at ground level, perhaps a camouflaged bowhunter concealed among saplings or brush who might have moved slightly and drawn the sharp eyes of a doe leading a small herd. She will stand some distance away staring intently at the "object" she saw move. If it doesn't move again within a minute or so, the doe stamps her foot, which may be another method used to warn her companions,

as well as to try to get the "object" to move again so that her suspicions of danger will be fulfilled.

Pronking, to use a South African term, is another trait among does that I consider humorous. I've most often seen does display this behavior when they want to go from Point A to Point B, but there is something new or suspicious in the way. The doe stares at the object, maybe takes a few small steps one way or the other, and then suddenly leaps high into the air, returning to earth about where she started out. Personally, I think this is a doe's way of draining off nervous energy, and may be a way to calm herself and perhaps other deer with her.

If you're going to bowhunt for deer, you're going to see far more does than bucks, on average. Are there really that many more does around than bucks? In a few isolated and hard-hunted areas, perhaps; but we all know that the buck marches to a different drummer at all times of the year, and he may use his own trails and bedding areas away from other deer except when the rut is on. Bowhunters in all states can take a doe if they wish, under the usual any-deer regulation, and there's certainly nothing wrong with that, old-time conservation theories notwithstanding. In fact, if a local deer herd is to be controlled in numbers, it makes better sense to take a doe than a buck because it is the doe that bears and rears the young, and to remove one doe by hunting also removes her potential offspring.

It's tough to say what an "average" doe may weigh, as this varies from region to region across the whitetail's range. However, an average doe whitetail in the Midwest will weigh from 110 to perhaps 140 pounds on the hoof. The

Early spring sees the deer's coat looking shaggy and rough This deer has begun the shedding process from the gray color of winter to the reddish coat of summer.

average doe getting enough to eat will bear one or two fawns during her first breeding year (usually when she is 1 year old), and twin fawns for about three years thereafter. If she reaches 6 years old, she may bear only one fawn for a year or two and none thereafter. A doe occasionally may bear triplets, but one of the three fawns will often fail to reach maturity because the doe has just two teats and only so much milk to give.

A friend of mine owns quite a large tract of land and got the bright idea that he'd like to stock it with deer. I warned

him that deer, like rabbits, don't take very long to fill the available habitat with their numbers, but he remained firm and I arranged for him to buy two fawns, a buck and a doe. Within 18 months the doe had produced triplets, two of which survived, and within two more years his herd had grown to three breeding bucks and half a dozen does. The original buck had been bottle-raised, had therefore lost all fear of man, and occasionally made a pest of himself come the rut by chasing his owner around the fields, apparently with great enjoyment. At last report my friend's land was overpopulated with deer, he couldn't open it to hunting because it lay within city limits, and he was considering opening the three gates to his place in hope the deer would wander away by themselves. I don't know how it turned out.

The doe, although she is quite a character, does lead the small herd she prefers to live with. The leader will usually be an older, woods-wise matriarch willing to take on the responsibility of her companions' welfare. They in turn give over control of their movements and travel to the leader, and it works out well—except when the lead doe spots a slight movement when you shift positions on a stand seat, or maybe try to sneak a hand up to scratch your nose. She will stop in her tracks, maybe stamp one forefoot, and fan her large ears in your direction. If at this moment she lowers her head, fans her ears and looks you right in the eyes, well, she's got you bore-sighted, buddy, and you might as well wave at her, take out a smoke, or maybe get up and stretch, because there is no way she will permit her charges to get close to you; as the cop shows put it, she's made you.

And if that little herd behind her contains a nice buck, either right among the other deer or, more likely, trailing along a safe distance behind, you won't see him either. He'll take a wide detour around the entire area, maybe head off in a different direction, and may or may not rejoin the herd tomorrow morning or whenever. It depends on the age of the buck and how deeply in the rut he is at the time. Bucks have learned to watch the does, using them as a sort of four-footed barometer of conditions up ahead. You can do the same in reverse, of course, keeping your eyes and ears tuned on the lead doe and her companions to test their mood at the moment, and perhaps pick up some sign that there may be a buck trailing along behind. Watch for the last doe in line to pause and look along her backtrail, as that can be a dead giveaway that a buck is back there somewhere. And if you luck out and one or more of those does in the little herd is in heat and leaving her tantalizing scent on the ground, chances are good that a buck may be close on their heels, no more than 10 minutes behind her, walking as fast as he can with his nose on the ground.

But buck or no, do watch the does, perhaps to stick one if you choose, or maybe just for the entertainment value they provide. Real characters, those ladies.

2

Scouting: The No. 1 Pre-Hunt Ingredient

I once asked an old and very successful elk guide what single factor was the *most* important for hunters after that big trophy. His answer was "dumb damned luck."

Maybe that's the single most important thing for elk hunters, at least in one old guide's opinion, but luck doesn't have a whole lot to do with success when you're after a wily buck deer with bow and arrow. Scouting is the most important pre-hunt ingredient for success, and don't let anyone tell you different.

The reason is simple and of overwhelming significance: Intelligent, complete scouting tells you where the deer are, and where they aren't. It will keep you from spending useless hours or days (or worse, entire bow seasons) in areas devoid of sufficient game. It gives the hunter, once a gamey area is located

and scouted, a real break in knowing ahead of time the prevailing wind direction, physical features of the terrain, the ease or difficulty of getting in and out of the immediate area via roads, trails or whatever means, plus some idea of the hunting pressure the area is likely to receive once the season opens.

An old yarn tells of a naive greenhorn who once asked a game biologist if it was legal to hunt black bear in New Jersey. "Oh, you can hunt 'em all you want to," the manager said. "'Course, you ain't gonna *find* many, but you go ahead and hunt 'em all you want." That's sort of the way it is when you try to hunt a new area without taking a close look at it ahead of time: You're hunting blind. Would you shop for hardware in a grocery store? Then why hunt deer where there aren't any?

Yes, scouting before the season does take more time than either hunting an area completely blind or, as often happens, hunting on another person's say-so. You know how that goes: *I looked over this area last week and found plenty of deer sign. You hunt up on the ridge and I'll take the valley and we'll meet back here for lunch.* This approach hardly prepares the visiting hunter for intelligently covering his assigned area, no matter how small or contained it might be. He can't know where all that plentiful sign is, whether it was made by bucks or does, where the local feeding or bedding areas are, etc., etc. In short, he's hardly better prepared than the chap who parks his car and goes tromping off into entirely new country without the help of so much as a friend's advice.

A good friend and bowhunting companion of mine has a very demanding job, one that requires frequent out-of-state travel. He and his family also have a demanding social schedule, so the time

Bob Cramer (left) and Jim Kunde examine a fresh buck scrape they discovered while scouting in an Ohio hardwood forest. Such scrapes can be hunting hotspots during the peak of the rut.

he has available to hunt, once the season opens, is limited to weekends, for the most part. Yet he has enough seasons behind him to know the importance of scouting ahead of time, so he splits his two-week vacation in half. He uses the first week for needed chores around the house, and he squeezes a couple of days out to do on-site scouting on the property he plans to hunt. This leaves him with one full week of bow-

There's no law against carrying your hunting bow and a few target arrows while scouting. Casual plinking keeps the eye sharp and the muscles toned.

hunting when the season opens, and since he's scouted the area no more than 10 days to two weeks ahead of the season, he already knows where to hunt, and how to hunt, before the sun comes up on opening morning. Not all of us have this flexibility, of course, as vacations are often devoured by family needs, but most of us can squeeze out at least a day or two.

What intelligent scouting does for the hunter, as much as anything else, is eliminate most of the surprises come the actual hunting season. You know what I mean by surprises: You find a spot where deer tracks lead into a picked soybean field, think you've got the local herd's feeding habits and travel routes nailed down tight, and then go on stand only to mournfully spot the same deer enter the soybeans from the far side of the field. I was once hunting brushland whitetails in southeastern Colorado and had been placed on stand by two local archers with many bucks to their credit. My stand was on the edge of a huge patch of shoulder-high cover, but atop a low knoll that allowed me to see in all directions. The dense cover, which lay before me in all directions, contained three deer trails used by the herd to move from feeding areas to a local lake used for watering. Both local experts advised me to remain quietly on stand and to keep my attention riveted to the west. "These bucks, one real buster and two smaller bucks, will move from the lake back in your direction along about dark," they told me. "They will use one of these three trails, and you can reach all three of them from this location. We'll pick you up after full dark—and good hunting!"

Oh, I had good hunting, all right. I

watched a high plains thunderstorm build on the western horizon many miles away, then watched a magnificent sunset in red and orange and blue form beyond the storm, and then I watched several dozen ducks trade back and forth in silhouette across the blazing sunset far off in the west. What I *didn't* watch were the three bucks that approached my stand directly from the east, or from directly behind me. In fact, I didn't spot them until I was reaching for a long-awaited smoke while waiting for the pickup truck to come rumbling and bouncing over the rolling terrain. And there stood the three bucks, the buster in the middle and his pair of 10-point buddies on either side, staring at me in the fast-fading twilight. Surprises. I hate 'em.

Don't rely on a well-intentioned friend's scouting job. By hook or crook or lying to the boss, get and take the time to do your own scouting. That means getting out of your vehicle, pulling on some comfortable walking and climbing boots, and getting out on the land you intend to hunt. Walk where the deer move, and keep your eyes split between the ground you're walking on and what lies all around you. Put yourself in tune with the surroundings. Think like a deer, which means knowing enough about deer habits to be able to look at two possible escape routes from a particular field or apple orchard or cedar bedding area, and, through proper interpretation of available sign, plus a sort of instinct that comes from a familiarity with how whitetails move, predict which route the deer will use and where they are headed when they move. Sounds like a tall order, doesn't it, thinking like an animal. It isn't, really,

Lightweight binoculars are a real aid in spotting feeding deer far across cropfields. Deer will often stand and look at a distant scout, or ignore him altogether.

and you'll be surprised how often you're correct in your interpretation.

Let's look at a particular situation. You've found abundant deer tracks in a grainfield and assume, since the tracks indicate that the deer, once funneled into the field by one or more breaks in the wire fencing, seem to spread out to feed rather than use the field as a crossing point, that here is where the deer are feeding or at least have fed in the recent past. That's the easy part, be-

Aging a deer track can be done, but it's a sure bet that tracks found in sun-hardened soil weren't made recently. Popular feeding spots, such as this cornfield, are often covered with tracks.

cause all you have to do to discern this is read the tracks in the field—where they enter and where they go after entering. Generally, a small herd of deer remains close together when traveling to and from a field, but tends to spread out somewhat while feeding to reduce competition for the available waste grain or whatever. This can make it difficult to determine precisely where the deer are leaving the field. What you need to do is make a slow (make that s-l-o-w) walking trip around the *entire* edge of the field. It's important to scout all of the fenceline, especially where the cropfield borders woods, in order to discover all of the spots the deer have used to leave the field after feeding. If you halt your scouting after finding just one exit location, you could, as described earlier, get no closer to the herd than watching it depart at a spot 150 yards away. Deer are not dumb. They are prey animals, just like rabbits or mice, and they know that to repeat past behavior patterns over and over is just asking for trouble.

You may discover just one entrance and exit point along the field's edge, and if so count yourself fortunate; for unless they are thoroughly spooked, deer stick to established routes that have been safe for them in the past. Does, especially, are never quixotic: They are forever practical creatures that very seldom get themselves into situations where they fail to control possible outcomes. In virtually all situations, they know ahead of time how they will react, and in what direction they will flee, before the situation occurs. They are extremely cautious creatures that are curious at the same time. They stick to routes and habits you know about right up to the moment you begin to rely on those habits to get close to them, and then they often change habits, seemingly just to foul up your day. This is where those hateful surprises come in.

The more you know about deer in any possible surroundings, in any situation you are likely to encounter while hunting, the better your chances of being able to out-think and out-anticipate those deer when the hunt is on the line.

This past autumn I was hunting in a party of about eight hunters on some 1000 acres of land owned by an attorney friend of mine. Each of us has hunted the place before, so we know it pretty well, even to the point of being able to predict where a certain buck, seen before but never collected, is likely to be found. One of our hunters, a likable chap named Kenny, decided to go after a handsome 10-point buck known to hang out with some does in a woods adjacent to a field of winter wheat. Smack across the middle of that field, joining at its ends two dense hardwoods, runs a narrow creekbed thick with second-growth hawthorn and black locust trees. The small herd there uses the creekbed to trade between the two woods while remaining in cover, so Kenny logically placed his treestand in a sturdy hawthorn's branches midway between the two woods, alongside the creekbed.

The deer showed up at dawn, right on time, feeding in a relaxed manner out into the bright green wheatfield, just as Kenny had anticipated they would. And when the early sun was well up the little herd of six does and the trophy 10-pointer started to depart the little wheatfield, again as anticipated. But as they were leaving, the lead doe suddenly stopped in her tracks, with the other deer quickly halting behind her—almost directly under Kenny's stand. *Oh boy*, thought the hunter. *Here he comes, here he comes, come to papa you big beautiful dummy, you!* Well, the lead doe gave some silent signal to the rest of the herd while she cantered out from under the bowhunter's stand and proceeded to prance in a circle around the wheatfield, ears all alert, head switching back and forth. Then she re-

When food is scarce, deer will browse on almost any foliage they can reach. Extensive browsing has left this pine stripped of needles to a height of four feet.

turned to the herd and continued along the original travel route that brought all of the does—but not the buck—within easy range of Kenny's tree. The buck, for reasons none of us in the party has been able to determine at this late date, simply went in the other direction and out of sight. Who would have thought the buck would abandon his ladies, especially when, Kenny insists, none of the deer could possibly have either scented him or seen him.

What caused the buck to depart without his ladyships? I tend to believe it was the odd behavior of the lead doe. Herd leaders (always experienced does, by the way) don't take chances; they take their responsibilities seriously, sometimes going to what seem to be ridiculous extents to investigate strange sights, sounds, even suspicions. I think that 10-pointer saw the leader, whose judgment he respected, acting as if she suspected something amiss, and even when the lead doe failed to find anything really out of place, the buck took no chances and departed in the opposite direction, alone but still in one piece. This sort of deer behavior is nearly impossible to anticipate, especially by lone standers. Any given situation and surrounding has just too many loopholes for the hunter to anticipate, much less put a hunter on each and every possible escape spot. So what the wise hunter does is read the situation as carefully and creatively as he can, then locate himself based on the total information his scouting provides.

Despite its natural wariness, the whitetail remains very much a creature of habit. You need only have one quick look at a deer trail so worn that its path lies several inches below the surrounding terrain, to have proof of how deer do the same things in the same places again and again. Provided that your scouting is accomplished shortly before the opening day of the bow season, you should be able to rely on the deer doing pretty much the same things as their sign indicates they have done in the past. If, for example, your scouting turns up fresh tracks in an old apple or pear orchard, you can expect the deer to continue to visit that orchard so long as the available fruit lasts. If the deer are pilfering a living by stealing corn still on the stalk, or perhaps hitting a wild grove of crabapples in some woods, such a spot will remain worth your time and effort until the food runs out—at which time the deer will immediately abandon it for better forage elsewhere.

Scouting a food source may be the best bet if you are unfamiliar with the area. All deer eat; all deer must go to the food to eat. It's an equation you can rely on. And since many food sources used by deer are either planted or nurtured by farmers or nurserymen, talking at length with the landowner is an excellent place to start. There are two hard and fast rules for good bowhunter-landowner relations that any responsible archer must adhere to. Rule One is, ask the owner's permission to hunt. Rule Two is, see Rule One, and then abide by the landowner's decision. Remember, it is *his* land. He can grant permission or he can withhold it at his discretion. Tap on his door at least six weeks ahead of the hunting season, introduce yourself politely, tell him where you're from and how you plan to hunt (with a bow, and with respect), and then pop the question. Engage the man in conversation; don't rush him into answering *the question* immediately after he answers the door. And if he gives his OK, ask for a slip of paper with his written permission to hunt, including your name and his, just in case one of those chaps in the green uniform with the patch on his shoulder shows up to check your license and so forth at a later date. Many states require written permission from the landowner of visiting hunters, and the farmer angered by trespassers can and often will press trespass charges

A close search for deer sign such as tracks, droppings and so on is only half the battle. Now you must find a specific spot for your stand that's both downwind and hidden.

if no permission slip can be dug out of a camouflaged pocket. A close friend of mine recently spotted a pickup truck suspiciously parked on a sideroad near his farm, and he jotted down the license number and reported it to the local game protector. A bit of official investigation revealed that a neighbor's son had sneaked onto the farm without permission, arrowed a big 8-point buck, and made off with it. When confronted by the game officer, the trespasser confessed and was fined a cool $500 for his misdeed. In telling me about the incident, my friend lamented, "If he'd just come and asked me if he could hunt, I'd have been glad to give him permission. But I won't abide him trespassing.

It's my land and that has to be respected." No questioning that policy. No arguing with it, either. Do things right. Get permission *first*.

But once that landowner's OK *is* obtained, the owner can be of tremendous help to get you headed in the right direction in your scouting. The farmer is out on his land nearly every day. He sees deer with regularity, knows where they cross and feed and maybe even bed down, and if he gives you hunting permission, it's likely he'll also give you invaluable tips on where to look for deer sign. I once attended a birthday party and was introduced to an older gentleman who owns a farm known to have deer on it. When he learned that I bow-

Orchards are always popular feeding places for deer, especially in midwinter when other choice foods are scarce. This orchard in Logan County, Ohio, is all tracked up by the local whitetails.

hunt for deer, he invited me to hunt his place that very fall. "I fly my own plane off a little grass strip on the place and several times deer have wandered onto the strip just as I was landing. I sure wish you'd come on up and hunt 'em, maybe get 'em to stay in the woods where they belong," he said. *Voilà*, I had a new place to bowhunt.

Once you have permission, spend every spare minute walking around the land, by yourself or with a hunting buddy (he'll need permission too!) who knows what to look for. Cover everything you can: potential avenues of travel from one woods to another; wide creekbottoms that deer may use as both travel routes and as feeding spots if the areas contain mast-bearing trees; ridges and valleys within the deer range; plus neighboring areas where you suspect concentrations of deer to be located. A friend of mine hunts a 200-acre combination woods and farm that has no resident deer population of its own. Instead, all deer seen on my friend's hunting land come from a neighbor's huge woods where dense pine growth offers bedding and relaxing areas. Deer hang out in this area between feeding hours, but move into and through my friend's hotspot to and from their daily feed in another woods, where there is also waste grain and winter wheat. The hunter doesn't have permission to hunt the big woods on his neighbor's place, but he can and does ambush deer when they move off the verboten land. So far he's taken a big 6-point and an 8-point buck in this manner. His neighbor raises the deer and protects them from severe weather, and my friend knows from scouting where these animals will move, and when they'll move, and he's there waiting

when the season comes in. A neat arrangement, and perfectly legal.

What To Look For

It's one thing to walk all over a new hunting spot, and it's quite another to do the same thing knowing ahead of time what is likely to attract deer come autumn. By learning a few facts ahead of time, you can cut your scouting time considerably.

Take favorite deer foods: If you know ahead of time what favored foods the land offers and where they are located, half the scouting is already completed. A landowner's advice can be invaluable for this purpose.

Acorns are among the chief foods preferred by whitetails as soon as the mast begins to fall to earth in autumn. And the single most important acorn where available is the fruit of the white oak tree. White oak acorns are slightly larger than most other species and are more palatable to the deer because of their relatively small content of tannic acid. White oak trees are easy to distinguish from other hardwood species; simply look for the rather light-colored bark in an otherwise dark woods. Second on the preferred acorn list is that of the red oak; these acorns are smaller than the white oak's and contain more acid. Deer will eat red oak mast, but only when the preferred white oak fruit has been gobbled up. If both types are available simultaneously, always scout for white oaks first.

And if you aren't sure you can tell an oak tree from, say, a hickory or a beech, you can always watch feeding squirrels. Bushytails know the difference between acorn species, and, like the deer,

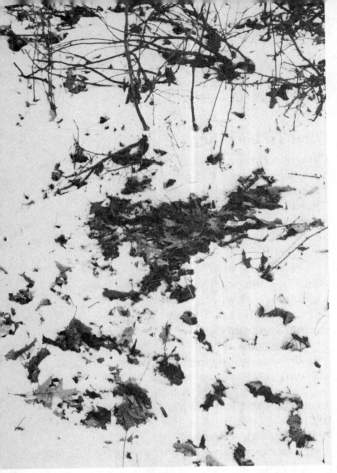

Snow makes pre-hunt scouting much easier. A deer scraped the snow away to search for acorns under the leaves.

they'll work on the white oaks first when storing against the coming winter. Remember, oaks must be at least 25 years old before mast production begins in earnest.

Other natural growths attracting deer include Japanese honeysuckle thickets, used for both feeding and bedding; sassafras groves; dogwoods and their red berries; red maples; poison ivy (among the first wild leaves to turn red in early autumn); blackberry leaves; thickets of

wild plum, used for both browse and cover; and of course field crops such as corn, wheat, soybeans and oats.

Regardless of which food source and/or bedding cover you discover and decide to hunt over, locating the source is only half the job. Now you must decide how the hunt will be set up, and this can come about only after you use the old noodle and correctly interpret what you're looking at. This is covered in more depth in the chapter on site selection, but suffice it to say here that you have to determine where the deer are coming to and departing the food source, and at what times of day (or night) these movements are made, and then where to specifically place yourself to get a clear, close shot when the big moment finally arrives.

Getting the Overview

There is no replacement for moving around on the ground before the season opens, but there are a few things you can do that will give you both an overview or "big picture" of the land and how it lies, and tips on specifically where to look for fresh, worthwhile deer sign when the time comes to get out on the land afoot.

One is to fly over the area you plan to hunt in a small airplane. Few of us own our own planes, but most airports and municipal fields offer rentals on an hourly basis. It costs a little money, sure, but the benefits of having an overview of the country are invaluable, and you can make sure you don't forget what you see aloft by taking some photographs out the plane's window. I've found that the single best time to fly over a proposed hunting area is mid-winter, especially when a light snowfall is followed by slightly warmer weather a few days later. At such times, you'd be amazed how deer trails show up as white tracings, distinct in the otherwise dark, dull woodlands. The overflight allows you to easily spot trails and converging spots, including some you probably didn't know about if you've hunted the area before.

Scouting on foot is a close-up sort of intelligence, great for finding and interpreting sign you happen across, but unless you really walk your legs off, useless for gaining an overview of how the entire region's terrain shapes up. Getting an overview gives you insight into the entire region's layout, and this in turn allows you to make intelligent guesses on how *all* the deer movements plot out on your map.

I hunted Ohio's Muskingum County several years in a row, doing all my scouting afoot and covering quite a lot of the country just ahead of the season. In four years I killed two bucks and missed another, and I thought I knew the area's deer movements completely. Oh brother was I wrong—and I didn't even know it until a friend with a Cessna 180 took me aloft for a 30-minute flight over the area we both hunted. Only then did I discover that just over a series of low, wooded hills that I hunted every year lay three positively *huge* cornfields, a natural area for deer concentrations since all three fields were completely surrounded by wooded ridges and hollows. Deer coming to feed on waste grain (or standing corn during wet autumns when the fields were too wet to permit operation of heavy harvest machinery) used every available creek-bottom and hollow to funnel into the cornfields every evening. Within 90 minutes after our little plane touched down on a local airstrip I was walking the edges of the cornfield nearest my former hunting spot, searching for a place where several deer with big tracks left the wooded hillsides to munch on kernels of corn. The spot I found was a natural: A tall ridge paralleling the fencerow surrounding the field was cut by an abrupt little hollow that fell off steeply until it met the edge of the field. On both sides of the hollow were thickets of second-growth saplings, an avenue from the deep woods to the corn that deer would naturally select. I hunted that area the next day, setting up about 30 yards off the little hollow, and by dark I'd seen 13 deer come walking and trotting down out of the hills to feed. The last deer I saw was an 11-point buck that scored a hair under 142 points and dressed at 196 pounds. He was fat and sleek and obviously well fed, undoubtedly almost entirely on field corn.

By not making myself aware of the major food source in that area (three big cornfields) when I decided where I'd hunt, I was actually working against my own success. The old stand I'd been using depended on deer trails to bring deer within visual range, but I now know that those relatively few deer I'd been seeing in seasons past were either on their way to or from the cornfields. Our little airplane ride revealed far more about the region's layout than nearly any amount of hiking could have uncovered, and it resulted in another fine deer trophy, plus some excellent eating, to go with those of seasons past.

As this is being written, I've just hung up the phone after talking with a friend who owns several hundred acres of prime hardwoods and hinterland crop-fields in the northern section of my home state. I've hunted this man's land sev-

A scrape recently visited by a rutting buck will stink with the animal's urine and the excretion from its scent glands. The soil may also be damp. *Michigan DNR*

eral times and he always provides me with an 8½-by-11-inch photocopy of an aerial photograph of his entire property. Because I've hunted here before and am familiar with the on-the-ground layout pretty well, studying the aerial photograph lets me figure out where deer are likely to move from one area to another when disturbed by other hunters, use my red marking pen to locate the stands of others in our party, and refresh my memory of worthwhile creekbeds, pine plantations and other spots where deer have been known to travel or otherwise be found. Alex, the landowner, never fails to bring me up to date on additional lands he's acquired in the past year, where small logging operations have been carried out and when, and where his employees have spotted notable bucks several days in a row. Alex used a wide-angle lens on a standard 35mm camera to photograph his entire property from an altitude of perhaps 1500 feet, and the one photo he uses year after year, with periodic updatings added with a felt-tip pen, does more to help him and his guests than all the verbal description he could offer. You know what they say about a picture being worth 1000 words. When it comes to aerial photographs, they're also worth an uncountable number of deer come bow season.

Topographical maps are another excellent source of overview, and they are available from a number of sources, depending on ownership of the land to be surveyed.

Federal lands such as national forests and parks provide topographical relief maps of the lands within their boundaries, and inasmuch as such public land is open to hunting, these maps can be especially valuable. States sometimes make topo maps available, and it's worth a letter or phone call to the state's geological survey just in case you can get a map or two of the area of interest. Failing all else, you can always drop a letter of inquiry to the U.S. Geological Survey, National Center, Reston, VA 22092, asking for a list of the maps of the area you're to hunt. Federally-supplied maps usually cost $1 or less each. They are printed on reinforced stock and last a long time, especially if you cover them with plastic lamination material.

Team up your topo map with a compass you know how to use, and then study the map carefully so you fully understand how to read it accurately. Once this is in hand, take both the map and the compass and go hike around your hunting area several weeks before the season. Do it thoroughly enough so that when a friend points out a particularly high ridge or wide valley on the topo map, you automatically know just what that feature looks like close up, where it falls off into a deeper creek bottom, or whatever. In short, scout the land well and know it before opening morning.

Scouting Smart

Smart scouting is my nickname for using more than your eyes, ears and nose while poking around prior to the bow season. Use your brain and try to think like that buck.

Here's an example: You're standing there looking at the point where a wooded ridge falls off steeply into a wooded creekbed maybe 50 yards below the ridge summit. Ask yourself this question: If I were a buck and either hunger or hunting pressure forced me off the point of that ridge, what route would I use to escape, and where would I probably go? If you do this mental exercise regularly, you will not only know your area thoroughly, but will have a firm handle on the behavior patterns of the deer within that area.

Rifle hunters can misjudge a buck's travel route by 100 yards or more and still reach way out to put that bullet into the buck's lungs, but we bowhunters have to get a lot closer to our quarry to be effective, and this is why smart scouting is so important. Smart scouting is really nothing more than thinking

Antlers took the bark strips off this small cedar. In early fall, bucks clean their racks of velvety covering by rubbing them against small trees. Later, such fresh rubs indicate a mature buck in the area.

like a deer thinks. If that sounds ridiculous, it's only because you haven't tried it seriously. Every physical condition of the deer woods is a puzzle to the human hunter encountering it for the first or second time, in terms of what a deer would do under similar circumstances. If a buck uses this narrow creekbed to escape hunters up the valley a ways, is he likely to come right down the middle of the creekbottom or will he keep to one side or the other in order to stay inside the cover? If a small herd of whitetails comes to this orchard (or oatfield or oak grove or whatever), are they likely to use the worn deer trail nearby, or would they probably have another entry as a backup?

The only way to determine this sort of behavior pattern ahead of time is to walk slowly over the land in question, using your head to set up possible answers to your questions and then confirm or abandon each by moving back and forth over the area until the available sign gives you the answers. Sometimes, however, you will find no sign to read, especially in an area suspected as an escape route. Deer may use such areas only when hunting pressure pushes them out of their normal patterns, which means you should be on hand when the maximum number of hunters is in the woods in order to determine what the deer do when spooked. It isn't likely you'll get a decent shot at such times,

The buck uses his forefeet and antlers to scrape away leaves and twigs to create his calling card for receptive does.

unless you're inordinately lucky, but you *will* be able to observe tracks left by escaping deer, and maybe even the deer themselves, once hunting pressure builds up. This casts other hunters in the role of playing dog for you as they move to and from their stands, wander

You must be able to shoot your arrow from stand to deer, but cutting away too much foliage may well alert nearby deer that something is amiss. Carefully choosing the stand site is extremely important to success. *Ohio DNR*

in and out of the area enroute to a lunch back at the truck, or as they briefly leave their stands to relieve themselves. Personally, I get a little kick when another hunter moves a deer past my stand. I mentally thank him for his effort on my behalf, even though he hasn't the faintest idea of what he's done.

Sometimes you'll end up scouting smart whether you want to or not. A couple of bow seasons back I was scouting a long, wooded ridge and at the top of the day I came on a buck scrape that had obviously been made that year but wasn't newly freshened and all skunked up—as if a day or two had passed since the buck had visited his calling card. I went on after noting the scrape's location, and came back a few hours later enroute to my car. Sure enough, the buck had been there after I'd discovered the scrape that morning, and 24 hours later I was tucked into my stand 25 yards from the scrape when the 5-pointer came back. He had just dropped his head to sniff for doe scent around the edge of the scrape when I released and sent a shaft thunking into his ribcage. He ran less than 50 yards before lying down for the last time.

Sometimes it happens like that, plain dumb luck, as that old elk guide put it, but the fact remains that I wouldn't have discovered the newly freshened scrape at all if I hadn't made a mental note to revisit that spot on my way out of the woods. Scout smart and score.

Scouting the Trails

Bowhunters make a big deal out of discovering one or more well-used deer trails in the field, figuring they've run across a veritable Valhalla of whitetail activity, and so they have. But you should know that your chances of seeing a buck for every doe on that trail are slim indeed, and here's why:

It is the doe that is the creature of habit, not the buck. If you find a well-worn deer trail winding through deer country, I can almost promise you that it was made by does, fawns and yearling bucks still traveling with their mommy's herd, and not by mature bucks. There are only two periods during any given year when a buck travels consistently with a herd of does. One is during the fall rutting season, when the buck is mating with one of the does in the little herd; and the other is after the hunting season is long over, when the buck has dropped his antlers and moved back with the local herd because doing so is easier and safer than striking out on his own. At this time of year (full winter), the buck looks much like his female counterparts except for body size. His swollen neck has once again returned to normal size, he carries no rack to mark his stature in the herd, and his testicles have withdrawn up into his body until next fall.

So, if you are after a buck and only a buck, even though most states permit archers to take any deer they see, should you hunt deer trails or not?

If the rut is in full swing, I'd say hunt the trails. Doing so will almost assure you of seeing deer, and there may well be a buck in the next little knot of deer that comes trotting down the trail right under your stand.

If you've located a well-used trail, by all means take a close look at the tracks you find there. Some folks say you can't tell a big doe track from a buck track, and that may be so, but any especially large track was made by an especially large deer, and there is at least a 50-50 chance that it was made by a buck—and that means it is worth your attention whether you are a bucks-only archer or not.

One last item on the subject of pre-season scouting. As a rule of thumb, I'd suggest that you scout up two or more food sources and plan to hunt them from dawn until 10 a.m. and from 3 p.m. until full dark. And back these up with some travel routes as determined by the behavior patterns your previous scouting has discovered. Undisturbed whitetails move to a food source before light in the morning, and move back to their bedding (and mating area, if the rut is on) late in the morning. The process is repeated late in the afternoon, with the deer moving back into their lolling areas well after nightfall. A buck deep in the rut will move directly on, or parallel to, established doe travel routes at any time of the day, in hope of encountering a receptive doe he can pair off with.

The more backup hotspots you've scouted ahead of the season, the less you must rely on a spot that looked good two weeks ago but fails to produce deer when the chips are down.

3

Deciding on a Hunting Site

The must successful bowhunters for white-tailed deer do more than put an arrow behind the shoulder of their buck every fall. Quite literally, they know their hunting area as well as they know their archery tackle. There is only one way to do this, and that's to use your own two feet, and as much time as you can squeeze out of your busy lifestyle, to get into the deer country and walk around. Use your eyes and ears, your nose and your brain to find a general area containing a good number of resident deer. Do this months in advance of the bow season, all year long if you can, until you can sit down and picture the entire hunting area in your mind's eye. Know where the deer bed down and when they bed, and the routes they take from day beds to food sources. Midsummer bucks don't hang around with the women and children; they remain mostly alone and aloof, wiling away the warm months as bachelors while their tender new antlers grow into the racks we all covet.

Once you have a firm and accurate mental picture of where the herd is and how it lives, begin to pare away those parts of the region with only minimal deer activity while concentrating on the smaller places offering more promise.

You may, for example, scout up a grassy ridge where fresh deer beds, much used, indicate that this is where a good-sized local herd of does and fawns spends the daylight hours. Concentrate on this herd until you discover the trail(s) used to find food, browse areas in the local area and so on. This will be your starting point for more concentrated scouting, hopefully to end up by knowing all the daily habits of Old Mossy Horns.

As a very talented bowhunter I know

told me, "Keep your eye on the ladies (does), because this is where you'll find the bucks. It's just like a bar," he said, using an example we can all understand. "The best and most fun bar in town is the one with the ladies. It's the same when you're looking for buck deer."

Midsummer bucks won't be found right in with the does and fawns, but you can bet that the animal you want is in a small area within a mile or so of the doe herd's haunts. When the fall rutting urge causes the buck to seek female company, he wants to be close enough to his home turf to include the ladies in his daily activities by expanding his range a little, perhaps even relocating his principal range if that's what it takes to breed the maximum number of does.

So, having found the doe herd, in which direction do you look for the bucks?

It's impossible to say, except perhaps to hint that the buck is likely to hang out in an area more remote than where you find the does. The only sure way to find that buck's territory is to get out on the land and walk it, every bit of it, until you pick up sign that shows your efforts are getting warm. In summer, the only sure thing to look for, short of actually spotting the buck himself, which seldom happens, is to look for his telltale tracks.

An average buck from 18 months to perhaps 2½ years old will have a track that looks much like the tracks left by a mature doe. It will be about 2½ inches long, measuring rearward from the point of the toes. If this is the buck you're happy with, the tracking job becomes tougher because it's nearly impossible to tell the track of an average buck from

a doe track. However, if you're strictly after a trophy animal, learning to recognize a buck track gets a lot easier. Here's a rule of thumb: If you find a deer track at least three inches long (toes only, not including the dew claws), and the track is relatively deep in pliable soil, you're probably onto a big, heavy-bodied buck. Look for these tracks along woodland creekbanks and other spots where the soil remains soft during dry summer months. Another clue, once you've found the big track, is to look for single deer beds. Summer bucks, es-

If you place yourself at the base of a tree, you run the risk that your silhouette will be seen by any deer approaching from the sides or rear.

pecially the big ones, hang out alone at this time of year, and this means they bed alone, often atop a grassy hill, ridge or knoll where rising air currents and a good view keep them informed about what's happening around them. You may find what appear to be several deer's beds; but if the beds are larger than normal and seem to overlap one another, you've probably found the spot where the buck beds down every day. This, when added to the big tracks you've found in the same area, gives enough circumstantial evidence so that you should plan to hunt this immediate vicinity come the season.

Once the bucks begin to clean their antlers of clinging velvet, of course, there will be more evidence of them in the area. At this time of year, bucks use small saplings, stiff-stemmed bushes and even fallen tree tangles to rub the now-drying velvet off their racks. If the individual buck does a lot of this chore by using just one sapling or bush, his efforts will leave the object scraped free of bark and small twigs; such rubs are easy to spot in otherwise dark woodland because of the white inner wood exposed when the bark is rubbed off. Depending on where in the country you hunt, this early rubbing shows up anywhere from late August into December and January, with northern whitetails showing this behavior earliest, and southern deer toward the end of the year. I've known Alabama bucks to hold off rubbing their racks until early January.

It's been my experience that rubs created to clean antlers are usually smaller and less damaging to the tree than those made just before and during the actual rut. After all, the buck is merely cleaning his tines and is not yet in the perpetual fighting mood that will overcome him during the rut.

Either way, the existence of cleaning rubs will certainly help you establish that the area you're scouting does contain antlered bucks. Now you can start looking for that big set of tracks mentioned earlier. Once those big slots are found, you can concentrate your scouting efforts to the immediate area—say a block of woodland and its surrounding half square mile. You should find the buck's core living area somewhere within this block.

Doug Crabtree, the expert bowhunter mentioned elsewhere in this book, and who has been hunting trophy bucks for 18 years, says he feels sure he has found the big buck he's after if he can locate two bits of evidence of the deer's presence. One is the three-inch tracks, measuring from the toe toward the rear, and the other is an exceptionally large rub.

"If the rubbed tree is about five inches thick in the trunk, and the rub starts at about knee level and comes up to chest level, I feel sure I've found the trophy I want to go after," Crabtree said. "Some smaller bucks under 3½ years old will sometimes make big rubs, but if I can locate the big tracks near a large rub, I'll abandon all other areas and concentrate right there."

Of course, the type of rub Crabtree is talking about is a rutting rub, a sort of signpost created by a very large, heavy deer with the rutting blood hot in his veins. The deer has long since cleaned his antlers. Instead, this rubbing activity is a ritual gone through every fall by bucks large enough to dominate all other bucks in the territory. Many such dominant bucks will tolerate the presence of other smaller males in the area, but they will drive out all lesser males that display rutting behavior. A boss buck is determined to be the only successfully mating suitor around, and he will search out, fight and overcome any resistance as the rutting season approaches.

Once you know the general area containing the buster buck, look for and discover where he moves, where and when he feeds, how he gets to and from his feeding area, and, once the rut approaches, where his scrapeline is located. A scrapeline is just what the name implies: A line of scrapes, usually found atop the spine of a wooded ridge, along the half-overgrown route of an old and long-abandoned woods tote road, anywhere near the doe herd that can be easily traveled and revisited by the buck on a regular basis. The scrapes will be located anywhere from 200 yards to a quarter mile apart, and there may be as many as a dozen or more individual scrapes in the line, all tended by the same buck once the rut is in full season. The scrape itself looks like a yard-wide spot of cleaned earth, usually located under one or more low-hanging branches of a tree or sapling. Almost invariably, these low branches and twigs show evidence of being horned by the buck; the twigs are broken and hanging only by strands of bark, and some of the bark itself will often be missing from the branches. I've found strips of freshly removed bark many feet away from the scrape, indicating that the buck unintentionally carried the strips tangled in his rack until the bark fell to the ground as he headed toward the next scrape in his line.

The buck removes the layer of leaves and other forest litter using both his feet and his antler tines. The same tools are used to gouge and plow up the newly bared earth, as if the buck instinctively knows that bare earth will retain the scent of his urine and his small forehead glands better than dried leaves would. Once the scrape is clean of duff and sufficiently disturbed, the buck urinates on the spot, often doing some more gouging once the spot is stinking with his smell. Scrapes are surefire spots to determine that the area contains a rutting buck, and at the same time you can estimate his size by looking at the tracks he leaves in the soft earth.

An area I hunt in southeastern Ohio's Wayne National Forest is very hilly with steep ridges and deep hollows. The area contains tangles of honeysuckle, thorn thickets, a devilish ankle-grabbing plant called greenbrier, and one helluva lot of white-tailed deer. The area was once heavily timbered and contains mile after mile of old tote roads, and I often locate fresh buck scrapes along these narrowing roadways. Once I find a single scrape, it's a sure bet I'll find more scrapes by simply walking on down the tote road. Sometimes these lines will go on for a mile or more as the buck expands his advertisement for does ready to mate, but soon he'll begin to concentrate his visits to just one or two core scrapes, as determined by the number of does that visit them over a period of several days or a week. It is the does, not the buck, that determine which scrape will do the best job of bringing buck and doe together. A ripe doe happening across a scrape smelling of a dominant buck tends to hang around that area until the buck returns. She may even add her own urine to the scrape to make sure her suitor-to-be is aware of her presence. When the buck next comes to freshen the scrape, his nose tells him of the doe's visit and he will abandon all else to track her down immediately. If that particular scrape continues to produce more does for the buck, he may abandon his other scrapes altogether, or he may visit them less and less as the rut continues. As the rut deepens and the buck becomes thoroughly involved in mating, chasing rivals and fighting, he also becomes less concerned with eating. In fact, you may never see the buck on his favorite feeding grounds once the rut commences in earnest, save for when the herd of ripe does he's staying with goes to feed, or perhaps late after dark sporadically during the rut.

If the buck is concentrating on just one scrape, the route he travels to and from that scrape daily may differ from the route used when he was tending all the spots in his scrapeline. You'll just have to look over the area, seeking the faint traces left by a single deer moving to and away from the spot, to discover how he moves and when he moves. One helpful trick you can use to find out when the buck is traveling a particularly faint trail is to stretch a length of dark-colored sewing thread between two bushes or trees astraddle the trail. The buck is used to stepping through low brush and should break the thread with his legs as he moves past; if you visit the spot a few hours later, you'll be able to determine approximately when the buck passed through.

But the best method of getting a shot at that buck is to be there at all possible times when he *could* visit, instead of when it's convenient for you to be on hand. Rutting bucks have been known to be out and about at any time of the day, and this includes high noon as well as the early and late hours of daylight. Remember, he is deep in the rut now, not concerned with eating but only with finding and mating as many ripe does as he can. The layers of fat built up over the late summer months begin to be consumed by the added physical exertion of his schedule of traveling and fighting and mating and chasing after some malodorous doe whose scent he's come across in the woods. Just how actively do some dominant bucks mate? A 250-pounder I nailed some autumns back had a six-inch-wide patch between his front legs where all the hair had been rubbed off. This was the buck's pivot point, used when he mounted a doe to mate, and he'd been so delightfully busy at the task of reproduction that he'd worn off the hide on his brisket. At least he died happy.

OK, let's run it down: Late summer scouting has located the doe and fawn herd, and you know that the most actively mating bucks, once the rut starts, will not be far away. You consequently pare down your scouting to perhaps a half mile in all directions from the home territory used by the does and youngsters.

You look for signs of big bucks, not the little 18-month yearlings, spikes, forkhorns and small 6- and 8-pointers still too young to be worthy of attention as true trophies. You want to find three-inch tracks and, as fall comes in, good-sized rubs on trees several inches in diameter. Through diligent scouting you locate the buck's bedding and traveling spots, where he goes to feed and what he's feeding on. After a while you get an overall feel for his movement patterns, and you can pretty well predict where he's likely to be at any one hour of the day.

As the rut approaches, you locate the buck's scrapeline and keep an eye on it until you find his core area containing the major scrape or scrapes. Once you know where these are, you're ready to start choosing one or two specific stand locations.

Notice I said *start* to choose. Before you put that ground or treestand in place, you still have a lot more homework to do.

Most of that homework will be determining just how the buck is likely to approach the scrape, or scrapes if he is still tending more than one. Is he likely to approach right down the tote road or ridge spine, or might he come in diagonally from the side? It's important to gain a knowledge of his pattern of approach, if possible, because the more you know about his habits, the better your chances of putting yourself in a position to get a clear shot.

I know one hunter in Georgia who plopped himself into the wide crotch of the very tree under which a large buck had made his scrape. The hunter sat there for days on end waiting for the buck to show up, but he never did. The hunter must have left some sign, some human scent in the immediate area that alerted the buck, which of course abandoned the scrape in fear of the human scent. No bowhunter worth his broadheads would expect a buck to revisit a scrape when man scent taints it. Don't you make this mistake.

A thermal is a very gentle movement of so-called dead air through the woods. We're not talking about true wind, breeze or even a zephyr here, but rather the natural movement of air on and over the topography of any given spot in the woods. It has to do with the temperature of the air in relation to the terrain: Warm air moves uphill, cooler air moves downhill. Any deer reads the scent on these thermals almost constantly; it's part of the animal's nature. The deer is always testing the air through its sharpest and most dependable sense: smell. The wind in the woods can be dead calm, but if you've hidden yourself in a spot where the thermals carry your scent to the scrape, you're not going to see deer.

And the only way to know ahead of time what direction the thermals will move is to eyeball the site and its surroundings very closely and with the knowledge of what the thermal currents are likely to do under various temperature conditions.

It's true, of course, that a persistent wind will wash your scent away, even if the thermal would normally take your scent to a deer. But I don't count on wind direction, or even the constancy of the wind at all, when determining where to place my stand, and neither should you. Plan on air thermals if there is no wind. And if hunting day arrives with a wind, allow for its direction in making a final selection of where your stand should go.

Doug Crabtree took his best-ever whitetail, a brute that scored more than 127 Pope & Young points, by placing his stand inside a bend in a ridge where the air currents were bent by terrain from a straight-line direction. As expected, the big buck approached from crosswind, and walked right into Crabtree's lap for an 18-yard heart shot.

If you plan to use a treestand, be it a commercial model or a permanent stand made of 2 × 4 timbers, keep in mind that the fewer alterations you make in the hunting site, the better the chances that

Installing permanent steps to a treestand makes for easy access, but it also announces the stand to others.

your buck will not be spooked by anything out of place. This includes cutting a so-called shooting lane from your stand to the spot where you expect him to show. I know some hunters who carry steel tree trimmers with them during stand construction and think nothing of cutting whole armloads of twigs, small branches and leaves from the foliage on a line to the scrape; they reason that the fewer twigs in the way to touch and deter the arrow in flight, the better their chances of a clean hit in the vitals of the deer. Well, I can't fault the importance of a clean hit, but you'll never get the chance for that clear shot if the experienced buck you're after notices that the site is somehow different than it used to be.

Maybe the deer can see more bright sky in the direction of your stand. Or perhaps there is more sunlight patterned on the woodland floor. Whatever he notices, it comes from too much trimming of foliage, or worse, the disposal of the trimmings too near the hunting site. Newly cut foliage carries its own scent, and what makes you think that an old and woods-wise buck won't pick up any new scent in his own backyard?

Sometimes you'll have no choice but to bend or break off a twig or two, especially if they happen to hang down smack in the middle of where you expect to come to full draw and aim if and when the buck appears. A twig or two will do little to alter the pattern of sunlight striking the ground, but expand your cutting all the way from stand to ground zero and you're asking for a day alone in the woods. *Completely* alone.

Ronnie Grooms, an experienced and successful bowhunter who lives in Flor-ida, and I were bowhunting for whitetails in Alabama two years ago. Ronnie had erected his portable stand in a medium-sized tree on the edge of a large food plot, and trimmed away two toothpick-sized twigs at eye level some 20 feet off the ground. I set up over another field 500 yards down the ridge. Sure enough, not one but two bucks showed up later that evening, one of them a 9-pointer that Grooms decided to collect. He raised his Bear compound, came to full draw, released and . . . his arrow ticked the one and only hanging twig he'd neglected to do away with. The arrow went far short of its target, plowing into the ground and spooking both bucks. Sometimes you can be *too* careful, overlook some minor detail that could come back to haunt you later. But I still think less is better when it comes to grooming a stand site.

There have been times when I've been very glad no one was around to see what happened to me in the woods. One embarrassing incident sticks in my mind in particular. I'd scouted my hunting area thoroughly, chosen a tree and humped my way up among the branches using a portable stand. The country thereabouts was hilly, but my platform was a good 18 feet off the ground and I considered myself adequately out of the game's ability to see and smell. I was wrong. Only after a yearling fawn traveling with his doe paused atop a nearby ridge and looked dead straight into my eyes did I realize that I was on the very same level as the nearby ridgetop. The yearling proved it by eyeballing my motionless form for a few moments, then slowly raising his tail, snorting and whirling to run, his doe in tow. I felt pretty stupid, and thereafter chose another spot to overlook the scrape below. This was pure oversight on my part. I should have noted the terrain and chosen another tree, on perhaps another level of that hilly spot, for my stand. But then life is full of should've.

After long experience in the woods, some hunters are convinced that deer can actually think, or at least reason out a dilemma. One successful archer I know was confounded by a particular buck a few seasons back when the buck always seemed to out-think him, day after day.

"I had discovered that the buck used two routes through a small hollow on his way to his scrapes," my friend told me. "He always seemed to use the trail I wasn't watching, even though I had a stand overlooking both trails and used each as I thought called for. Finally I got so frustrated that I put a dummy in my other stand, and that did it. The buck came to the fork and paused a few moments, and then he came on down the trail I was sitting over and I stuck him when he got within range."

This is an odd situation, no question; in fact, it's the only time I can recall when a bowhunter used two stands to get one deer. But it brings up an interesting point about selecting the site where you will hunt: Can deer really *think*, and if so, what effect does this have on the spot where you're going to hunt?

Science insists that deer don't actually think, at least not in the same way and on the same level as humans. Rather, the deer react to human hunters with sharply-honed instincts. We are, after all, the only consistent predator hunting deer today in most parts of North America, so it's little wonder that in the past two centuries or so the prey species has developed instincts based on avoiding men in the woods come autumn.

How can an animal that makes decisions based on facts gathered by nose, eyes and ears, plus years of experience, practically walk right into a bowhunter's lap when the rut is in full swing? And the next month, how can it once again become a wraith of the woods, never to be seen by human eyes again until next summer, when the sweet corn ripens?

Could a creature that actually *thinks* be so much of a Jekyll and Hyde when it comes to behavior?

I'm convinced of it. Truly big, mature bucks can be the ultimate frustration for even serious bowhunters; yet on another day, these same deer seem to have lost all natural caution, ignore the wind, and apparently walk where they please, nose to the ground, completely oblivious to any and all around them, including hunters. How else could I explain the antics of a buck that showed up directly downwind from my ground stand a year ago and spent 20 minutes playing hide and seek with me on two sides of a row of pine trees? I first saw the buck when his head and neck suddenly showed up 50 feet away, sticking out to one side of the pine trunks. We eyeballed each other for a few moments, and since the buck didn't provide me a clear bowshot, I slowly leaned to my right on the other side of the pines. The buck followed suit. I leaned the other way and, moments later, so did the buck. This went on until, I suppose, the animal tired of the game and, snorting, went humping off through the pines. I never saw him again. I've never again played hide and seek with a mature whitetail buck, and it makes you wonder if bucks perhaps do have thinking capabilities. And maybe a streak of humor as well?

Even the possibility that deer can think, or at least instinctively reason, puts a whole new light on selecting the spot where you'll hunt. Let's say that despite your best efforts, you've still left some of your human scent in the woods prior to opening day. The buck comes along, detects your scent, and files its location away for future reference. On the following morning, you're all set up on your treestand, bow in hand, and no deer has shown up by noon. You decide to tough it out, stay on your stand all day, and still see no deer by dark. Did that deer intelligently avoid the spot where he smelled human scent the day before, or did his normal daily habits take him elsewhere? In short, how important is it to out-think your buck in trying to come up with just the right spot to erect your stand?

I don't think that's a question we can fully answer until scientists know more about deer. It's tempting to think that a deer that uses this trail every day of the autumn, *except* the day when you wait for him there, simply used his gray matter more than you did, and therefore avoided your broadheaded arrow for another day. Personally, I think deer react to stimuli more than we give them credit for; this is certainly true of old, mature bucks which, unlike does, seem quite willing to go miles out of their way to avoid even a suspicion of trouble. Examples of this are legion: Bucks never cross a line of human scent on the ground, but does often do. Bucks suddenly abandon the pattern you've

scouted for them every day for the past two weeks, and they do it for reasons unknown to us. But then we're not deer, are we?

All of this points up the importance of being willing to change your hunting site after a few days if the spot has produced nothing. Why sit over an unused trail when you could be seeing (and maybe getting shots at) deer somewhere else? Certainly all that preseason scouting and careful effort to find just the right spot for your stand is useful, and no one likes to see it go to waste, but the object is to get close enough to whitetails to make a bowshot worthwhile, so don't be afraid to take your stand out of the tree and try somewhere else.

It could be that you're inadvertently leaving your scent around while scouting or moving to and from your stand. If so, no new location is going to help matters until and unless you correct the error. A full and working knowledge of the best ways to keep your scent out of the deer country is the first step, and then going the extra mile to avoid broadcasting your scent is the next step. Take a look at Chapter 14 on scent, for some helpful hints.

It could be that you're sitting over a buck scrape that has been all but abandoned by its maker in favor of another scrape that's producing more female company for the buck. If this is the case, simply move along the scrapeline looking for a lot of fresh deer sign in and around one scrape, and relocate your stand there.

And although we all hate to admit the possibility, it could just be that another hunter has picked off the buck you've been scouting for more than a month. It often happens that another, lesser buck will take up the daily vigil of visiting the scrapeline of a recently killed buck, but this possibility is pretty remote. Better to look for another worthwhile spot to stand over. Another buck *could* show up, of course, but do you want to stake the rest of the bowseason on it? Neither do I.

It's also possible that you haven't patterned the big buck's movements as well as you thought. He's going about his daily routine undisturbed, but you don't know enough about the pattern to put yourself in a spot to intercept him. This calls for more scouting and a sharper eye. This runs the risk of alerting the buck to your presence in his bailiwick, of course, but you don't have much choice if you hope to put the trophy on the wall. Wear rubber-soled boots, use a little masking scent now and then, and use your head. If you've scouted this deer since last summer, you should already know both his primary and secondary travel routes. (Secondary routes are those used by a buck that for some reason suspects aliens in his territory; he abandons his normal routes to save his skin, which is how he got to be so big and old to begin with.) Maybe your buck has been spooked by something, and the only way you may get a decent shot is to relocate your stand over a secondary route.

This is when your knowledge of the buck's approach routes, as determined by good scouting, comes into its own. It may well be that the buck is still using his scrapes, bedding area and food sources as usual, but he has altered his approaches to these spots. He may have detected your scent or that of another hunter, or perhaps someone took a shot at him, making him even more cautious than ever about moving around and exposing himself. Whatever the reason, you must alter your methods somewhat or forego the chance to get a shot at him.

Bob Byrne, an avid bowhunter who heads up the bowhunter education program for the New Jersey Division of Fish, Game & Wildlife, was on stand last fall when he spotted a big doe running toward his stand from about 150 yards away. Moments later Byrne could see a very large buck on the doe's trail, and if things went apace, the doe was going to lead that buck smack under Byrne's treestand and within easy bow range. But good old Murphy's Law intervened and the doe spotted something, veered off and took the trophy buck with her. "Maybe she saw something around my tree, or maybe I moved a little," Byrne lamented to me later. "Whatever it was, the buck and his lady ran off into the woods. But I know where he is now and I plan to meet up with him again."

Of course, a buck trailing a ripe doe is liable to go anywhere the doe takes him, making it all but impossible to predict where you and he can cross paths. The best you can do in a case like this is to pick one or two heavily used doe trails and select a spot downwind from where you hope the deer will show up. If the local herd is deeply in rut, every buck worth a place on your wall is out after a little sex, and to get it they must find willing does. The only way for them to do this is to leave scent around and stay active all day long. If a buck finds the trail of a doe in heat, he'll probably abandon whatever he's doing and follow her. And it follows that if the doe is moving along an established trail in her home range (much more likely for does than bucks in fall), you stand a good chance to see a good buck by standing over that trail. Setting up by the intersection of two trails can often double your chances, because you can get deer coming from four directions instead of two.

If you intend to watch deer trails, you'll have to be familiar with the herd movement patterns in order to be successful. I found that out the hard way a couple of seasons back while hunting in West Virginia.

The terrain where I was hunting was quite hilly. Deep, wooded valleys were crowded between quite tall and steep ridge spines. I'd found a well-used trail running just under the lip of one of those ridges and decided to put up a stand so I could watch the trail. My host, another archer with much local experience, said he'd stand over a trail located halfway down the ridge, and we were to meet back at camp after dark.

As it turned out, I came back to camp toting a flashlight while my partner showed up toting a bloodied arrow and a big smile. The wind had been up all day and my companion knew from past hunts that the deer switched their routes to and from feeding areas from open to protected trails, and he'd been in a perfect position to intercept a small doe herd as it moved along the lower trail down the ridge face from me. I had no complaint; he'd given me first choice of stands and I'd simply chosen the wrong one, leaving him the better spot. You've got to know the territory when it comes to choosing a place for your stand.

If you've had your eye on a particular buck, as a result of your earlier scouting, and that buck changes patterns on you, don't despair. You should be able to rec-ognize his track by now; if you cannot, you didn't do enough scouting on him when you should have, before the season opened.

So, assuming you know what his footprint looks like, get out and determine what he's doing *now*. If he hasn't shown up over his scrapeline for a few days, or if his tracks in the beanfield are old, then he's obviously off his former pattern of movement. This may sound like the odds are totally against you, but he has to be *somewhere*, and it's up to you to find out where.

Revisit his bedding area. Look for fresh beds among the trees and weeds. If you see sign that he's still bedding in that spot, make ever wider circles through the surrounding cover until you cut fresh sign, then follow it until you can figure out his new pattern. Like largemouth bass in a hot new reservoir, buck deer establish patterns; either you match the pattern or go home skunked. Those unwilling or unable to determine the right pattern go fishless or buckless, or both.

If the rut is on, it could well be that the buck has changed his pattern somewhat because he's found does hitting his core-area scrape; this is especially true if your buck abandons his other scrapes in favor of the one getting all the attention from the ladies. In this case I suggest you revisit all of his scrapes you know about and look for a concentration of sign, including those big tracks that have become so familiar to you. And if you're able to relocate his comings and goings in this manner, it's usually an easy matter to set up your stand so that you're on hand when the buck comes around.

If it's early in the rut and your buck is still in the process of establishing dominance over other male deer in the area, it may well be that the deer will remain warier than you'd prefer. Unfortunately, this can't be helped. Keep in mind that he is still driving other mature bucks away, and he's alert to any sound that might indicate the presence of a rival. If the rut is at its peak, however, the buck has already put his mark on all possible rivals, and he's likely to be more relaxed, with his attention more on sex than on combat.

These two factors—sex and combat—seem to go hand in hand in bringing about a full rutting mood in bucks. This seems especially true for big, mature bucks; the smaller bucks in the area (forkhorns, spikes, small sixes, etc.) have to content themselves with whatever they can get away with, away from the dominant buck's attentions. I once watched a little herd of four does and a big 10-pointer in Tennessee. The five deer were feeding among some oak trees, nuzzling the leaves for fallen acorns, when a small 2-pointer I judged to be about 18 months old came sidling through the oaks, ever closer to the does that fed on with unconcern. The little buck pretended to be feeding, but it wasn't difficult to see that he was trying to make off with one of the does, right under the nose of the dominant buck. Well, that big old boy let the little squirt pussyfoot within 20 yards or so of the nearest doe before reacting. All he did was raise his head from feeding, stare hard at the forkhorn, and then shake his handsome antlers once. That's all it took. The little buck turned up his white tail and took off through the woods. The big buck went back to feeding, as if what had just happened was an everyday occurrence.

That's the way it is for an immature buck in a bigger buck's range: The two must co-exist to an extent, but if the smaller animal is to mate at all, he has to do it away from the bigger buck—which isn't always possible if the dominant animal has all the ripe does within his care. I once saw a big 12-pointer chase a nice 8-point buck clear across a huge wheatfield because the squirt came too close to the buck's doe herd.

It can be tough to hunt small bucks during the rut because their daily movements are so erratic. They wander here and there throughout the region, trying to mate here, getting run off there, and all without sticking to any sort of pattern. The best you can do, if a smaller buck is to your liking, is to stand over established doe trails and hope one of these smaller males will trail along with a doe or two as the females move about during the day.

On the morning when I killed my best-ever buck whitetail to date, I'd seen two other bucks in the immediate area before the big one showed up. One was an 18-month-old 2-pointer feeding by himself, and the other was a surprisingly large 8-point rummaging for acorns along an oak-studded hillside. Despite the 8-pointer's size, I decided to wait for a larger trophy. The big buck showed up within 150 yards of where I'd seen both smaller animals, yet he was clearly the largest buck of the three, and his swollen neck showed him to be fully in rut. Why did he permit these other bucks in his area? I think he'd so cowed those deer that they no longer offered any threat to his successful dominance over them, and he just forgot about them. So long as the small bucks didn't try to take part in the reproductive rituals of making scrapes, fighting, chasing does and actual mating, I think he was willing to let them remain. I suspect you'll agree that seeing three antlered bucks before 9:00 a.m. on opening day is exceptional, but it can and does happen when your scouting puts you into a good area with lots of buck sign.

Of course, sometimes the amount of scouting you can do, and therefore your available choices of stand locations, will be limited by things beyond your control. I have permission to bowhunt several farms near my home, none of which is larger than 300 acres. In doing my preseason scouting, several times I've noticed that only part of a particular buck's scrapeline will be on land I can legally hunt. In a case such as this, I have to make do with part of the buck's line and set up my stand in the best available spot in hope that Mr. Big will come by while I'm there. Sometimes that happens, and sometimes it doesn't. When it doesn't I'll happily make do with a big doe, if that's all I get a shot at, since my home state (Ohio) allows only one deer per year per hunter, regardless of seasons. Such was the situation as this was written, at least. I'd rather end the season with doe meat in the freezer than with no venison at all, and this is why active doe hunting sometimes ends my season in Ohio, as it might end your season wherever you live. Some states (Maryland and New Jersey, for example) permit bowhunters to take more than one deer in a season, and if this is the case where you hunt, you might take your buck early and end up with doe hunting, or vice versa.

When you specifically go after whitetail does, you hunt the apparent sign. The doe is a creature of almost strict habit; she will travel the same routes morning and evening day after day to and from food, and finding a spot for your stand is much less of a problem than for bucks-only.

I'd strongly suggest you hunt the trails, those often inches-deep paths leading through the deer woods. Bucks don't travel the same paths frequently enough to make deep trenches, but does do. If you already have an overview of your hunting region, look for food sources (cropfields, orchards and so on) and then for large, grassy fields and woodland edges where deer are likely to make their day beds. Then concentrate your trail scouting between these two points (beds and food), and you'll locate several doe trails leading between the two.

Another nice thing about hunting for does is the fact that they usually travel in small herds—unlike the buck, who is found alone most of the time in fall and winter. If your stand is set up overlooking a doe trail and you see game, it will probably be three or more does, or maybe two mature does and two or three yearling fawns. Naturally, this gives you more than a single target from which to choose.

When hunting these small doe herds, I try to take the lead animal if possible. This is usually a mature old doe, who may or may not be barren, but who is almost always the largest doe in the herd. This largest doe gives me the maximum amount of venison and deer hide for my efforts. The lead doe is also the first deer to venture into a particular clearing, or come down a given trail, so you will be shooting for the first deer to come along, which lessens the chances of being spotted or scented by her companions. She *is* the lead doe, however, and this

What's missing here? The bowhunter is climbing into his stand without a rope to pull bow and quiver up after him. *Michigan DNR*

means she will be more vigilant and warier than her companions, but if your stand is well placed and camouflaged, you should get the sort of shot that puts deer on the ground.

If you hunt the doe trails, look for stand sites where you can predictably keep your man-scent *away* from the expected approach of the deer. Don't rely on how the wind was blowing the last time you were here; if the wind has swapped directions, move your stand downwind. Keep face and hands and bow camo covering complete, and don't move around while waiting for deer to show. The lead doe can spot movement 75 yards off through a dark woods. Believe it and stay still.

Weather oddities can sometimes make deer do weird things, and you'll have to abandon the accepted standing methods to get your shot. More than once I've had does approach my stand from an unexpected direction; and, consequently, I've been forced to oh-so-slowly climb down out of the stand and stalk closer to get a clear shot through the trees. High winds seem capable of making doe herds temporarily abandon their normal trails in favor of routes through dense cover, perhaps to shield them from the bitter wind. Anticipate this when the wind is up, and be ready to alter your hunt plan at the last minute if needed.

High wind sometimes lets you move much closer to unwary deer than on quieter days, however. At least twice I've been able to sneak within 60 feet of unalerted deer in a January woodland— on six inches of crusted snow, no less! Sure, the snow crunched every time I stepped on it, no matter how light my tread, but the persistent wind through the leafless trees let me get close by covering the sounds of my footsteps.

Of course, if I hadn't been standing near an active doe trail at that moment, I wouldn't have seen the deer or had the chance to try to stalk close enough for a shot. Never underestimate scouting, even when you're after the female of the species.

4

Treestands

You hear all kinds of things about treestands, and some if it just ain't so. I've heard (and until fairly recently believed) that using a treestand keeps your scent above the deer under all circumstances, and that tree platforms are so effective because deer never look up. So I went on using stands and having good success with them. I was fat, dumb and happy, but my success was due to facts about treestand hunting that I was unaware of at the time. Similar to the alchemists of the Middle Ages who tried to concoct a medicine by adding red coloration. The medicine worked, but not because of the red color; the iodine used for that red color made the mixture effective, not the color.

I suppose something like 90 percent of today's bowhunters after deer use treestands of one kind or another. Plat-

forms in trees, perched atop wooden or steel poles, or designed to be portable, account for thousands of deer taken every year, and for one good reason: They work.

Just *why* they work so well is open to question, at least as far as I'm concerned, but there are several possibilities. Elevating yourself does help keep your human scent above deer level, at least in the immediate area of your stand, assuming the terrain is fairly level. If you don't move around much on stand, you give any deer near the spot little reason to look up. Being on a relatively small platform 15 feet off the ground will stop almost anyone from: (a) walking around; (b) making much noise; and (c) lying down to sleep through the best hunting part of the day. Treestands have a way of keeping people alert, although Bob Cramer, a hunting buddy of mine,

54

Using a broad limb as a platform saves erecting something more time-consuming. But such a perch makes it tough to turn side to side and take an accurate shot.

once fell asleep while on his stand and toppled over backwards into a rock-lined creekbed. Surviving the fall, he found he had broken several ribs and was forced to crawl a few miles until his brother heard his shouts and got him to a hospital some hours later. I once dozed off on a stand in Kentucky, nearly fell out of the tree, and spooked two nearby deer in the process. Some of us do a more complete job of screwing up than others. I'm occasionally one of those people.

There are about as many variations on the treestand theme as there are hunters to dream them up, but a few rules apply no matter what your platform preference. One of them is to raise

your stand at least 10 feet above the ground; any closer to terra firma puts you smack in the vision level of the average deer, and you might as well stick out your hand and say howdy, for all the good a too-low stand will do.

Another good rule is to not locate your platform above low-hanging limbs, if you can avoid it; in some cases those limbs will also be the upper limit of any browse line caused by deer feeding on tree leaves and twigs. If you can't see through tree foliage, you can't very well get a clear shot through it, either, and if you use a tree trimmer to clip the limbs off, you'll probably advertise your presence to all deer that pass this way often.

It's obvious but worth repeating that

Practicing your shots from an elevated position can help you hit when the season opens. This archer needs to work on his release form.

despite the scent-reducing nature of most treestands, the platform must be located *downwind* from the expected approach of any deer. This was pointed out to me during bowhunting school I attended a few years ago. The instructor insisted that no matter how high your stand, any deer located downwind from that stand and some distance away is going to detect your scent and make itself scarce. "You might as well ignore the corridor of your scent downwind from your stand, because you won't see any deer there," he told me. I made it a point to check this out during subsequent hunts, and he was right. Human scent *will* settle to ground level from a treestand; exactly where and how quickly depends on air temperature (colder weather, faster settling) and wind.

A good friend of mine prefers to build what he terms permanent stands in trees. He uses scrap lumber and sometimes adds a bit of carpeting to the platform surface to quiet foot scuffing. He also nails ladder-like steps from the ground to the platform. All this sounds great until you actually get up in one of this chap's stands. It's not something you want to do again real soon.

Most of his stands are so small that the number of square inches is barely more than the measurements of the bottom of your boot soles. He often chooses slender trees as stand sites, and every time a slight breeze blows the tree, the stand and bowhunter go swaying back and forth like the tail on a friendly dog. I've seldom been willing to unhug the tree long enough to draw and shoot out of one of these homemade stands, for fear of taking a header over the side, and no one can be an effective hunter when he thinks he may pitch into space at any

moment. This same chap, by the way, now has a 200-acre farm of his own with both deer and very comfortable stands on it, but he doesn't take credit for them. They were there when he bought the place.

Tree platforms that are too small are not only unsafe; they simply do not lend themselves to effective deer hunting. Neither do permanent or portable stands so old and creaky that you're more concerned with keeping quiet and keeping airborne than with being alert to any deer within the area.

Old stands can be dangerous. The friend of a friend of mine had just climbed into his stand when his buddy's platform support 2 × 4s gave a loud crack, followed by a scream from its occupant as both stand and bowhunter tumbled to the ground. I've never had a stand give out on me (so far), but I have suffered the frustration of having a buck hear the creak of old timbers and rusty nails in my stand when I was slowly turning around to take a shot. At first the deer moved away only 25 feet, ears all alert, when the stand creaked. But when it happened a second time, the deer had heard enough and hightailed it out of there.

Portable stands can also be dangerous, with some types more so than others. One that relies on the hunter's body weight to anchor it in place can be downright wiggly at times, and its side-to-side movement even when ideally placed can ruin shots that otherwise might go where they are aimed.

I guess I'm just a little afraid of heights, but I'll be damned if I enjoy deer hunting when in the back of my mind I'm worrying about my stand collapsing, skidding down the tree trunk, or oth-

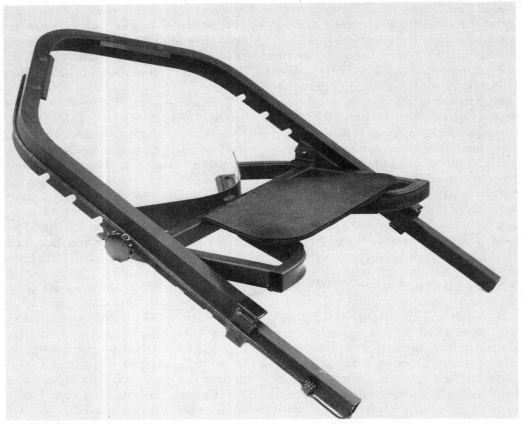

The Quick & Quiet Seat Climber is very lightweight, provides a seat for the hunter, and is adjustable for tree-trunk diameter.

erwise not doing what it's supposed to. Any stand I'll use more than once had better be firm, and I mean jumping-up-and-down firm. I don't want it to wiggle, not even a little, and I want it safeguarded against making squeaking or creaking noises at just the wrong moment. Perhaps the steadiest treestand I've ever used was the Andy Stand provided for bowhunters on Burnt Pine Plantation about 60 miles east of Atlanta. This stand is locked onto the tree by means

of draw-tight chains, then the stand platform and the separate seat are raised to horizontal position, forcing steel teeth into the outer layer of the trunk and further tightening the stand. I tested this stand by jumping up and down on it, then hanging from the front edge of the platform by both hands; it would not budge. At all. Now *this* is my kind of treestand.

Another gripe I have with many portable stands is that you often have to tote a whole hardware store into the woods with you. The manufacturers provide shoulder straps to make the job easier, sure, but why should the straps be necessary to begin with? Recently I needed to shoot some photographs of a portable stand to illustrate a magazine story I was writing, so my wife, Arlene, and I toted the stand into some nearby woods. The stand wiggled on the tree trunk so much that I had a deuce of a time getting Arlene to stay up there long enough for me to shoot all the pictures I needed. The platform was properly installed on the tree, all the wingnuts were tightened, and the trunk was of the right size. The stand is fine for a lot of things, I suppose (firewood, for one), but I'll be darned if I'll trust it come deer season. Maybe I'll attach it to a backyard tree and Arlene can use it as a planter.

The point is, *any* treestand can dump you, and any treestand *will* dump you if it isn't erected properly. This goes for portables and homemades. The idea is to put them up right, and if you've done everything the manufacturer tells you to do in the directions and the thing still doesn't feel right, either augment the erection technique or leave the stand in your car trunk and hunt without it. Don't trust any stand you don't trust, in other words. It's your life and limb, and the biggest buck in North America isn't worth a stay in the hospital or, worse yet, funeral bills.

I have to smile at the way some stand makers hedge their bet when it comes to stand safety. On the one hand they insist their particular stand is the steadiest and the safest on the market, and then they turn around and recommend that you buy and use a nylon safety belt just in case that super-safe stand dumps

you into space. I think there is something a little odd about a hunting method that requires you to go into a woods before light, climb into the branches and then tie yourself to a tree. What happens if you fall while you're tethered? I've never had the experience, but it must feel a lot like a World War II paratrooper whose chute tangled in the trees and left him dangling, unable to climb back up and too far off the ground to cut the strap holding him, so he just hangs there like a worm on a hook. There are literally dozens of people in the world I'd hate to see me in that predicament. It would confirm too many suspicions.

In the chapter on site selection I discussed how to locate your hunting site for best results, but there are some particulars on the topic that apply only to treestands. Let's look at them here.

Obviously, if you think there's any chance of deer coming by your stand on ground at or near the level of your treestand, your chances of being spotted by those deer are too high to risk. Some hunters make the mistake of paying attention only to the spot they want their stand to overlook, ignoring a nearby ridge or hillside from which any deer could see the archer on his perch. This has happened to me and it has made me feel pretty stupid. I should have chosen my stand location with more care. So should you.

In deciding which side of the tree your platform should hang on, keep sun and shade in mind. If you're in the sun while up on the stand, you may well be a little warmer on a cold day with sunlight on your shoulders, but you will also make yourself easier for deer to see. Better to move that stand around the tree into the shade; you may be a bit chillier out of

This casual perch is fine if a deer approaches from the bowhunter's left, but he'd have a hard time shooting, or even detecting, deer passing behind or to the right.

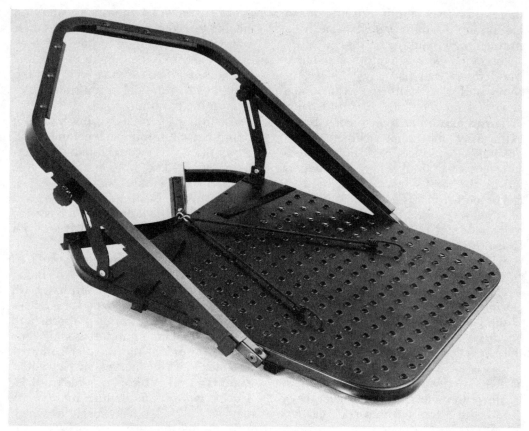

Holes in this Quick & Quiet platform reduce overall weight and give the hunter's boot firm purchase.

the sunlight, but you've lessened your chances of being spotted, even if you sit bolt upright and dead still. Move around at all and you increase the chances of being seen dramatically.

Doug Crabtree, an excellent bowhunter mentioned elsewhere in this book, is a firm believer in using a stand with a mesh platform surface, rather than one made with solid wood planking. Doug hunts trophy whitetails almost exclusively, taking great pains to locate their hangouts and then using equipment designed to minimize any sign of his presence while hunting. According to Doug, "A big buck in his home territory is very aware of even small changes in the appearance of that territory, and this includes his spotting a solid block of shadow on the ground where there used to be unbroken sunlight. A mesh stand doesn't create a solid black shadow, so that's what I use." Crabtree believes that big bucks can and will look up to try to see what's causing a heavy shadow on the ground, and this is what causes him to see the hunter in some cases. The Clearbrook and Amacker Bowhunter Lite stands are two stands offering mesh platforms; it could be that mesh is stronger than planking for this purpose.

I do much of my bowhunting in hardwood forest that has never been timbered, and this results in a wide choice of very large, thick-trunked old oaks, hickories and other tree species. Some of these behemoths have trunks five feet in diameter and the first limbs, themselves two feet thick where they depart the trunk, don't appear closer than 15 feet or more from the ground. Using these big trees as treestands often doesn't require any sort of platform, simply because the tree crotches themselves are so wide and roomy that I can sit or stand comfortably without added support.

That's the easy part. The hard part is getting up into the tree safely to begin with. The owners of the land where I bowhunt are hunters themselves, and they have used the same trees as stands in past seasons, so the nail spikes used as steps up the trunk were placed there by the landowners. I would never drive a nail into a tree without specific permission from the owner; doing so can kill or injure the tree, and if that trunk is ever sawed up for timber or pulp, a hidden nail can play havoc with anyone using a chain saw.

There are quite a few devices available to help hunters reach the right height on trees. Commercial tree steps, using either wood-screw type anchors or short nylon ropes or leather straps, can be helpful, but when the trunk of the tree is five feet thick, using these steps effectively can be iffy. Rope ladders with solid wooden rungs are good, provided you have a sure way to anchor them before trusting your body weight on the steps. I've seen bowhunter's shinny up smaller trees that have fallen against their stand tree, using rope to haul the bow and quiver up once they're in the tree, but this is a little iffy as well; it's too easy to fall from a slanting tree you're attempting to climb.

An Indiana hunter I know bought a brand-new aluminum extension ladder, spray-painted it a camo finish, and permanently spiked it to his stand tree overlooking the intersection of three deer trails. The camo paint does such a good job of hiding the ladder that a passerby can stand within 20 feet of it and not see the ladder at first glance.

Some commercial treestands, such as the Apache Ladder Model and the Baker Platform Ladder, come complete with their own metal ladder. The ladder gives easy access to the hunting platform, and provides half of its support as well. This makes for one of the sturdier commercial stands on the market, but the ladder standing well out from the tree trunk is, I believe, a bit too obvious for all save heavily forested, brushy locations where surrounding foliage helps conceal things.

One of the better commercial stands with its own ladder is the Forrester, made by Forrester Marketing of Buford, Georgia. This model consists of two tubular steel ladder sections that join together for a total height of 10 feet. The platform section consists of a sturdy wooden platform and padded seat joined together using the same tubular steel, and when in place the seat is about 13 feet off the ground. Both sections of the assembly (ladder and seat-platform) attach firmly to the tree through the use of small chains. This is a very firm, comfortable stand that allows the archer to take shots in all directions except on the side of the stand opposite the platform.

One of the sturdier one-piece climbing treestands that I know of is the Woods and Water stand known as Quick and Quiet. Made of aircraft aluminum and finished in a non-glare black, the stand weighs 9.5 pounds, and, once the support arm has been adjusted to the tree thickness to be climbed, the hunter makes his way up the tree using two rope foot stirrups. A matching hand climber weighing three pounds is also available. The Quick and Quiet relies on the archer's weight to anchor it in place in the tree, but its strong construction and overall sturdiness make it a good choice if you're in the market for a self-climbing stand.

A treestand can sometimes be as casual as scurrying up a handy trunk that happens to have usable climbing branches in the right places. I was photographing whitetails in central Kentucky one Saturday morning when the guide told me to hide while he walked through the far side of a hardwoods in an attempt to push deer in my direction. When he'd left, I looked around and quickly climbed 12 feet up a nearby pine with low branches. As luck would have it, I'd no sooner gotten comfortable when a fat doe came mincing through the woods. I raised my camera and telephoto lens just as she paused in a bathtub-sized spot of sunlight. I snapped half a dozen pictures of her before the click of the camera got her attention and she moved off. Such casual treestands are OK for short periods of time, but the hunter planning to remain in the woods for several hours at a time will need more comfortable accommodations.

Using a Baker stand, Arlene Bowring clears away a twig that might get in the way of a bowshot. Such trimming should be kept to a minimum.

Maybe you can stay alert and contented while a beech limb etches its every bump in your butt, but I can't. Bowhunting's supposed to be fun, the last I heard.

I think that far and away the most comfortable type of tree platform is the permanent one built by the hunter himself, using whatever scrap materials he can gather. The usual self-built stand requires driving large nails into one or more trees, and this of course demands the landowner's permission. It's also

The Deluxe treestand from Golden Eagle is made of heavy-duty structural foam and comes with a safety belt and four strap-on climbing steps, plus a built-in seat.

possible to use nylon rope; such a rope or line is pretty rot-resistant, will keep well-designed stands firm and steady for years, and doesn't harm the tree.

If your bowhunting area contains no really large trees that will accept all of the stand-support task by itself, then look for two or more smaller trees standing side by side and use both, placing the stand platform on 2 × 4s spanning the distance between trunks. I can't stress too much the importance of making dead sure your supports are firmly placed, regardless of how you anchor them (nails or rope). Once this is done, I like to use a piece of one-inch plywood cut to size, nailing this in several places to the support 2 × 4s. To this I add a scrap of carpeting; this not only gives me firmer footing while on stand, but also quiets those little sole movements that cause loud scuffings in an otherwise quiet woods.

The carpeting is tacked down so it stays in place, and then I add at least two rails made of more 2 × 4s about waist-high on both sides of the platform, regardless of the platform's shape. This serves two important purposes: The rails are handy for holding my bow with nocked arrow, and they also let me tie on some brushy, small limbs to help hide my silhouette. This screen of brushy limbs lets me move slightly from time to time without advertising my presence to any whitetails in the area.

How roomy should the homemade stand be? That depends on the tree or trees you'll use, and just how roomy you want it to be. I like to add some sort of seat to my stand, even if it's only an old milk bucket that's been turned open end down, has padding added for comfort, and is then tacked in place.

A permanent stand I used while bowhunting for black bear in southwestern Manitoba overlooked a dead Hereford bait that was 40 yards down the fire break trail. The stand was triangular in shape and was large enough to comfortably hold me and Doug Raynbird, a friend and fellow hunter from Winnipeg. The platform was made of plywood and covered with carpeting and was roomy enough for both of us to sit down. As it turns out, we both had books to read while we waited for a bruin to show up. After an hour's sitting my legs needed stretching, so I quietly got to my feet and stretched while Doug continued to read. I happened to glance over my right shoulder and spotted a large bear coming along the trail from the rear, so I slowly raised the bow, waited until the bear moved to within 18 yards of the stand tree, and put a shaft deep into the area where the neck meets the shoulders. The bear let out a blood-curdling roar and fell over backwards, and poor Doug, oblivious to the whole thing until the bear sounded off, just about had a baby. Hunting with a second party in the tree with you can be fun under certain circumstances, but scaring the daylights out of him with a very steamed black bear may not be the way to do it. At least Doug didn't think so.

Personally, I like my stands roomy. A floor platform of, say, three feet by four feet can be safely supported in most trees, and this gives me room to move around a little, change positions, maybe store some extra gear or a sack lunch. I insist on side rails for any stand I build myself, and I'll add some concealing pine or hardwood foliage if I think the situation merits.

I also like to add a hanger hook or

It's true that deer seldom look up, but you can help yourself see more deer within bowshot range by wearing camouflage clothing even when you're located above ground.

two, so I can hang my bow, bow quiver (removed from the bow for ease in shooting and silence), a spare jacket, small backpack containing lunch, thermos and so on, binoculars, whatever I happen to have along. These hooks can be made out of tailored sections of metal coathangers lashed to the tree with twine, or simply a couple of large nails the landowner has given me permission to put in place. The hook holding my bow, in particular, must be within easy reach and positioned so that I can get the bow and its nocked arrow in hand without making noise or undue motion. If the situation allows, I'll sometimes rest my "loaded" bow atop the two side rails; then all I have to do is reach out and pick it up and I'm ready to shoot.

As mentioned before, it's never a good idea to do much twig and limb trimming in the vicinity of your treestand. Any deer native to the area (and that means almost every deer you'll see) has been past this spot dozens of times; he or she knows what the spot looks like, including the rough pattern of sunlight reaching the woodland floor. Trim away much foliage and you let more light through, and this *can* spook a wary deer. I know it sounds remote, but it can and will happen. You must have a clear shooting lane from stand to anticipated target area, of course, but not so much that you have to clear a highway from one to the other. Besides, it's smart to do a little neck-craning and decide on maybe three spots where your deer is likely to be walking or standing when you shoot, clear a very narrow lane to those spots, and pretty much ignore the others. Reading the tracks and other sign near your stand will help you determine where these spots are.

A tip mentioned in Erwin Bauer's fine

This stand from Scientific Atlanta is extremely sturdy and offers its own climbing ladder. It's one of the author's favorites.

illustrated deer book, *Deer In Their World*, is to use the whitetail's own droppings as a scent mask in the immediate area of your stand. The idea is to gather fresh droppings while scouting or when enroute to your stand, and then distribute them on the ground in a rough circle around your stand. Deer are used to scenting their own species' body waste, and this is a good way to help them miss any human aroma re-

Gary Behnker shows the proper use of an all-fiberglass stand with its own carryall satchel attached.

maining around your stand. Don't worry about touching deer droppings with gloved hands either. They won't bite you.

A virtually costless yet effective treestand is simply a one-inch-thick two-by three-foot board with a shallow V cut into each end. Drill a hole in each of the board's four corners and fit each hole with a stout piece of rope. The idea is to wedge this board into a handy tree crotch and then lash it tightly into place. I make sure I take several yards of extra rope, lashing it back and forth on the far side of the crotch where the board platform is to be used. The rope gives me a backrest and added security and I lash it back and forth, sort of like the backrest of a rattan chair. This casual treestand doesn't offer a place to sit down, of course.

Some stands, particularly the old wooden stands that have been in place for several years, weather poorly, split, and just don't remain safe. For this reason, Westervelt Lodge in Alabama insists that any visiting hunter desiring a treestand must provide his own portable stand. I believe the decision was made for insurance purposes. Having clients fall isn't the best advertising in the world.

But old stands don't have to fall to ruin your day. They can just as easily remain standing and ruin your day. An old wooden platform I'd scaled on Kentucky's Lexington-Blue Grass Army Depot, near Richmond, did enough creaking and squeaking to keep a very respectable 12-point buck inside some maple saplings and effectively screened from my arrow. He was content to bed down there, face in my direction, and try to figure out what was making those funny little sounds when old wood planks rubbed against rusty nails. I stayed in the tree and fumed. The buck remained in his bed and chewed his cud. He was happier than I was.

I've heard experienced hunters insist that treestands are most effective when other hunters are in the woods. I think this is true except during the peak of the rut. Before and after the peak, it may take the movements and crashing of other hunters moving about to get an appreciable number of deer to move during the middle of the day; and in this way the bowhunter who stays put right through the lunch hour and early afternoon can see deer while others are walking out to lunch and a warm dinner.

During the very peak of the rut, however, there's no predicting when that big buck is going to move through his home territory in search of does. I've seen them do it at high noon and you probably have too. Bucks in rut, particularly the larger dominant animals, move about their range night and day and spend little time feeding or resting, so strong is their sex urge. So it's evident that the more time you spend on your treestand during deer season, the better your chances of seeing Mr. Big. Oh, I know you've heard that time after time, and it always sounds as if someone is trying to get you to invest your time in something with an infinitely small chance of succeeding. The only thing is, it's *true.* As Doug Crabtree said, "You can't kill that buck in your living room or garage." You gotta be out there on stand.

An old book on bowhunting insists that all bowhunters get bored on stand and soon lose their mental sharpness. On the contrary. There are ways to avoid boredom, and I've used them.

The best way is to put your attention

Ronnie Grooms, an avid Florida bowhunter, took this nice 8-pointer when it came to feed under Grooms' stand in a hardwood tree. *Westervelt Lodge*

on what is going on around you in the woods. There is always *something* you can watch—a chickadee hopping among the deadfalls, a fox squirrel in search of last summer's morsels of nuts, maybe a red-tailed hawk flying high overhead. I've always found something to watch, and it helps until deer show up.

One time I had a chipmunk crawl all over my left gloved hand and arm, maybe thinking them a strange sort of log. And a friend of mine from West Germany,

Elert von Müeller, was positively enthralled by a red-breasted little songbird that landed on his boot while he was stand-hunting in central Ontario. There's always something to watch. Your job is to discover it and keep the boredom at arm's length. And by the way, Elert came back to camp with a filled game tag that evening, but it was the bird, not the trophy, that filled his tale that evening.

At least half of the white-tailed deer that fall to bowhunters each year in North America are taken by hunters in one sort of treestand or another, be it a big old oak tree or a commercial platform you shinny up a hickory bole on the edge of a cornfield. Perhaps the best single benefit of any sort of treestand is that it forces its user to stay in one place and use his eyes and ears instead of his legs for a change. And when you think about it, that isn't all bad.

5

Ground Stands

I'll take a ground stand over a tree platform any time I feel the ground position won't hinder my chances to see deer within bowshot. I know this bucks the commonly accepted idea that elevated stands are best, but my reasons for preferring ground stands are at least worth mentioning here.

In the first place, I simply feel more relaxed with my feet on the ground. I'm not particularly fearful of heights, but of all the tree platforms I've used over the years, only half a dozen or so were roomy and sturdy enough to allow me the precision aim necessary to put that arrow exactly where I want it: behind the shoulder and into the lungs of a whitetail or mulie. And because stand hunting means silent, near-motionless waiting for hours on end, it's vitally im-

portant to be relaxed and alert; for me, this means on the ground.

When you stand at ground level, all of your shots are likely to be at targets on your own level. This eliminates having to allow for the downward angle of a shot taken from a tree. There have been times when I've forgotten to allow for this angle, only to see my shaft either miss the deer altogether or tickle his withers as it sailed high of the lung area. Several years ago I was bowhunting an Army installation in central Kentucky from a treestand, and for more than an hour had watched four doe whitetails and a 10-point buck feed in an open oak woods behind me. The animals finally moved closer to my tree until the buck was broadside, head down as he nuzzled the leaf carpet for acorns, no more

Ground stands are tougher than treestands because you're right at deer level. Yet this is the author's favorite way to bowhunt deer because it calls for woodsmanship and stealth.

than 15 feet from the base of the tree. I slowly drew my recurve, came to anchor, took a steady aim and released— only to see my arrow fletching brush the smooth hair atop the big buck's withers. He bucked like a mule, ending up 30 yards from my tree but screened by some maple saplings. The does stared at the buck as if he'd gone crazy, then continued to feed as if the whole thing hadn't

happened. That was only the first of several times I've misjudged the angle of arrow flight from a treestand, and now I hunt on the ground when I can, secure in the knowledge that I can indeed see deer at close range without having to climb into a tree.

But what about human scent, I can hear you thinking. The whole purpose of treestand hunting is to get the man-scent above ground level, isn't it? And doesn't ground-stand hunting spread scent around?

Not if you're careful. In the first place, treestand hunting does little to keep your scent away from downwind deer. Scent tends to spread as it moves away from its source—so much so that you might as well forget about seeing deer within decent range downwind from your location, regardless of whether you're in a tree or on the ground. If the area you're hunting has a prevailing wind direction, then by all means add this to your planning when scouting and building your stand. The scent carried by even the gentlest breeze forms a sort of corridor along which any deer with half a nose is going to detect your scent and immediately leave the area. You might as well know this in advance and use that corridor to travel to and from the stand, being careful to touch little or no underbrush, tree limbs and so on while enroute. And since it's nearly impossible to remain fully alert to a full 360-degree circle around you while standing, you can forget all thoughts of seeing deer directly downwind. It simply won't happen, unless you catch a glimpse of a deer's tail or antlers as it bounds away. Concentrate on those areas and vistas upwind and on both sides, for that is where you'll see 99 percent of the game.

What makes a good, productive ground stand? In a word, *cover*, but this word has two meanings for the ground-standing hunter. Not only must you be able to cover the surrounding area with your eyes without having blind spots caused by natural obstructions such as dense thickets, logpiles and so forth, but you must be in heavy enough cover to hide your silhouette and small move-ments from the ever-sharp eyes of deer. Sometimes selecting the right spot for a stand means using a large fallen tree trunk, because of the cover and elevation it provides, and sometimes it means selecting a stand *below* the surrounding ground level, such as just over the edge of a wide creek valley. Let's take a closer look at a few typical situations calling for ground stands of various types.

Let's say the area you hunt is fairly level and lightly wooded, perhaps on the edge of a cropfield of corn or soy-

If you're a careful (and lucky) watcher, you'll see wall-hanger bucks such as this one. *Ohio DNR*

beans known to be visited regularly by deer. There are no abrupt terrain features that might offer natural site selection, such as a low hill, so you have to make do with what you've got. Through a little scouting, you've already determined where the deer are entering and departing the cropfield and you want to locate your stand within easy bow range of one of these travel points. Check the wind so you can set up your stand downwind from the deer's expected line of approach; no sense alerting them to your presence, right? Once you've determined the downwind side, you've begun to locate your stand site by the process of elimination. Now you should look for natural spots where you might set up your ground stand. Look for small clumps of bushes or saplings, a little stand of cedars, perhaps, or a few large tree trunks growing close together. What we're looking for here is some natural feature that's large enough to conceal your presence, something the deer are used to seeing there and are therefore not afraid to approach. Maybe, upon entering the field, the deer pass close by a thick little stand of willows or sassafras trees. Remember, the cover you're looking for needn't be much larger than the approximate size of a phone booth, just large enough to hide your standing figure.

It can also make sense to stand in *front* of some natural feature as opposed to standing behind cover. Your silhouette, even on a dark, overcast day, is apparent to wary-eyed deer because it's out of place. You're hunting in the deer's backyard, a place they know like you know your living room, and if you don't take measures to disguise that shape of

yours, the deer will pick it up and depart. Period.

So, depending on the situation, stand in front of something larger than yourself—a wide tree trunk, a dense thicket, maybe a large, bulky bush, anything that will help your silhouette blend into the area.

If you stand in front of a natural feature, there should at least be some light cover between you and the deer, to allow for the minimal movements needed to turn your head from side to side, ever so slowly, as you look for approaching deer, and of course the movements needed to come to full draw when the big moment arrives. The better job of camouflaging yourself you've done before going afield, the less cover you'll need between you and the deer. Camouflage is covered in detail elsewhere in this book, but I mention it here because how well you blend into your immediate surroundings is a factor in choosing those surroundings to begin with. This is especially important if your stand is directly at ground level, at eye level with the deer.

Another choice open to the ground-standing hunter, provided the area offers it, is what I call the upground stand, which is sort of a compromise between a treestand and a ground stand. Simply put, the upground stand means utilizing whatever large, solid object nature provides. It could be a large fallen tree trunk, an abrupt, small hillock, perhaps a large, flat-topped trunk stump—almost anything that'll give you a bit of elevation above the surrounding terrain for a better field of view.

I first used an upground stand while photographing whitetails in Kentucky

Although this hunter stands in a small opening, he is almost impossible to see distinctly because of the camo he wears from head to toe. Bow camouflage would help here.

The Johnny Stewart Pop-Up Stand serves well when located amid surrounding brush. Be sure to take a folding camp stool along for those long between-deer waits.

for a magazine article. I knew the deer would approach through an open hardwoods, and there was no way I could remain right at ground level without being seen, so I found a spot where a mature maple had toppled into its neighboring tree. The fallen maple's trunk provided a handy slanting ramp and I scampered up the trunk and remained still among the tangle of limbs where the two trees met, camera in hand and ready. Sure enough, along came a fat doe that not only walked unalerted well within camera range, but stopped as if on cue smack in the middle of a spot of sunlight filtering through the overhead branches. I got the photos I needed and the deer was never the wiser. The only clue she had to my presence was the clicking of my camera every time I snapped another frame—and the deer looked in every direction except at me, less than five feet off the ground and no more than 15 feet away from her.

A nice thing about fallen tree trunks as upground stands—especially those that have been lying on the ground for a year or so—is that the deer have become so used to seeing them every day that they often ignore them. One early morning in Nebraska I had a buck not only walk directly up to the fallen trunk on which I was standing, but actually make his bed among the tangle of limbs and fallen leaves almost at my feet. I admit that I didn't put an arrow in that buck. I was having too much fun taking peanuts from my pocket and dropping them, one at a time, onto the bedded buck's back. The buck would snort and his hide would shiver every time a peanut tickled his withers, and when my supply of peanuts was about exhausted, the buck got up, looked all around him, and went to find a less annoying spot for his day bed. I had a heck of a time trying not to laugh and give myself away.

Another time, in Kentucky, I was perched atop a rather large old beech trunk. My hunt had begun before first light and I'd driven nearly all night to arrive on time, and my eyelids got heavier and heavier as the dawn got brighter. I must have dozed, leaning as I was against a beech limb, and when I awoke I was staring directly into the eyes of a whitetail fawn that had me positively boresighted. Moving along near my stand with its mother, the young animal had hopped atop a low hill that put it on a level with my position, and it had caught the slight movement of my breathing. The fawn's white flag slowly came up as it stood and watched me. The doe quickly picked up her youngster's signal of alarm, and the two of them went bounding away across a large meadow. I hadn't noticed that little hillock before. If I had, I wouldn't have chosen that particular tree trunk for an up-ground location. This sort of experience illustrates how important it is to look around before making final selection of a place to wait for deer to come by. You wouldn't choose a treestand with a tall hill directly behind it, because deer moving along that hill would be at eye level with you. The same principle applies to a stand at or near ground level: Assess the surroundings before making a final choice.

Last autumn I was hunting a military installation in a southern state. The place was packed with whitetails, and in one afternoon's standing I saw a total of 27 deer, many of them within reasonable bow range. I used just two locations on that hunt, both of them consisting of fallen logs on which I sat. One was very large and offered cover in and among the limbs of the tree itself. The other was right out in the open, in a spot where a tiny brook formed a U around a two-foot-thick log that had fallen years before. The large trunk allowed me some freedom of (slow) movement, but when I moved to the more open location I had to sit completely still. It worked. During the 90 minutes or so that I sat on the completely exposed log, five deer walked to within 25 feet of my location, and although several of them stared hard at me for a few seconds, none saw me so much as blink and all of them quickly

dismissed me as an odd-looking part of the terrain and continued about their business. When the buck I wanted finally came along, in the company of two does, I had a heck of a time bringing my bow up to shoulder level and then coming to full draw without them seeing me, but the deer helped me out by walking on the far side of a little copse of saplings, allowing me a moment's unnoticed movement. The shot was level, relaxed, and at a range of exactly 26 yards (I later paced off from ground stand to point of arrow impact). I should add that I helped myself a bit with a few drops of scent on my boots and pantlegs while using the open stand location, but the fact remains that a standing hunter *can* remain in the open if he watches wind direction and manages to sit or stand still when deer are in the area.

A variation of the ground stand that I've used successfully is called creekbed standing, for lack of a better term. It requires a bit of a special terrain, but this sort of ground feature is common enough to be useful almost everywhere.

What you need is the sort of woodland creekbed that's been a part of the landscape long enough to have dug a pretty wide little valley for itself. To illustrate what I mean, let me describe a creekbed that I hunted on Georgia's Burnt Pine Plantation.

The creek itself wasn't more than five feet wide, and was fairly shallow. The water ran through a six-feet-wide natural trough, but the creek apparently flooded with some regularity because it had carved out a 30-yard-wide secondary bed that was perhaps six or seven feet below the level of the surrounding terrain. Middle-aged mast-bearing trees grew in this secondary creekbed as well as in the surrounding woods, and it was my hope that deer would either come here to feed on the acorns, hickory nuts and so forth, or perhaps use the wide secondary bed as a travel route offering some cover. As it turned out, I was correct on both counts.

I took a friend, a non-believer in my creekbed method, along with me that morning, and we got down into the secondary bed with our backs against a couple of large hickories when dawn was just a hint off to the east. Each of us sat on the hickories' protruding tree roots and we tried to keep our movements and sounds to a minimum. I remember glancing at my partner's face in the dim predawn light and seeing a smirk of disbelief there. If ever I prayed for deer to show up, it was right then. I knew my creekbed method worked, but my companion didn't, and nothing would wipe that smile off his face like the appearance of deer within bow range. We sat and listened to the dew drop off the trees, pattering lightly onto the leafy carpet all around us. A gray squirrel clawed its way down a nearby pinoak, eyed us momentarily, and humped off through the leaves on some errand. Then the deer showed up.

An 8-point buck and four does, all heads down, noses nuzzling the leaves for mast hidden beneath the carpet, showed dimly in the early half-light off to our left. At first all I could make out was a little gathering of dark forms that moved independently, but then I was able to identify the shapes as deer moving slowly down the secondary creek valley. A doe picked up her head, and, eyes and ears mildly alert, briefly scanned the area before her, trim jaws munching on acorn meat, then dropped

her head to locate more food. I stiffened involuntarily, touched my companion's knee while nodding slightly off to our left, and pivoted on the hickory root in order to face the deer. My partner was all eyes and ears at this point, the smirk forgotten. Funny how a few deer can make a believer out of just about anyone.

The little herd of whitetails fed closer and closer. When most of the deer were on the far side of some poplar trunks, I quickly raised the bow and came to full draw. There was my buck on the far side of the little herd; if only he'd separate himself and give me a clear broadside shot! As it turned out, I had to snake my arrow between two does to reach the buck's boiler room. When the shaft smacked home, all five deer scattered. One spooked doe nearly ran the two of us down as she fled in our direction; she leaped over us and the hickory roots and thudded out of sight. The buck tried to run up the opposite side of the little valley, changed his mind and went bounding off to my right. We found him 20 minutes later, piled up against an oak trunk, stone dead.

That very evening I could have arrowed a second buck, this one a hefty 6-pointer that came snuffling by, hound-like, after a doe that had passed us a few minutes earlier. Once again, both the doe and the following buck passed by two hunters sitting in full view just under the lip of the little valley, maybe 50 feet from the edge of the creek. Both of those deer approached us directly from the rear; the doe was close enough for me to touch her with my bow limb when she passed, and neither she nor the buck had any inkling that man was anywhere about.

If the creekbed method had worked

The ability to return to a remote stand location is helped by the use of a compass. This clip-on model weighs little but provides you a constant directional check.

just once or twice, it would be easy to write off such success as a fluke, something not worth trying. But I have used it time after time, season after season, and there is no good reason why you can't take advantage of the same method in your hunting area, for whitetails or mule deer.

In fact, you don't really need a bona-fide creekbed at all, if none is handy. I've done well using just the base of a hill for my ground stand.

To illustrate this point, two instances in Kentucky come to mind. Late one morning I took up a ground stand at the base of a little dropoff in terrain, where the ground level fell rather steeply from one level, down perhaps 20 feet to a lower level. As I moved into place beside a couple of medium-sized hard-wood trees, I noted where the autumn leaves on the ground had been disturbed, marking a casual path of sorts directly down the little hillside, as if one or two deer had come running over the lip of the hill and down the slope. The disturbed leaves were only an arm's length away from me, and I remember thinking, "Boy, if a buck comes running down this path while I'm here, he'll just about run me down." That's exactly what happened too. Five minutes later I heard a disturbance above me and a 7-point buck came galloping over the rim of the hill and by me close enough to touch. The buck stopped 15 feet away to take a closer look at whatever it was he'd just run by, and the two of us stared at each other in complete, disarming amazement. He bolted away when I raised my bow, and my arrow sailed somewhere over his back. As luck would have it, however, this same buck ran under a hunting companion's treestand moments later and fell to one well-placed arrow through the lungs.

An hour later, I was seated on another hillside about 75 yards from the first when a 4-pointer came sidling out of a wooded draw and stopped, broadside, about 60 yards in front of me. I had plenty of time to put the 50-yard pin on my bowsight a few inches above his back while he stared off across a long meadow. The Easton shaft went true, passing all the way through the buck's lung area, and he ran only 30 yards or so before piling up.

Both of those deer came well within bow range, and neither saw me until it was too late. On each occasion I was situated on a sidehill with little or no cover around me. True, I moved as little as possible, and when I did I moved in super-slow motion, but I *was* in plain view, especially for an animal as sharp-sighted and attuned to movement as the whitetail. In each case (and this is im-

portant), I was located in front of something large that broke up my silhouette; I am sure that even the human eye, with its ability to discern color, would have had a tough time spotting me until I moved. In fact, my hunting experience tells me that undisturbed deer are most anxious to get on with their daily activities, moving slowly and normally from place to place along established routes, provided the hunter blends into the surroundings and doesn't call attention to himself. Success at blending in, in deed as well as in appearance, is extremely important for all deer hunters using the bow, and especially so for the hunter using a ground stand.

At the beginning of this chapter I stated that a ground stand is steadier than almost any treestand. Besides making the hunter feel more comfortable, and therefore a better, more relaxed shot, comfort, at least as far as balance is concerned, is only part of the story. It's likely you've hunted from a tree platform from time to time, so the following won't come as any great surprise.

Treestands age. The nails holding the 2×4s in place rust and loosen, wooden supports and planks shrink and crack, even the wooden steps often used to provide access become unsafe and noisy. More than once I've had the platform on which I was standing pick precisely the wrong moment to shift position slightly or, worse, give a loud squeak just when the buck I'd been watching for 15 minutes was about to move within range of my bow. More often than not, such an out-of-place little sound is all it takes to send that wary trophy trotting off, through little or no fault of the hunter above. Treestands just *do* that.

With a ground stand, on the other

hand, I *know* that my footing is solid. I can relax physically while keeping my mind, eyes and ears alert to the surroundings. I avoid noise on ground stands by clearing away dry, noisy leaves, twigs and other forest duff before I take up position. If any little branch or twig threatens to scrape bow, arrow or sleeves on stand, should I need to turn left or right to face an oncoming deer, I determine this ahead of time and trim away the offending foliage with a pocketknife. Be sure you remember to deposit all tree, bush and other trimmings well away from your stand, too. Trimmed branches and such that are left in the immediate area can alert deer that all isn't as it should be. Keep in mind that a deer knows its home bailiwick as well as you know yours, and a pile of freshly cut greenery will be noticed as out of place, and it will be avoided—often to the extent that you won't see deer in the area at all for at least a few days. Deer can smell freshly cut twigs and so forth without actually seeing them, so do yourself a favor and keep cuttings well away from your stand.

Soft-finish outer garments are also a must when hunting on the ground, and this is true for still-hunting as well as stand hunting. Hard-shell jackets simply make too much racket when scraped against branches, weeds and so on. The same applies to nylon jackets, leather-fronted hunting pants, most leather gloves, and the popular but oh-so-noisy hard-finished hunting caps. The deer woods are not silent, by any means. Birds, small mammals and even the deer themselves make small noises from time to time, but abrupt and unnatural scraping noises will send wary deer to parts unknown if you don't dress quietly.

I once managed to spook a small herd of Rocky Mountain mule deer because I was wearing a heavy jacket with a hard finish, and because it had been several days since I'd shaved. I was on stand inside a little copse of jackpines when I heard the deer approach through the woods to my left. I slowly turned my head in that direction, but my chin whiskers scraped against the jacket collar, upturned against the cold. That's all it took. The deer heard the scraping sound, paused, and then skedaddled over the mountain and out of sight. I agree that it was a rather freak way to *not* see deer, but I spent the rest of that day trying to get the guys in camp to believe me. Little sounds mean a lot. Prevent them any way you can.

There are some stands that are called ground stands because those who use them don't know what other moniker to use. A friend of mine has arrowed two decent whitetail bucks through the sagging open window of an abandoned farmhouse. He discovered before the season opened that deer were passing within 15 yards of the window enroute to an old orchard on the place, and he simply put himself inside the house and stuck his two deer right through the window. I suppose this is a sort of ground stand, but you'd have to arrange for the deer to make house calls before it'll work.

Another hunter friend of mine who lives in southern Alabama noticed that a certain buck, accompanied by a pair of does, came meandering through his brushy side yard every evening when it got to be about half dark. He made sure nothing disturbed the deer's travels and waited for the season to open, and when it did he was waiting behind the corner of his garage when the threesome came pacing across the road and through his property. "There's some who'd say I got that venison unfair, but when it prac'ly walks into my kitchen, I ain't gonna turn it down," he later explained. We shared a venison roast a few evenings after the event, and I honestly couldn't tell the difference between his deer and those I'd spent long hours seeking in some distant woodlands. Not on the fork, anyway.

Southern deer hunters, and those in a few Canadian provinces, have long employed the use of specially trained deer hounds to push game before waiting hunters. On the hound hunts that I've shared, the hunters remained smack at ground level while the hounds rousted the deer and got them moving. I agree that a pursued deer isn't as vigilant of his surroundings as is the deer moving slowly through his habitat, but the fact remains that southern hunters take a lot of deer every year, and many of them do it with both feet planted firmly on the ground. Hound hunters seldom resort to raised platforms to see deer and get their shots. The same can be said for still-hunters and those who drive their deer with hunting buddies. All of which serves to prove that you don't have to get above the deer to get on top of the sport and be successful at it.

If there is one short fact or statement to be distilled from all of this, I believe it to be simply this: Be flexible. Look at your hunting situation thoughtfully, balance the physical conditions of your surroundings, deer movements, and so on against your personal preferences and physical health, and then come up with what is best for you. Hunting from the ground is relatively easy and non-exertive, and it is successful much of the time. I know of no hunting method that needs more argument than that to make it a regular part of a successful technique.

6

Still-Hunting: The Ultimate Challenge

Still-hunting equals supreme woodsmanship. Write that across the back of your hunting bow's upper limb so you won't ever forget it.

Still-hunting means moving slowly —s-l-o-w-l-y—through suspected deer hideouts in hope that you'll see and get a shot at a normally very alert animal before it sees you, smells you, hears you and even suspects you're anywhere around.

Still-hunting means sharpening your own senses to the point where you'll pick up the tiny sound of a deer walking some distance away in a quiet woods. It means noticing the tiniest flicker of a bedded doe's leg as she reaches to scratch with one hind foot, or the flop of an ear when the afternoon insects descend on that little herd you've been trying to locate all morning.

An accomplished still-hunter is, in my humble opinion, the very best deer hunter around. He knows when to move and when not to, and for how long. He knows how to use weather conditions to help him move quietly and unseen among deer, and he just as readily knows what types of weather don't lend themselves to this kind of hunting style, so he either changes his style for the day, or he stays home in bed.

Some still-hunters get into the woods a month or so before bow season opens. They move through all the best deer cover, bedding areas, travel routes and so forth until they pick up one particularly huge set of tracks. From this point on, all other deer might as well not exist, because for this hunter in this season, it will be Mr. Big—this *particular* Mr. Big—or no deer at all. A serious

Deer tracks in an old woods road. Deer often use these abandoned roadways to travel to and from feeding areas, making them ideal for the hunter who's studying whitetails.

still-hunter will then spend even more time in the woods, following those big tracks day after day, getting to know over several weeks where the buck beds, where he goes to feed, and when in each day's 24 hours the buck chooses to move and make himself available. And very often, when season's end rolls around, that particular Mr. Big is drawing ooohs and ahhs in some taxidermist's workshop.

Other still-hunters pick up a big set of tracks and stay on them all day, two days if necessary, until hunter and buck meet within bow range. It takes more than luck to stay on a buck's trail and finally kill that buck. It takes woodsmanship.

And other hunters of the still art merely move slowly through areas they know to contain deer, spotting some deer, some bucks, but holding out for something worthy of a place on the wall. Perhaps they spot a good buck 80 yards off through the woods or in the edge of a clearing. They know how to use stealth to get within clear range, and then how to pull that bow without spooking the trophy.

Most hunters use stands, either on the ground or on platforms built in trees that overlook deer routes. Most hunters do this for two very sound reasons: It works, and it's easier than still-hunting or even driving. In fact, the question can be asked, why still-hunt at all if other hunting methods work? Why not perch on a treestand like everyone else?

The same reason applies to fishermen who restrict themselves to the use of flyrods and feathered lures: The method adds an extra measure of challenge and excitement to the sport. Still-hunting doesn't always produce physical results. But that's to be expected because it is, I think, infinitely more difficult to sneak up on a buck than to let that same buck amble unawares to the spot where you're hidden. *Let the game come to you* is an old and good hunter's axiom, but for the still-hunter, the "game" is how you get close to the deer, and not seeing the buck only as a dead trophy to be loaded into a pickup truck and toted home.

I still-hunt now and again because it lets me move. I'm a person who can quickly become cold, bored and discontent on a stand, be it on the ground or in a tree. I long to get up on my feet, move around, see new places and maybe, just maybe, spot a deer before it sees me. If I can get within range of the deer and it still hasn't seen me, it makes no difference whether that animal is a 6-month-old doe or a 12-point buck. I've counted my personal coup, beat the beast in its own backyard, and my day is complete—whether I shoot it or not.

I know few hunters who still-hunt exclusively; most in my acquaintance combine standing with a little still-hunting when they've been on stand for what seems like years, nothing of note has ambled by, and whatever they're sitting on has grown a lump or a knot that's paining the old butt bone. So they get up and move around, stretch cramped muscles and do a little still-hunting.

Dave Borgeson, chief of inland fisheries for the state of Michigan's resources department, gets his whitetail buck every year, most of the time from either treestands or ground stands. But, as with most of us, it feels good to get up and walk after a long time in one spot, and this is when still-hunting methods come into use. "I'll still-hunt occasionally," Borgeson told me. "But if you're going to still-hunt you have to stop a lot. If you don't stop a lot, the deer are going to see you before you see them. I don't think any hunter can do a good job of looking and listening for deer while he's walking." Borgeson said he uses the sandy backroads threading through much of Michigan's forestland for still-hunting. "The sand lets me move pretty quietly, and occasionally I'll see

Here's lookin' at ya! This buck heard my camera's click and ambled over for a closer look. I never see them this way during bow season.

some nice deer before they see me. I've gotten pretty close to some of them, too." Borgeson carries a powerful bow, a pocket compass, wears old and soft camouflage clothing, and is one of the best bowhunters I've ever hunted with. He works hard at it, and his record of sticking his buck every year is proof of the pudding.

Dave Morris, who operates Burnt Pine Plantation in Georgia, also likes to use old forest roads for still-hunting, espe-

Where to look for deer can be a problem. One solution is the public hunting area. Ask the area manager for specific locations.

cially when it's been raining and the woods are quiet.

"When the ground and the leaves are wet, I like to sort of slip through the woods on some of our old roads," Morris said. "With the leaves on the ground quiet, I can slip up on some pretty good bucks without them knowing it—close enough to take a shot with my bow. I tell some of our visiting bowhunters to try the same thing because it's an effective way to get close to deer."

I've used the same method elsewhere, hunting old woods roads from time to time. These old roads were built for the smaller, narrower vehicles in use earlier in this century, and they are often perfect for the quietly moving archer. With screens of trees on both sides, I can slowly ease along, stopping every half a dozen paces or so to look intently into the woods on both sides for any sign of movement, or a patch of color, that's out of place, something to give away a deer's presence. Because these roads are partially overgrown and seldom used by vehicles, deer have no qualms about crossing them as they browse, or even bedding down on their brushy edges. Finding what looks like a fresh set of deer tracks in the roadway is always reason to stop, determine the deer's direction of travel, and then do some especially intent looking and listening off the road in the proper direction. If you can see the deer before it knows you're around, you can keep an eye on it and try to ease up on it for a shot.

I spotted a bedded forkhorn within 20 feet of a Georgia tote road some seasons back, and, by keeping one eye on the deer and another on where I was putting my feet (there are rattlers in those woods), I was able to get within 25 yards of the deer without letting him know I was there. Then I was confronted by a problem: The buck was bedded smack in the middle of some sparse waist-high weeds, and there was no way I could snake an arrow to him without ticking a weed or two. So I came to full draw and then gave a little whistle; he got to his feet and began looking in every direction except mine, and the shot was an easy one taken at a completely relaxed animal.

While it's true that any bowhunter who wishes to move through deer country on his own two feet is, by definition, a still-hunter, it's also true that you can adapt your tackle and your outfit, not to mention the right kind of weather conditions, to help make your efforts successful. Let's look at some of the things you can do.

Use the Weather

The quieter you can remain as you still-hunt, the more effective you will be. Naturally, damp weather moistens fallen leaves, twigs and so forth, making it much easier to walk silently or nearly so, so choose damp weather for the still-hunt if you can.

Deer also seem to be less alert in a light drizzle, the kind of penetrating moisture that can make an improperly dressed hunter miserable beyond words. Yet it's a fact that whitetails often react to light rainfall by herding in small groups. Sometimes these little herds gather in tight cover and stay there until the weather improves, and sometimes they seem to ignore the wet and get on with the business of feeding. Only a deer could explain the differences in reaction, but it's nonetheless true that deer

You can also use a telephoto lens for close-up looks at distant deer, with the added advantage of snapping a picture of the animal.

in rain are less alert, perhaps because the damp woods make less noise or because the patter of light rain on leaves and other objects makes sound detection tougher.

Of course, no sooner is the hunt-the-rain suggestion made than along comes the objection that rainfall washes out blood trails and risks lost deer. This is certainly possible. Jim Kunde, an avid archer, and I were hunting in Kentucky a few years back when he arrowed a dandy 8-pointer in a light misting rain, tracked it for a good quarter-mile, and then felt his heart hit his shoes when the blood trail ended, washed out by the rainfall. It's a risk to take a shot at a deer in the wet woods, especially if more rain is predicted for that day, but if you do a good job of still-hunting, you'll be close enough to the buck to place your shaft carefully through his pumphouse, he'll bleed out quickly, and drop only a short distance away where you can find him easily.

A large tract of riverbottom land that I hunt can quickly be under the spreading floodwaters of the river nearby, and when this happens I know from past experience that approaching floodwaters will concentrate the deer on a few pieces of high terrain in the area. This naturally makes the still-hunter's job a lot easier. This sort of temporary concentration is unnatural or at least infrequent for the deer, and has been known to make them nervous and tough to approach, but few are the hunters who would pass up the chance to try for a lot of deer in a relatively small piece of woods. Like salmon concentrating in one pool of a spawning river, flood-crowded deer are the sort of bonus that nature provides once in a while.

Clothing Choices

The usual head-to-toe camouflage clothing used by most bowhunters serves fine for the still-hunter, with a few minor adaptations.

Footwear is important because whatever you wear on your feet touches the ground, and whatever touches the ground makes noise. Soft-soled footwear makes less noise than the usual leather hunting boot with cleated or smooth soles. A friend uses knee-length leather moccasins with tough but relatively soft soles; such soles let him get a feel for what lies underfoot during a stalk, and this in turn enables him to avoid noisy forest duff such as dry twigs or clusters of crunchy fallen leaves. The high-top length of the moccasins, which he calls Apache boots, probably would offer some protection against snakebites. He can also spray foul-smelling masking scents on his boots until the cows retch, since he always stores his hunting gear in the garage, away from the family's dainty sniffers.

Besides these advantages, the moccasins' outer surface is made of soft-tanned moose hide, which is quiet in the woods. Moose hide, by the way, is a soft but extremely tough leather containing large natural pores that admit air and let the feet and lower legs breathe, even inside heavy hunting socks.

I'd rule out tennis shoes and similar footwear for still-hunting because their canvas construction and low profile offer little or no foot protection, they can become saturated with water the first time you have to cross a creek or step on wet leaves, and even their color (normally all white) is a giveaway. Far better to invest in the right kind of footwear, even if it is somewhat expensive, and give your feet and legs proper protection and your still-hunt skills a chance to succeed.

Your outer clothing—and normally this means camo shirt and pants and maybe a jacket of the same design—should be soft to the touch so it doesn't scrape when you ease your way through a sapling thicket or bramble jungle. I remember seeing the jacket photograph on a bowhunting book that was published some years ago, and among the many errors illustrated by the so-called hunter's clothing was a bright yellow nylon shell jacket, complete with chrome-finished snap closures, and faded blue jeans. I believe the photo pictured the book author, and it made me wonder if the guy had the first inkling of what it takes to move quietly in the woods. A nylon shell jacket, or any outer garment with a relatively hard finish, might as well be a siren and flashing lights in deer country. The garment scrapes loudly every time it's touched by tree limbs, leaves, bushes, downed timber, you name it. Shoot, the darned thing even makes noise all by itself when a sleeve scrapes against the side of the jacket, or when the hunter's three-day-old chin stubble scrapes against the collar. The blue jeans worn by the "hunter" had been machine washed so many times that they were nearly white, and in a dawn or dusk woods, or even at full dark, such washed-out jeans show up like an airplane's landing lights. If it weren't for such things as infringement of copyrights, I'd run that jacket photo in this chapter with the simple caption: Don't Do This. But authors and book publishers are touchy people and have other people arrested for things like that.

But don't *you* be that knucklehead bowhunter. Think QUIET.

Because the still-hunter does move pretty much all day long, interspersed with periods of immobility while he looks, listens and thinks like a deer, excessively heavy clothing usually isn't necessary because movement encourages body heat and therefore comfort. You should wear enough clothes to remain warm and dry, however. A few types of the new long underwear are designed to keep body moisture (sweat to you pigs out there) away from the skin's surface. The fabrics actually wick moisture away from the skin, keeping the skin dry, and this lets natural body heat maintain your comfort, even when you exert yourself and work up a bit of a sweat on the uphills. When I was new to bowhunting quite a while back, I hunted the thick pine woods of New Hampshire with a friend, using snowshoes. We hiked around all morning, and when we stopped for lunch I began peeling off outer garments until my upper body literally steamed in the cold air. It didn't take long until I was chilled clear through and miserable the rest of the day because of it. Layered clothing, removed if you're too warm and added again if you become chilled, is the way to go if you move around while hunting. This can be important even in mild weather.

Last season I bought a warm camouflage-finish waist-length jacket. Because of its design, it's perfect for still-hunting. The sleeve cuffs and the collar are made of stretch-type material that doesn't get in the way of pulling a bow or the release, and the jacket contains four large pockets plus a jacket-width game pocket with zippered closure

If you can see the buck, the buck can probably see you, so choose your deer-watching locations carefully. This curious 8-point walked to within mere feet of my location, and all I had was a camera.

Hiding Your Face and Hands

A new bowhunting book just out as this is written pictures a fully camouflaged hunter pulling his compound. There's one problem, however: His face has no camouflage. The hunter is white and his face shows up among the foliage like a paper plate in a coal bin. He's also wearing sunglasses, which reflect every tiny point of light and defeat all of his other efforts to fade into the brush. He might as well shout "Here, deer!" at the top of his lungs, for all the game he's likely to see.

Don't forget the face and hands. They show up like beacons, particularly because the face and hands are the most often moved and fidgeted-with parts of the body. Some hunters like face nets, such as those worn by turkey hunters, but I much prefer odorless face paint that can be washed off with warm water and soap. Such face paint comes in green, brown and black; by blending these three colors, you can make your face fade right into the terrain. Tubes of special face paint are available from several manufacturers and are available at most sporting goods and archery tackle shops.

I prefer face paint rather than a mask or the like because the paint is right on the face, rather than hanging down over it, and paint doesn't get snagged when I duck under a limb or try to lose myself in a thicket. Also, even the best and thinnest face net impairs vision to a certain degree; this is especially true of peripheral vision, and how many times have you first spotted a deer out of the corner of your eye? I know of one archer who nearly had his scalp torn off when the nock of his chin-anchored arrow somehow became entangled with the

across the rear that's good for toting nylon rope, a plastic sack for heart and liver, a sandwich and maybe a small thermos of hot soup. The jacket's outer surface is soft, and I wear an extra-long arm guard on my bow arm to make sure the sleeve's rather bulky material doesn't catch string slap when I shoot. I paid about $35 for the jacket and it's the best cold-weather garment for still-hunting I've ever found.

face mask he was wearing. When he released the arrow the elastic lanyard holding his mask zipped up and over his head and nearly scalped him. No thanks. I'll go with paint, thank you very much.

Whatever method of camouflaging face and hands you choose, however, I strongly suggest you do *something*. Remember, the still-hunter is down at deer level, which means he is just that much more visible to the game. The hands are best covered with camo-finish gloves made of cotton or some other soft fabric, which can also serve to protect your draw fingers from the ravages of a released bowstring.

The Stop-Step Method

When an animal moves through the woods, it seldom moves as a human does. People generally move at a steady pace, and the sound of that movement is sim-

This appears to be a deer family à la *Bambi*, but it isn't. Bucks remain with the does only long enough to mate, then return to a solitary life. The two deer on the right are yearling twin fawns.

ilarly steady, such as the regular sounds of footfalls in the leaves.

An animal's movements, on the other hand, are seldom regular. The animal changes pace, pauses to test the air or sniff this and that, and generally uses a stop-start rhythm of locomotion. There are few animals in the wilds whose pace approximates that of a walking man; the wild turkey can and often does sound like a man in the woods when it comes striding through dry leaves, but most other creatures do not. It's the same with deer, whose ears are sharp enough to hear each other walking at amazingly long distances. Deer are members of a woodland community of wildlife, all of which use the same areas, so the deer are used to hearing sounds made by these creatures. The flutter of a bird overhead is no cause for alarm to a deer, nor is the scratch of squirrel claws on tree bark.

The still-hunter does far more looking than moving. He may travel only 50 yards in an hour in a very careful attempt to see deer before they spot him. This archer hunts through a Morris County, New Jersey, hardwoods.

Knowing what is likely—and unlikely—to spook deer is vitally important to the still-hunter, because no matter how hard we try, our movements in the woods do cause sounds. The trick is to tailor those sounds as much as possible to approximate natural sounds the deer are used to hearing.

If you still-hunt and therefore move through the woods, you will make noise—with your feet, by ducking under low branches and so on. I'd say the single most important factor in successful still-hunting is to extend the immobile moments, times when you're standing in one spot and using your eyes, ears and reasoning powers. You're not making noise when you stand in one place, and this in itself is reason enough to do more looking than walking. But when you do walk, completely abandon the natural pace of human walking; that is, the steady step-step-step rhythm. Deer know damned well that other deer don't walk that way, and when they hear you coming they are long, long gone before you ever know they're around. Break up your pace. Take three or four or perhaps half a dozen steps, then stop. Look around —*all* around, including back over your shoulder in the direction you came from. If you don't see movement that might be deer right away, make it a habit to look back at the same vista a minute or two later.

Intelligent use of the eyes is important because it lets you see more than you think likely. Let's say you have a strong belief that since deer in fall and winter are a sort of dullish brown-gray color, every deer you see will be that same color. This is fine if every deer you see is standing in broad sunlight, and standing in such a position that its rather shiny coat reflects no sunlight. If every deer stood out in the woods like this, every deer you see would in fact look dullish brown-gray in color. But what about those deer you first spot perhaps 150 yards off through a dark hardwoods, where the tall trees shut off much of the sunlight reaching the ground? These deer do not appear in any color at all, but rather as black (or nearly black) silhouettes. Intelligent looking doesn't lock the looker into seeing any one thing to the exclusion of all others. Very often the first view I've had of deer was the

A good set of binoculars is a must for the deer watcher. They permit you to watch unalerted deer from a safe distance, and they let you look *into* cover instead of at it.

slightest bit of movement in an other-wise quiet scene. Deer passing between tree trunks 100 yards away appear as brief flashes of dark color, and the far-off flick of an ear can easily be missed unless you tune your eyes to see the movement, and tune your brain not to automatically dismiss such tiny move-ment as irrelevant. Sure, that little bit of movement might have been a squirrel just peeking around a tree trunk or a brown leaf fluttering in the breeze from a low-hanging twig. But, it *might* have been part of a deer. Don't dismiss any

movement until you know what caused it, and the only way to do that is to look at it long enough and often enough to see it for what it really is.

Seeing deer movement is important, of course, but even more important is the ability to see a standing deer in a silent, motionless woods. The deer is immobile and so are his surroundings, which is why immobile deer are the toughest to pick out and identify.

Bucks, in particular, seem to spend a great deal of time doing exactly what the good still-hunter does: They stand

Easy does it. Attempting to sneak up on a buck without giving yourself away makes a hunter humble most of the time. *Ohio DNR*

A buck usually voids himself directly in his daybed upon getting to his feet. This nice buck, one of a dozen deer in a fenced area, displays the same behavior as free-roaming deer.

in one spot and use their senses to find out what's happening within range of their eyes and ears and nose. Traveling bucks—those moving from bed to feed, from feeding area to scrapes—are in no hurry unless they've been spooked. They pause for minutes at a time to sense what lies ahead, and have patience beyond description. They just don't move much in any given time period. Because this is how they'll be most of the time, it's important that you be able to see deer that are stock still.

When I hunt in mature or nearly-mature woods, the tree trunks of course resemble vertical lines; they grow up from the ground, and no matter how large or small the tree trunk, it describes a vertical object in the woods. Deer, however, appear as horizontal lines in the woods; the trunk of their bodies from withers to hips, the line of their back or belly line, all describe horizontal lines. Sometimes I've mistakenly stared at a fallen log 150 yards away, thinking I was perhaps looking at a standing deer's body line, and at other times I've looked briefly at a horizontal object across a field for a minute, dismissed it as a log, and then had the "log" walk out into the open and suddenly turn into a whitetail. You won't see every deer this way, but you'll sure see a lot more if you generalize your vision and know

ahead of time that you just aren't going to see the whole deer. You'll see bits and pieces of it as it passes on the far side of some tree trunks, or maybe you'll see just flashes of dark color as a buck walks slowly through a sapling thicket on the ridge behind you. Deer that haven't been disturbed literally slip through

This hunter would help his efforts by using camouflage clothing and some camo paint to cover his face. *Michigan DNR*

their habitat. They move silently and slowly, with their natural camouflaging nearly matching the colors and tones of their environment. The bowhunter who has programmed himself to this will see far more deer.

You've probably read magazine stories in which the author claimed he first spotted an antler's flash in the sun, followed by the entire buck as it moved into a clearing. Sometimes it happens this way, but most often it doesn't. Seeing deer is an inconsistent art: Sometimes the first thing you'll notice is a patch of color that doesn't look exactly like the colors around it, and other times you'll be staring at empty woods when suddenly a big deer walks into your view with all the apparent stealth of a mailman on his delivery route.

I was bowhunting in the Midwest a few seasons back, and when full darkness came I headed toward my car by crossing a long, open field. As I stepped out of the woods into the field something made me look well off to my left, and there stood a big doe right next to a patch of timber. There was very little light to illuminate the deer, plus she was partially hidden by the dark woods behind her. Yet there she stood, stock still and making no noise, and still I saw her immediately. She watched me watching her for a minute or so, then snorted and bounced off to the woods at her back, the flash of her white tail and underparts disappearing into the gloom. I think that the main reason I was able to see that deer under far less than ideal conditions was that I was on my way home, my mind was wide open, and I hadn't locked myself into seeing what I unconsciously wanted to see. I just looked around and there she stood,

as big and as identifiable as any whitetail I've ever spotted—in the dark, 60 yards away and standing nearly inside a dark woods.

Don't Look 'Em in the Eye

If you still-hunt long and well enough, there will be moments when you are suddenly aware that there is a deer, or a number of deer, standing and looking right at you from as little as eight feet away. They have long since identified you as a predator, but instead of running away have decided to play cat and mouse, and, like a cottontail that lets the hunter walk right by, wait it out until you've passed before moving. If you're like a lot of hunters who walk through a deer woods and see nothing of interest, you'll just crash on your way and never know the deer are there at all. But if you've tuned yourself to see deer, even immobile deer, you'll turn your head to the left or right and *Holy cow, there's a deer!*

Whether it is one deer (most likely) or several, believe that every eye is on you as you spot them, because to coin an old hunter's term, the deer have you boresighted and can count the number of cigarettes left in the pocket of your jacket.

Do not, under pain of blowing the chance, look these deer directly in the eyes. There is something about direct eye contact that triggers a hidden animal. It suddenly realizes that it is no longer hidden, no longer secure. You have in *fact* spotted him for what and where he is, and all he can do now is depart as quickly as possible.

I've heard turkey hunters say the very same thing about eye contact. Tom Kelly,

There's seldom a lack of willing hands when a big buck is to be hung up. This dandy 10-pointer from Gallia County, Ohio, fell to one shot after being jumped from its bed in a honeysuckle patch.

an excellent gobbler hunter with 40 years and about 100 toms worth of experience, tells me that he's come across gobblers hiding among fallen brush less than 20 yards away, often less than half that. "Sometimes I'll get a shot at a bird in that situation, if I can convince him that I haven't seen him and can get my shotgun into position," Kelly said, "but it's a really tough thing to do." Kelly said that his body language—the rhythm given off by how he's moving when he sees the game—cannot change much or the tom will know he's been spotted and depart. "And I know this sounds like something out of the Twilight Zone, but I can't look a hidden gobbler in the eye and expect him to stay where he is," Kelly said. There is just something about direct eye contact that tells a hidden creature that he's been spotted, and that the cat and mouse game is over.

The same thing applies to bowhunters who see game that see them: Don't look 'em in the eyes. Try this experiment on your housecat or dog. Wait until the animal happens to be looking at you, and stare directly and intently into its eyes. In all probability, the animal will very shortly look away, and perhaps move out of the room entirely. Deer react to eye contact in the same manner, except that their reaction is more dramatic because they are wild creatures depending on their senses and instincts for survival. Deer don't question their instincts; they respond to them. In the case of deer seen at very close range, about the only thing you can do is to come to full draw as you walk by the deer, then smoothly pivot, find your aim and release, provided you have a clear shot into a vital area behind the shoulder. The key word here is *smoothly*. Deer, like so many wild animals, react to quick movements more swiftly than to rather slow, smooth movements. There is an outside chance that a smooth draw and pivot and release will find the deer still frozen in the belief that it's still hidden. The deer will usually flush when you pivot, but enough will stay put another second or two to at least make the effort worthwhile.

Hours in the Woods

There has never been a deer that has walked up on anybody's back porch, tapped on the door and said "Shoot me." You can't hunt deer in your bedroom, your living room, your basement or your garage. You have to go where the deer are or you're not going to see game, much less reduce it to possession.

The more time you spend still-hunting, the better your chances of seeing game, maybe even that huge buster of a rocking-chair buck whose track you spotted this morning. The beauty of moving is that you don't have to depend on the deer happening to walk within bow range of a stationary stand. You create your own movement, your own chances, by going to the deer.

And if you are a diligent hunter, you do this endlessly. You're out in the woods, bow in hand, when you have only 45 minutes to hunt before you're due at work. You make use of weekends, half-weekends, those long evenings of daylight in early autumn, even the frigid January mornings when anyone with a lick of sense has packed it in and is watching pro football on the tube. You are still out there, the diligent hunter, giving yourself a chance to arrive at a certain spot when the buck's there too.

Doug Crabtree, an archer with 22 whitetails to his credit since 1967, says the single most important part of successful bowhunting for deer is hours in the woods. "In the early part of the season, I think the morning hours are best. Later, when the weather gets colder, midday and evenings are best," Crabtree said. "But don't get the idea that you can pare your hunting hours down to only these prime times and still do the best job of hunting possible," he added. "The best and often most successful hunter hunts as much as he can whenever he can during the season. You never know when you'll see that buck, or even where you'll see him, and if you spend a lot of time in the woods your chances are just that much better." Crabtree, who—with his bow—once took a 224-pound (field-dressed) whitetail buck scoring a total of 127 2/8 by the Pope & Young method, is strictly a trophy hunter for most of the bow season, and he firmly believes in spending a maximum amount of time hunting. It just makes sense.

Position Shooting

The best shooting position for accuracy with the bow and arrow is with the body facing at a 90-degree angle away from the intended target, feet positioned just so, weight evenly balanced on the balls of your feet and so on. But for the still-hunter, this ideal positioning just isn't possible that often. More likely you'll just have stepped over a collapsed wire fence, or bent under a low limb, and there will be your shot smack in front of you, and you'll have to make that shot *now* or forget it.

For this reason the still-hunter/archer must learn to draw, aim and release his tackle in a variety of body positions. I was hunting a hilly piece of woodland a year ago, stopping every few feet to look and listen, when I happened to catch a bit of movement directly behind me and some distance off through the woods. A 6-pointer was walking up the hillside, and I could see that his path would soon take him across my scentline right in the middle of a sapling woods. I had to shoot within the next minute or the buck would enter the thicket and detect my scent, either of which would mean I'd get no shot, so I waited a moment for the buck to put his head on the other side of a large tree trunk, pivoted and came to full draw. I shot when he walked out from behind the tree, and the shaft took him at the base of the neck on his left side and severed the jugular vein. I paced the shooting distance at 58 yards, longer by twice the range that I prefer, but it was the only shot available if I was to shoot at all, and I felt I could make it. I had to bend over slightly to get the upper limb of my bow to clear a low branch, and although I've practiced odd-position shooting endlessly, I still think I was lucky that the shot went as true as it did.

Let me make a plug right here for bowhunting ethics. It applies to the still-hunter and to any other type of deer hunter using bow and arrow. Don't take marginal shots. You know the ones I mean: The deer is walking in a jungle of sapling trunks that a snake would have trouble entering. A deer is some distance off through the woods and walking directly away from you, something like 70 yards away with only its butt as a target. A couple of whitetails are walking across the far end of a long field at least 80 yards away, and there's a crosswind to push any arrow off its aim.

Most marginal shots miss their targets completely. A very few actually hit the deer, and those that do are usually in the foot or tail rather than in a vital area. And anyone seeing you shoot under these circumstances has to believe you're either a complete idiot or that you're someone who doesn't have the faintest idea what his tackle or talent can do. You look like a complete novice, in other words. Bowhunting gets a bad enough name because of things over which the ethical bowhunter has no control, such as mythical tales of scores of wounded but lost deer, hunting arrows that wound but don't kill, ad nauseum. Don't add to this ill-fueled fire by using poor judgment in the field. If you have a good shot within your range of effectiveness, by all means take that shot. But pass up everything else, regardless of how anxious you are and the fact that you're alone and "nobody will see." Turkey hunters sitting over a field of rye or wheat grass first walk off 45 or so yards in three directions from their stands in a sort of fan pattern, placing sharpened sticks in the ground to mark the maximum effective range of their three-inch turkey loads fired from a full-choke shotgun. Any gobbler within those marker stakes is fair game. And any gobbler beyond that little line of upright sticks is off-limits because a shotgun's range is limited, just as a bowhunter's talents and tackle are limited. If you're a really good still-hunter, you can perhaps get yourself into range of that buck you've spot-

ted way the hell and gone through the woods. And if you're not yet a good still-hunter, just watch that buck as he moves out of sight, learning from how and where he moves, and then plan to alter your route through here tomorrow in hope of catching him at closer range. But don't go arching fruitless arrows off through the woods in hope that God or somebody is going to guide it into his boiler room, because it just ain't gonna happen.

Mapping It Out

Accurate topographical maps can help both the standing hunter and the still-hunter. Doug Crabtree, mentioned earlier in this chapter, joins forces with his brother Dennis in plotting deer hotspots that they've found during their year-round scouting efforts. After just a few seasons, the Crabtree brothers have a very good handle on where the deer in their hunting zones are moving, where they bed and go to feed, and how to intercept them come bow season. They pretty much know where the big bucks hang out, and have an idea what the bucks' habits are, before they go afield to actually hunt. This cuts down on a lot of dead time in the woods and lets them concentrate on only those areas that contain good animals.

The still-hunter can do the same thing if he hunts the same general area season after season. State geographical survey offices usually offer topo maps of at least fair detail, and if you hunt national forestland or parkland, the administering agency (U.S. Forest Service, National Park Service and so on) should be able to provide you with topo maps. And failing this, you can always pop for the cost of an hour-long flight in a small plane, directing the pilot to fly at, say, 800 feet or so over your hunting area while you use a 50mm lens to shoot aerial photos for later use. Blow up the best of these, establish some landmarks and which direction is north, and then use the aerial photo as you would a topo map, carrying it with you and marking scrapelines, bedding areas and so on with a red pen or pencil. In time, this will let you go directly to the areas where you're most likely to see game.

As a rule of thumb while hunting, if you must choose between a route between ridges or hills, and another route along the spine of those ridges or hills, go with the latter because your eyes will serve you better from a position above the surrounding terrain. You can look down into those valleys and hollows and creekbottoms. If you see deer down there, it's likely they haven't spotted you yet and you have the chance to put yourself in a position to take a shot. Hunting high also keeps your scent above the game much of the time; this is especially true in the afternoon when the air is warming and the air currents (thermals) are rising along the contours of the hills.

But most important of all, *enjoy it*. It's exciting to move slowly through deer country, using all of your senses to the limit of their capabilities as you hunt for North America's wariest and toughest bowhunting challenge.

7

Where to Hit Your Deer

The arrow jumped off the string, the bowstring twanged loudly, and I knew I was in trouble.

The big doe had been quietly feeding in an open field of grass and a few saplings no more than 25 yards away, but the unsilenced string on my recurve bow gave the shot away and spooked the doe into "jumping the string," an archer's term for being startled into nervously jumping forward a few feet. My worst fears were realized. The cedar shaft tipped with a Razorhead smacked dead center into and through the whitetail's ham, the 45 pounds of the bow driving the shaft completely through the deer's hip, out the other side and another 10 yards, where it buried itself in a small cedar. The doe, along with her two companions, quickly fled the little field and disappeared over a small rise, into some

deep timber. I mentally kicked myself for using less equipment than I should have. String silencers would have made the shot perfect, with the arrow taking the doe just behind her right shoulder where it belonged. As things stood, I had a long tracking job ahead of me, and the fact that I eventually found that deer dead of blood loss and shock hardly excused my oversight.

No one intentionally shoots a deer in the rear or in the leg or even in the viscera-rich paunch. It sometimes happens because we forget to allow for the downward shot angle from a treestand, we underestimate the force of a crosswind, or maybe we take a shot that we shouldn't. The reasons are as numerous as hunters in the field, and when one of them results in a wounded-but-uncollected deer running across a high-

Notice the arrow's entry hole in the buck's near shoulder. This still-hunter placed his arrow carefully and well despite heavy brush.

owe this respect to the deer, to ourselves and to the sport. Anyone unwilling to pass up shots because they are marginal should be horsewhipped with a freshly waxed bowstring and then lashed to a honey tree in a woods full of bears. The error in judgment is that bad.

The vital area on a white-tailed deer, be it buck or doe, is roughly circular in shape, or I should say spherical. It's as if the deer carries a pie plate-sized ball in its chest area. From any angle—top, side, even the bottom, should this angle somehow present itself—this area of the deer's anatomy is where you want your shaft to penetrate. Stick that deer anywhere else and you will be tracking until dark, and maybe not finding the deer when the blood and sign run out.

There are three major organs in this area, any one of which can be damaged to the point of death for the deer. They are the lungs, the liver and the heart, listed in order relative to their size and availability, and therefore in the order of interest to bowhunters. These organs are full of blood and susceptible to a well-sharpened broadhead capable of punching/cutting its way into the chest cavity and then doing damage to the organ. Severely cut any one of these organs, and your deer will bleed out relatively quickly, probably within five minutes of the arrow's impact. Tear a hole in the membrane between the deer's chest cavity and stomach cavity, and the lungs will collapse because the balance of pressures between the two cavities has been disturbed; lungs (really just bellows) depend on just the right air pressure to operate. Mess up this pressure and the animal will suffocate quickly.

way where passing motorists can see a shaft sticking into its hip or neck or whatever, the public relations losses are tremendous and irreparable, and all too often the deer is uncollectable. The animal may eventually die of its wound, but that death may well occur a mile away where you'll never find it. Such a death does no one any good.

So, what can we do about it?

We can and must put that arrow into a vital area of the deer's anatomy *every* time the bow is pulled and released. We

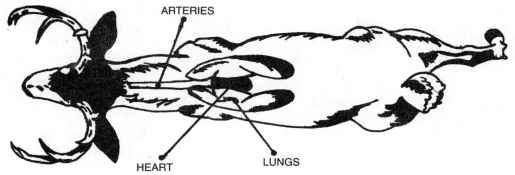

ARTERIES

HEART   LUNGS

Know where the vital areas are from every angle. A deer walking under your treestand offers this angle for a vertical shot, one of the toughest chances in bowhunting.

Imagine your deer is already down and dead and you have a tin pie plate in your hand. Find a spot midway between the deer's brisket (forward belly area) and his withers (top of the shoulders). This should give you the correct vertical positioning for the vital area. Now find an area between the *rear* edge of the shoulder bone and the third rib on the deer, starting with the deer's first rib (closest to the shoulder) and counting ribs toward his hindquarters. Center the pie plate where these two lines cross, horizontally and vertically, and you've located the prime place to put your next arrow—from a *broadside position*. It would be handy if the best spot to shoot for remained the same regardless of the angle of the shot, but it just isn't so. Remember, you're shooting for a spherical ball that has height, width and depth, and your arrow must strike the ball squarely whether you're shooting from the side, slightly above or slightly to the rear of the animal. The shaft also has to penetrate the deer's ribcage with all of its cartilage, if you shoot from the side; or it must punch through the forward

area of the paunch if the deer is angling away from you. And if that buck is angling *toward* you, your shaft must

Two chances here. The best (No. 1) gets your arrow into the lung area, while No. 2 seeks the neck arteries and perhaps the spine.

either strike nearly dead center in his chest, or just miss the large shoulder bone while sliding through the ribcage enroute to the pump room of heart-liver-lungs.

Think of the vital area as a ball wrapped in armor that is impenetrable here, susceptible there to a well-placed arrow. Hit that ball and the deer is yours. Miss the ball just a little and you have a long tracking job on your hands. Miss it by a lot and maybe you won't eat venison this winter.

The exact spot to hit your deer—midway between top and bottom and ahead of the third rib—is the spot considered prime by Doug Crabtree, the Ohio archer with 22 whitetails to his credit and a student of trophy-only bowhunting. Crabtree says he's seldom had a deer run far when stuck squarely in the pump house, and that he usually finds the an-

The optimum broadside shot. Don't be fooled into shooting at the entire deer. Go for the shoulder, the largest single lethal target.

imal within 50 to 75 yards of the spot where it was shot. Crabtree discards the notion that hunting arrows do not cause shock when an animal is struck. He uses an 80-pound bow and Easton 2416 shafts and a forward-cutting, fixed-blade broadhead. Most of his arrows pass completely through his deer, leaving a double blood trail to follow. Crabtree claims that his shafts do cause shock, and he's had experts test for shock and verify it.

"I had the kinetic energy of my bow/arrow combination tested by engineers and they determined that my arrow strikes the deer with the same force as a .38-caliber bullet from a pistol," Crabtree reports. "Anyone hearing the sound a deer makes when an arrow strikes it wouldn't doubt that the collapse of its chest cavity causes shock. The deer gives a loud *Whoosh!* when he's hit, and I've had them fall down within a step or two." Crabtree has used this same bow-arrow combination successfully on mature black bear and obtained the same results, so it's difficult to doubt his argument that shock does result from a powerful and well-placed shot.

While most shots into a whitetail's boiler room are made from the side and, if the hunter is in a treestand, from slightly above, it's entirely possible to reach the vitals from directly above the deer. Bob Cramer, a hunting buddy of mine, killed a mature 7-point buck a few seasons back by driving a heavy aluminum shaft toting an MA-3L head vertically through the buck's back. The head ticked the spine, broke up both lungs and a corner of the liver, and exited the deer's chest cavity at the brisket. The buck ran about 10 feet before

On bowshots at running deer, hold for the shoulder with a good lead.

collapsing, which was all the more amazing because the deer was at full leaping gallop at the moment of release. Cramer was 18 feet up in a treestand at the time and shot a 76-pound compound bow.

So it's possible to reach that "ball" of vitals from almost any angle. It's a matter of having a heavy enough bow, a heavy enough arrow and an efficient enough broadhead, if you must enter the buck's body at something less than an ideal angle. Do not, however, take the type of shot that a friend of mine did three seasons back while bowhunting in Wisconsin.

He had carefully still-hunted just within bow range of a bedded buck, only to have the buck leisurely get to his feet and start to amble away. With only half an hour of daylight left and the deer moving directly away from him, the hunter drew and released. The sharp broadhead went perhaps 10 inches low, neatly trimming off the buck's testicles

and a handful of belly hair before plowing into the soil in front of the buck's snout. The buck ran off (probably screaming in falsetto), but was later found stone dead from blood loss. Whether the hunter retrieved the buck's lost anatomy, I've never been able to determine. I don't know how he'd mount something like that, anyway.

The brain shot is practically nonexistent; in fact, I doubt if any bowhunter intentionally shoots for this vital organ, which is quite small compared to the chest cavity organs. There is nothing located around the brain that, if struck by a broadhead, will cause death or even severe injury—and who wants to carry a deer out of the woods with an arrow sticking out of its head?

A close friend of mine, who shall remain nameless, has killed not one but two whitetails by hitting each in the head, doing brain damage and dropping both on the spot. In each case he was hunting from a treestand and had a broadside shot at his deer. He used the usual aim just to the rear of the shoulder, but in each case the deer looked back the way it had come, and the movement of its head and neck put its head right where the arrow went. I like to joke about this chap's extreme accuracy with his hunting bow, but in neither case did he intentionally choose a brain shot. It just happened that way.

Quite a few deer are taken by the arrow striking the spine or the large artery just beneath the spine. The spine itself is relatively small in diameter and runs just under the deer's hide along the middle of its back from the base of the neck to a point near the base of the tail, decreasing in diameter as it goes. The spine is most often hit by treestanding

A buck standing in tall cover offers little, but maybe you can punch an arrow through those weeds and into his neck.

gathers in the lower level of the chest cavity will exit through the same path taken by the arrow, leaving a good, heavy blood trail for the hunter to follow.

A hit in the heart, if the head's cutting edges cut both ventricles, is a good one because the shock of this hit transmits itself throughout the deer's body very quickly and internal blood loss is rapid. There are two points to consider before holding on the heart, however. One is the small size of the organ, which is only slightly larger than a man's fist,

archers, although a hunter on the ground trying for a chest cavity hit may hold a bit high and catch the spine-artery area by mistake. Taken from above, a spine hold is a good one because of the possible hits. Of course the arrow may strike the spine itself, or the artery just beneath it, either of which will bring a clean kill. If the arrow penetrates to the left or the right of the spine, you may well catch one lobe of the lungs, the liver or even the heart if penetration is excellent. Out of a powerful bow, a heavy arrow striking the deer in this area from above may even go completely through the animal's chest cavity and end up imbedded in the ground beneath the animal. This is an ideal situation. The entrance hole permits cold outside air to enter the lungs and lung area ahead of the heavy membrane, and any blood that

The head-on shot offers two targets: No. 1 gets your arrow into the heart-lung-liver while No. 2 tries for the spine, arteries, or both.

This nice New Jersey whitetail fell to one arrow through the ribs and into his vitals, angling from rear to front.

and the fact that deer carry their heart well down in the chest cavity, almost between the uppermost part of the front legs. This can be a tough region to reach under many hunting conditions. Additionally, many heart-shot deer run amazing distances at top speed immediately after the shot, even though the sharp broadhead has skewered the heart squarely. A 6-pointer I heart-shot last January ran almost 300 yards before piling up, and he did so in great leaping bounds resembling the gait of an antelope. His chest cavity was full of blood when I opened him up for field-dressing.

A deer hit in the paunch area will almost always die of the wound, but death comes much slower than had the vitals been penetrated and bled out. Personally, if I'm unfortunate enough to stick a deer in the paunch area, I wait at least six hours before starting to track the deer. This allows for the slow process of blood loss to take place inside that deer, as it can take a long time for the deer to feel sick enough to lie down, stiffen and die. Most often the paunch is hit when you fail to allow for the quartering angle of the shot presented, such as when the deer is walking diagonally toward or away from you. Even the ideal broadside position can result in a paunch-hit deer if the arrow strikes too far back in the lower rib area.

Hits in large muscles can kill a deer quickly because most large muscles in the animal's body are well oxygenated by large arteries and blood loss can be severe, bringing relatively quick death. The deer's hams are one such spot, and this is of particular interest when you take a shot at an animal facing directly away from you. The ideal hold in this situation is just under the deer's tail-

bone, in the vicinity of the anus. A precise hit here from a powerful bow allows the arrow to penetrate slightly above the viscera area of the paunch and on into the area of vital organs in the chest area. With this hold, your arrow may well catch one or the other lung or the liver; if there is a slightly downward angle on the arrow's path, it may even strike the heart. Hitting a bit higher than hoped from the rear may sever the artery just under the spine, or it may strike the spine itself. Hitting slightly to the left or right of the anus puts your broadhead into one of the deer's hams; bleedout is slower here, but most such hits cut large arteries and bring death.

The words "powerful bow" recur above because, although a 40-pound bow can and will take deer if you use sharp broadheads and quality arrows, a bow half again that draw weight lets you use arrows with heavier shafts. These heavy shafts, shot from a bow matched to their stiffer spine and tipped with a forward-cutting head, are a combination that is tough to beat. The heavy bow delivers more penetration energy, and the cutting head reaches more vitals inside the deer and, very often, leaves the hunter with a good, strong blood trail—sometimes even two of them running parallel, when the arrow passes completely through the deer and exits the far side. Pull the heaviest bow you can handle accurately and then aim for precise entry spots.

Some consistently successful hunters say they aim for certain individual organs, most commonly the lungs because the lungs are the largest single vital organ offered. Even when shooting from an elevated treestand, it's a good idea when shooting for the lungs to hold

This huge nontypical whitetail buck, formerly Ohio's record deer, turned out to be poached and the record was withdrawn. Its full body mount is on display in southeastern Ohio. *Ohio DNR*

slightly above an imaginary centerline drawn front to back on a deer's side. Because of the downward angle of the arrow's flight when shot from a tree-stand, hitting the deer just above this centerline drives the head down into the middle of the lungs, usually catching both lobes of the lungs at the same time, an excellent hit.

One of the toughest shot placements to make correctly is on a deer quartering toward or away from you. All too often the hunter remembers broadside deer targets used in practice and forgets all about the angle of the deer's body. Hit that deer at the same point of impact you'd use for a broadside animal and you'll entirely miss the lungs, perhaps hit the liver, and just maybe strike the heart. You may also have a wounded animal that can and will put a lot of distance between it and you before it slows down.

A deer quartering toward you, if the angle of approach is severe, should be taken in the chest area in order to reach the vitals. This hit has a very good chance of taking one or both lungs, the liver and just maybe the heart if the hold is low enough. A deer quartering away from you must be struck well back in the rib-cage so that the shaft will drive forward into the vitals. A quartering-away shot should enter the animal's ribs about two-thirds of the distance from chest to the rear edge of the hams. If penetration is good (up to your arrow's cresting, at least, or all the way to the fletching), the shot should catch the far lobe of the lung and perhaps the liver.

Sometimes—in fact, most of the time —you have to take what the deer and the physical circumstances give you. Your buck may be standing in saplings,

A deer bedded in short cover and among trees reduces the available targets, but in this case a neck shot is presented. Shoot for the center of the neck.

bushes or other cover of medium height, and all you see for a clear shot is the top of his back, his neck and head. The book on this sort of situation insists you should wait him out until he moves into a better position. This is good advice as a rule of thumb, but you and I both know there's a good chance that the buck is going to move where you'll have no shot *at all* unless you take what you can get when you can get it. In a case such as the one described, the neck shot is your best bet. The neck contains two targets, either of which will do a quick job if you hit it. One is the spine, which is midway between the top and bottom edges of the neck when the buck is broadside to you. And the other is the jugular, itself a lethal target.

Quite a few old-time hunters believe that the deer's white throat patch makes a good and consistent target, but I believe this is more the case for rifle hunters than for bowhunters. The throat patch of even a large deer is quite small. I like to take a neck shot well back from the head, near where the neck broadens and joins the chest and shoulders.

A fellow bowhunter in Kentucky shot a very nice 10-point buck in the side of the neck some seasons back. The deer trotted by me, his head canted to one side and the arrow still in place. At first the blood spots were very few and far between, but then we were able to locate a second drop of blood and thereby had a line along which to look for more spots. Within 25 yards I came on a small leafy opening in the woods and the entire clearing—perhaps 25 feet wide —was covered with blood; the arrow lay there too, also greasy with blood. The buck was down only a few yards away, dead from blood loss. I think the buck paused to attempt shaking the arrow from his neck, and when the shaft came free, the punctured jugular pumped blood all over the place in all directions.

You could try for this buck's neck, but a better bet would be waiting until he raises his head, presenting a larger target.

As thick as some whitetail cover is, you'll likely be presented with the neck shot, so don't be afraid to take it. You'll either hit spine and drop the deer where he stands, hit the jugular and have a short and easy tracking job, or you'll miss altogether and save that deer for another day. However it works out, you're a winner.

Most everyone whose arrow strikes a deer knows immediately where he has hit the animal. You either see the arrow enter the deer's body, or catch a glimpse of it being carried away as the deer runs or walks away.

There are times when the bowhunter just isn't sure, however. Maybe the angle was odd or the deer moved just as the arrow was released. But, it's possible to determine where your arrow struck the deer if you can find the arrow after the shot.

Blood from the lungs, whether found on the arrow itself or on the ground, is usually bright red and frothy. The lung tissue is gorged with both blood and oxygen (which make the lungs top choice of where to stick your deer), and this will be apparent in any blood you find after the shot. A high oxygen content accounts for both the bright color of the blood and the tiny bubbles it often contains.

A muscle hit usually results in uniformly dark blood, and the drops you'll locate will usually be singular rather than in small pools or groups of spots. Muscular blood is dark because the deer's body has already depleted much of the oxygen content of the blood, and the blood was on its way back to the lungs for rejuvenation when your broadhead interrupted things.

A hit in the paunch area leaves little blood for you to follow, by and large,

but if you can find your arrow you'll be able to determine where the shaft struck. Often the shaft of the arrow will be clotted here and there with half-digested bits of food, carried along as the arrow passed through the deer's stomach or intestinal tract. Such an arrow often smells bad, and this is also proof of a hit in the paunch area.

If you do hit the lung area as hoped, remaining quiet immediately after the shot can often help determine the success of your aim.

A lung-hit deer suffers severe blood loss almost immediately inside his chest cavity. The blood-filled lungs pump free blood into the chest cavity, and some of it is sucked into the esophagus as well, and the hunter who is quiet immediately after the shot can sometimes hear his deer's reaction to the glut of blood as it tries to breathe. In an otherwise quiet woods, a lung-shot deer sounds somewhat like a human with a

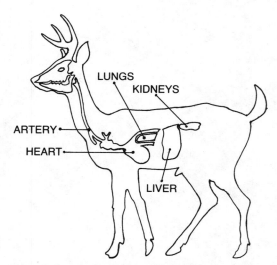

The vital organs are relatively small in comparison to the overall bulk of a deer, but they can be reached if you know where they are and then place the shot carefully.

severe head cold; the animal's breaths come in snorts and chokes and there may be a wheezing sound at the same time. Remember, blood from the lungs is being breathed out, then in again by the deer. You'll often be able to hear this right after the shot, and again when you follow the animal up if he hasn't died yet. If you hear these sounds, stay alert and well back from where you think the sounds come from. Let that animal lie down and succumb. Moving in too soon merely puts him on his feet when he could be lying down, and you'll have a longer tracking job.

Bowhunters who can hit the bull's-eye every time at 30 yards on the practice range often can't do the same when the target is a whitetail buck standing 20 yards away. There's something about *The Moment* that shakes the draw-aim-release regimen required to hit where you want to. Buck fever, some folks call it. It can not only ruin an otherwise easy shot: It can ruin a whole season if not corrected.

A bowhunting friend of mine, the female half of a husband-wife team who hunts very often every fall, ran smack into a bad case of the fever on her first-ever whitetail hunt. She was alone in her treestand and a large doe came ambling up and stopped just 20 yards from the stand. But poor Judy got a case of the shakes.

"I'd look at that deer and try to draw my bow and I just could *not* get it back all the way," she says now with a smile. "I just couldn't look at the deer and pull my bow, I was so nervous. So," she continues, "I finally turned completely away from the deer, drew the bow to full draw,

When a trophy buck like this is on the ground, put there by your arrow, you have a right to be proud.

and then turned back and took my aim. I had no trouble shooting, but getting ready for the shot seemed impossible so long as I faced the deer." Her shot went high—a clean miss.

Buck fever can cause us (you *and* me) to shoot for the whole deer instead of the best spot available. But all of us have to hit where we aim, and aim to hit the right spot, every time out. The serious hunter will do this.

8

Tracking a Wounded Deer

There is a certain old beech tree standing beside a field of foxtail in the hardwood country of far western Kentucky. Among the tree's huge lower limbs, perhaps 12 feet off the ground, rests a sturdy tree platform made of 2 × 4s and spike nails, and it was on this platform I stood one frosty October morning when all the hardwood leaves had turned colors and my breathing showed as white plumes in the dawn cold.

I shot a whitetail buck from that tree-stand, a medium-sized 8-pointer that ever-so-slowly ambled within bow range along with half a dozen does hungry for the nuts lying hidden under some fallen leaves. The deer stood almost perfectly broadside when the arrow went its way, the shaft taking him a bit lower than I'd aimed, although later examination showed that the broadhead neatly cut

the heart's upper surface before exiting the body on the far side.

That buck did what nearly all heart-shot deer do right after being struck: It leaped away from the base of the beech and went galloping and jumping out of sight into the hardwoods behind the beech, trailed by the little herd of puzzled but obedient does. Three seconds after the shot I was completely alone, wondering if I had perhaps imagined the buck and the does and the shot, after all. That is a natural reaction for any bowhunter, too. Lord knows it's tough enough getting within bow range of a big, wary whitetail, not to mention actually getting a decent chance for a shot. No wonder bowhunters (you, me and everyone else) blink a couple of times at that moment and silently ask ourselves, *Did it really happen?*

I think it's very important to put a lid on thoughts such as that immediately because negative thoughts can cost you deer. If I had to put a label on the right philosophy for successfully finding deer you've arrowed, I might call it the Norman Vincent Peale Approach: positive thinking, every time.

There *were* deer under your stand, you *did* get a good sight picture, your shot *did* fly where aimed, taking the buck in the vitals, and you *will* locate that deer, down, dead and beautiful, within a very short time after leaving your stand to begin tracking.

You get the idea. And it's not all psyching yourself, either. If you did actually make a good hit on the deer, he's going to lie down, stiffen and die if you let him. All you have to do is find him. I am convinced that the most important part of successfully locating that buck takes place before you ever leave the stand. The head part, using your noodle, you know—*thinking*. If you will apply your intelligence you will not only really find that deer, but you'll do it with far less time and effort as well.

Positive thinking is important when tracking your buck, mostly because the hunter who is certain he'll find his deer will be more tenacious in searching for sign, taking note of every scrap of information available, and will make use of hunches when there isn't a blood spot or a tuft of cut deer hair to be found. If you're that tenacious bowhunter, you'll not only look for signs of which direction the deer fled, but you'll make every effort to find the arrow, unless it's impaled in the deer, checking the shaft, head and fletching for blood or other matter. Sometimes you'll find only meager sign, and if this is enough to make

you give up and leave a perhaps mortally wounded deer in the woods to die, wasted, after a long period of suffering, well, then you'd better give up bowhunting and take up some other pastime.

I recall one cloudy November afternoon in Pennsylvania a few seasons back. I was still-hunting across a semi-open field dotted with saplings when the head of a whitetail doe popped out from a cedar thicket 50 yards away. I froze in place, one foot in the air, the other shakily trying to keep my balance. Somehow I stayed still and the doe, after staring at me for about three lifetimes, walked into the open, followed by three other mature females. They began to nose their way, left to right, past my tenuous position, and since I'd seen no bucks at all that day, I decided to take one of these does if I could.

The lead doe nosed her way to within perhaps 35 yards when I slowly drew the recurve 45-pound bow I carried at the time, found her shoulder over my fist and released a cedar shaft and Razorhead. I didn't use string silencers in those days (I was a semi-rookie to bowhunting) and the doe jumped the string, bolting forward as soon as she heard the *twang* of the released bowstring. The shaft hit her squarely in the left hip, instead of behind the shoulder, and she took her three companions on a leaping retreat down a slope and into the cedar woods.

There was no doubt that my arrow had in fact struck the deer; I'd watched its flight from bow to target, and I'd seen it disappear in the doe's hip. I'd also heard the soft, moist sound of the broadhead as it punched into the solid meat of the hip. When the deer were out of sight I walked to the spot where they'd

If all sign seems to have disappeared, look under the leaf cover. Tracks can often be detected in the soft soil beneath.

been standing and, sure enough, found a fistful of deer hair, neatly cut to length on one end by my broadhead. Then I spotted the arrow. It had gone all the way through both of the deer's hips, flown another 10 yards, and then buried itself halfway into a sapling trunk. The arrow was covered with blood from neck to head; the blood was dark red and smooth, indicating that my arrow had struck muscle tissue, and not the artery I'd hoped for.

This was a real complication. An artery hit would have bled out my deer in relatively short order, but a muscle hit, no matter how solid, meant that she could still motor well enough to stay on her feet indefinitely, and I'd almost have to get close enough for a second shot to put her down for good.

I set to work tracing an imaginary line between the last spot I'd seen the deer, and the spot where I'd originally shot her. That gave me a line along which to begin looking for more sign. Fortunately, upon entering the thick cedar woods, the doe had left a small smear of blood on two low branches. This not only gave me an extension of the search line but also meant that the doe was bleeding from both sides of her body, not just one. Following a twin blood trail is easier than following just one, and it also meant that the doe was losing blood at an increased rate. I was hopeful that she would soon slow and perhaps lie down in some thicket where I could stalk up close and stick her again. I was able to move through the little cedar woods quickly after finding a few more spots and smears of blood, and then the trail led across a little opening and toward a jungle of honeysuckle-wrapped saplings and downed branches and trunks. "I'll bet she's in there and maybe already lying down," I thought. "Just hang back here a minute and have a smoke. Give her time to stiffen up a little." So I stayed well back from the tangle, sitting on a locust log and just waiting.

As it turned out, the doe had been lying down when I approached, standing up only when I was almost on top of her. She moved at a slow trot diagonally away from me, and it was an easy matter to put my follow-up arrow into her neck and end things right there. In cases such as this, where the deer you're following isn't yet down for good, you must remain fully alert at all times because deer, especially mobile wounded deer, are not always predictable. Getting a solid second shot is part skill in knowing where to look, and a whole lot of luck.

There are rules of thumb, allowing some predictability for wounded deer, for deer hit solidly in the lung-heart area just to the rear of either front leg. Deer so struck by a modern hunting arrow feel shaky and sick. All they want to do is go off a little ways by themselves, find some thickly overgrown spot for some privacy and quiet, and lie down, much the same as a human would feel when

hit with a case of the queasies. It's your job to know the immediate area well enough to be able to predict where that deer is likely to head, and this isn't as tough as it sounds.

For openers, wounded deer seldom if ever head directly uphill, simply because doing so requires too much effort inasmuch as they're already feeling shaky and perhaps suffering from early symptoms of shock. Given a chance, deer fleeing from the spot where your arrow went home will choose a route either across flat terrain or downhill. If there is dense cover nearby, and that location happens to be slightly (but *only* slightly) uphill from your spot, the deer may take this route in order to gain the security of that thicket, honeysuckle tangle or whatever. But for the most part, you can disregard most routes uphill from your stand, because the deer will probably do the same thing.

Sometimes the headlong galloping flight of a stuck whitetail can have nearly tragic consequences. A good friend of mine was bowhunting with two companions when, along about noon, he decided to hike up the hill to their stands for a little comparing of notes. Unbeknownst to him, one of his friends had just arrowed a 7-pointer which was even then heading downhill in great leaps, directly toward the oncoming hunter headed uphill. The two of them met in a little clearing and the buck took one quick look at the startled man in front of him and jumped right over the hunter's head, his rear hooves passing just east and west of the poor man's ears. The hunter went over backwards, dropped his bow in a pile of dead leaves and scattered the sack lunch he'd been carrying all over the hillside. He did

Deer tracks may initially appear similar, but a really big buck will leave a larger and deeper track than the average doe, especially in snow.

not, it was later reported to me, have much to say when his buddy came pacing downhill a few moments later and asked the innocent question, "Did you see a buck come by here just now?" He pointed with one thumb, from his prone position among the weeds, in a general downhill direction, and the dead buck was quickly located. If I recall correctly, he gave up hunting and spent the rest of the day in camp trying to get his heart restarted.

So look downhill for your buck, or at least for the first sign he's left behind. Failing that after a diligent search, look crosshill for sign. Wounded deer dislike

wasting their dwindling energy on uphill runs.

Occasionally, but not frequently, you'll arrow a deer and the darned thing won't run away. He'll just stand there, maybe take a swipe at the shaft in his hide, and then, I swear to God, drop his head and go back to nuzzling the leaves for acorns.

An acquaintance of mine had this happen a few years ago in Michigan. He'd set up a ground stand with camouflage netting and ended up sticking a little 8-point buck smack in the boiler room behind the shoulder. The buck skittered sideways a few feet when the shaft struck, then darned if it didn't go back to feeding alongside the other deer in the group. To hear my friend tell the tale, at that point he was damned if he knew what to do.

"The buck was less than 10 yards away from me and every once in a while he or one of his does would lift up a head and look at me, then go back to eating. I had one or the other of them staring at me all the time, and I was so close I couldn't even reach for another arrow."

Finally, the buck's internal hemorrhaging took its toll and he began to wobble on his legs, and finally he lay down where he stood. He died shortly thereafter, and still the does stayed around, one of them actually nuzzling the buck's inert body as if trying to get him back on his feet. Obviously, a case such as this requires no tracking job, only the ability to remain stone-still and silent—and maybe a Valium or two back at camp.

Let's look at a more typical tracking situation from string release to field-dressing, and see if we can't come up with some usable rules to help you find your deer with a minimum of time and effort.

Before You Shoot

This is the *single most important* time in the tracking job, as far as this bowhunter is concerned. If you've done your homework in choosing your stand, you already know the layout, terrain and local covers in the immediate area, and it should therefore be an easy matter to predict where a deer will run after the arrow has hit. A good bet is along the deer's backtrail, a reverse of the route it used to reach your stand area. This is especially true if you're standing over a food source, because deer most often approach a food source along a route offering cover.

Before your deer ever comes into sight, you should be looking around for possible routes it might take when escaping after the shot. Maybe the nearest dense cover is a sapling thicket across the soybean field, or maybe just downhill from your stand in a copse of pines or field of standing corn. If you know ahead of time that wounded deer head down- or crosshill when hit, you can crane your neck a little with this in mind and spot one or two places that may come in handy if you have to do some tracking later.

You've perhaps heard that an arrowed deer always heads in the direction he's standing when hit, but I don't subscribe to this for a minute. In the first place, I've never known deer to *always* do anything. And secondly, I've seen too many newly-stuck deer wheel and turn and head in a direction of their choosing, and not where they were pointed when the string went *twang*.

Of course, you could guess wrong. The deer could thunder off in a direction you thought the least likely when you did your pre-shot analysis. I've seen it happen, and so have you. And in this case all you can do is wait those 20 or 30 minutes, then move to the last spot where you saw the deer and look for sign to follow.

But let's assume that you have a clear line of route taken by that buck, you've waited a minimum of 20 minutes after the shot, and you're ready to start tracking. I sometimes find it helpful to shoot an arrow into the ground to mark my starting place. This is helpful in case you lose the trail before locating the deer and have to come back to start over. Do this where you start tracking the deer, whether that's next to your stand, the last spot you saw the deer running, or wherever. This gives you an anchor spot to work from, no matter what you encounter later. If you're hunting with friends, an arrow in the ground near your stand also serves to let them know you're off tracking a deer, and they can then plan their next moves accordingly.

If the arrow went completely through the deer, or if it came loose while the animal was running away, finding and examining the shaft can tell you a lot about where the deer was hit and what it is likely to do. Let's say that arrow of yours is covered with gray hair and carries a foul odor. In this case, it's likely that the deer was gut-shot and it's best

to wait at least two hours before following it up. Gut-shot deer feel sick, but if pushed can and will travel long distances, pumping their system full of adrenaline and making the venison strong and sometimes inedible.

If the arrow is covered with bright red, frothy blood, it's likely that you hit one or both lungs. Lung-shot deer bleed internally and seldom travel much beyond 50 yards. They also tend to leave heavy blood trails and are easily followed up. Again, however, it's important to give them time to stiffen and die —20 minutes at a minimum, 30 minutes even better.

As mentioned earlier, dark, smooth blood on the arrow shaft indicates your arrow pierced muscle tissue, and unless your broadhead damaged a major mus-

When tracking your deer, overlook nothing, even something as small as this bit of arrow-cut deer hair.

cle or similar supportive tissue, you may have a long tracking job on your hands. It may even be necessary, as it was for me, to enlist the help of a second party to help push the deer into range for a second shot.

A second advantage of punching that shaft completely through a deer is that you'll probably have two blood trails to follow instead of just one. Sometimes this situation makes itself known by leaving two drops of blood 18 inches apart on dead leaves, flat rocks or other backgrounds. More often, however, you'll notice spots or smears of deer blood perhaps two feet off the ground on trailside leaves or brush through which the deer passed after the shot. Deer bleeding well from both flanks, shoulders or neck seldom go far because they're losing vital blood at an accelerated rate.

That bowhunting school I attended in Alabama wisely stressed the practice of looking and listening intently all through the tracking process, from beginning to end. It's amazing what you can sometimes detect by halting in your tracks and just paying attention.

Eyes, Ears and Noggin

While hunting in Michigan a season back, I arrowed an average 9-point buck, and although the animal leaped away and thundered out of sight when the arrow struck, I was fairly sure I'd made a good hit right behind the shoulder. After a decent wait I climbed down from my platform in the hickory tree and took up the trail, easily following the line of flight by drawing imaginary lines from blood spot to blood spot. At one spot in the woods I had some trouble finding the next bit of sign, and I stood in one place for a moment just looking all around me. Then I heard it: a sort of low gurgling sound, as if something was having trouble breathing. It dawned on me that I was hearing my buck's last gasps as his lungs filled with blood. The sounds stopped in less than three minutes, and after another minute or two I moved in the direction of the sounds. I soon found the buck, the rear end of my arrow still showing an inch behind the point of his shoulder, quite dead.

You aren't likely to hear a deer, wounded or otherwise, snap a twig in a woods, but some hunters who listen while tracking have heard their deer stumble and fall, occasionally taking a full header down steep hills. I had a wounded 4-point buck nearly roll over me in Arkansas a few years ago; another bowhunter had arrowed the buck, and when it got to the top of the steep hill I was leaning against, it lost its balance and tumbled, smashing small bushes and brush right in front of me. He was dead when he stopped rolling, but the whole event really shook me up.

Heart-shot deer are a mystery to me, even though I "know" how deer shot in this vital organ can move so far so fast after the shot. Here is a large animal with its pump gone and out of commission, and it goes streaking off like some African antelope chased by a cheetah. If your shot entered the deer low in the front of the chest cavity —tight behind the upper front leg, for example—and if the deer takes off like a streak, chances are you've stuck him in the heart and that he'll eventually die, probably more than 50 yards away. This past fall I hit a deer dead center in the pump and he ran 300 yards before piling up, dead, while trying to leap a wire fence. Fortunately, the arrow went all the way through and I had twin blood trails to follow, which made eventual location much easier. Perhaps heart-shot deer have inordinate amounts of oxygen in the brain that gives them such a long surge of life after being mortally shot. Whatever the reason, it's an unusual deer that drops dead less than 200 yards from the archer if that broadhead severed his heart muscle.

If your arrow hits high on a deer standing broadside, you aren't likely to find blood immediately. This is because the deer's vital organs are mostly in and around the belly cavity, or low in the body. In this case you must rely on other signs to tell which way the deer went; this is when the woodsman's skills come into play.

Deer cannot move through normal woods without leaving sign of some kind. This is true whether you can detect that sign or not. You have to know what to look for, and how to look for it, and then be able to put the pieces together to form a line along which you'll find that deer.

On a recent hunt, I arrowed a white-tail and found absolutely *no* blood at all, anywhere. Yet I saw the arrow enter the deer's vital area and knew he was hard hit despite the apparent lack of blood. What was I to do? The only thing I *could* do was to go looking for sign along the line of flight I guessed the deer had taken. My plan was to look for 30 minutes, and if the search turned up nothing, to look in another direction, and another if necessary, until I did locate the deer. I knew I'd hit him hard, knew he was out there somewhere, and I tried hard to know I'd eventually find him.

So I started looking. I went to the spot where he'd disappeared from my sight into the cover and made ever-widening circles in search of sign, *anything* that would give me a clue. The first thing I found was a bit of bark knocked off a hardwood tree down at foot level. I examined the bark closely, on hands and knees, and could find no clue as to what had made the mark. Lacking anything else to go on, I was forced to assume that the deer, passing this tree at a run, had nicked the tree trunk with one hoof and dislodged a small chunk of bark. So I lined up the last spot I'd seen the deer with the barked tree trunk, and looked a little farther, maybe 30 yards.

I came to a farmer's barbed-wire fence and, in walking along it, happened to notice a tiny tuft of what looked like deer belly hair impaled on one of the rusty barbs. I plucked the tuft off and took a closer look. It was deer hair, but there was no way I would know how long it had been hanging there. So, once again, I had to assume it had come from my deer jumping that fence and miscalculating its height. I went on a little farther and spotted a thicket of overgrown hawthorn trees draped in honeysuckle. In the middle of that pile lay my buck, dead as yesterday and lying on his left side. My arrow had passed through his right shoulder and was still in place, pointing at an upward angle. The arrow had stayed where I shot it, effectively plugging the wound and, this time at least, keeping the wound from bleeding enough to leave a blood trail.

You'll agree there was precious little sure sign left behind by this deer, even after a good hit in the heart-lung area. Despite this, I'd found it less than an hour after starting. Such a situation can happen to the best bowhunter in the woods, and if you don't apply a little noggin work and make some assumptions, if you just look a little while and write it off as a poor hit and a lost deer, you'll never find those whitetails that leave no sign. You have to be willing to put two and two together to get four, even when you have to contribute all the numbers yourself for a while.

Sometimes you have to play Daniel Boone to find some slight sign left by a wounded deer that has left no apparent blood sign behind. Maybe you spot a leaf without dewdrops on it, when all the others in the immediate area are wet. Maybe a bent tuft of green grass catches your eye, perhaps bent down by your buck's hoof. Disregard even the freshest droppings when looking for that arrowed deer; I've never known a deer carrying an arrow in its body to pause to relieve itself. Fresh droppings are left by calm, uninjured deer, and if you find droppings while tracking your trophy, you've happened across sign left by some other deer.

I once wrote in a magazine article that getting close to deer is easier during a light rainfall because deer aren't as alert as normal at such times. This basically is true, but a letter I received from a bowhunter who'd read my article brought up an interesting question: How do you find a blood trail during a rainfall, when the rain itself washes away the blood?

Good question, but not impossible under actual field conditions. Deer wounded in rainy weather react the same as when the sun is shining: They go to deep cover and lie down, provided the arrow wound is severe enough, and provided they aren't disturbed for half an hour or so. The difference is that with no blood trail, you must be able to predict where that deer will head, using the last spot you saw it as your last physical hint or clue. In cases like this, several hunters I know simply stand where their deer was last seen, and crane their necks for the nearest thick cover. If they spot more than one thicket (or similar cover), they try each one in turn until the deer is located. If the deer is only lightly hit, however, it may or may not head for thick cover. It could keep on moving well out of the immediate area before stopping. In this case, and to be candid, your chances of finding that deer are slim indeed.

A great-uncle of mine hunted cottontail rabbits quite a lot and taught me one way to find rabbits that had been hit by the shotgun load but were not in sight. "Head for the nearest trail, no matter how faint, and you'll find your rabbit," he told me many times. It worked. Maybe wounded rabbits find it easier to run along open trails than to buck brush through thick cover. Whatever the reason, I recovered more than a few "lost" rabbits along small trails after that. The same sort of rule applies to deer that have been arrowed but unrecovered: Look in the nearest thicket for your deer, and if it isn't there, look in another thicket, and yet another, knowing all the time that it *is* here someplace. All you have to do is look in the right place.

Let me add a word or two here about the right way to approach a small clump of cover where you suspect your deer might be located. There's no guarantee your deer will be stone dead when you arrive, and so-called dead deer have been known to revive, leap to their feet— injuring the hunter in the process—and go thundering off out of sight. One chap I know, hunting Colorado whitetails with an expensive compound bow complete with arrow-filled bow quiver, lost his bow et al when his supposedly "dead" buck ran away, bow and quiver entangled in his antlers.

So, first of all, approach that thicket from downwind and move slowly and very quietly. Your deer may well be standing just inside the cover, recovered from the original shock of taking a hunter's shaft in his hide and alert to scent and sound. Secondly, be alert to seeing and identifying *parts* of your deer. Maybe you can see only the black hoof on one leg, or a horizontal dark line of the deer's back in an otherwise vertical pattern of tree trunks, or maybe the slight flick of a tail or ear. Keep an arrow on the string at *all* times, and be ready to draw, sight and release at a moment's notice because that deer is no longer relaxed and unalerted. Far from it, in fact: He's been stuck with your arrow, he knows very well that everything's not normal, and a sloppy approach will put him into high gear if the wound permits. So go slow, use your eyes and ears, and be as alert as the animal you're hunting.

If you find your deer already down, it's still important to keep an arrow on the string; you'd be surprised how many "dead" deer get up and scoot when touched. Approach your deer from the rear, and actually walk toward his back, assuming he's lying on his side. A sure way to tell if he's really dead, or simply stunned or shocked into temporary immobility, is to lightly touch his exposed eyeball with a branch or long twig held in your *draw* hand. This is very important, because if you do things right, that hunting bow and nocked arrow are in your *bow* hand, where they can be put to use instantly if needed. Should you touch the deer's eye and see it quiver or blink, immediately drop that twig and put a second arrow into the deer's neck or lungs to anchor him where he lies. Even a deer deep in shock cannot prevent the twitching of its eye when the eyeball is lightly tapped, and I've never seen this test method fail.

Once you know that your deer is definitely dead, don't get so excited or eager to start field-dressing that you fail to quiver that arrow you've been holding ready for so long. One luckless chap I know placed his bow and nocked arrow on the ground, finished gutting and draining his deer, and then reached for his bow again without looking where he was reaching. It took 19 stitches to close the deep cut in the heel of his hand caused by his grabbing the sharp inserts on his broadhead. Only a quick tourniquet and a nearby friend prevented his likely death due to blood loss. And to rub salt in the wound, by the time the hospital was finished with him, neither he nor his friend could exactly recall where he'd dropped the deer, so he lost both deer and bow due to carelessness—not to mention a quantity of blood. Make it your business to replace that arrow in its hooded bow quiver before you do anything else—including counting antler points or drawing a belt knife.

String Your Deer Along

As an alternative to the chore of tedious tracking, you may elect to just string your deer along by using a Game Tracker.

The Game Tracker involves attaching a very light nylon line to your arrow just behind the broadhead; the line goes to a spool attached to the front or side of your bow and is pulled from the spool as the deer moves away from where the shot was made. With this, all you have to do is follow the line from stand to deer without having to search for tracks, blood sign, bits of hair and so on.

I've seen the Tracker in use and it does have its advantages, when all goes as planned. However, having a loop of line hanging between broadhead and bowlimb invites occasional tangles, treestands and other locations not being the roomiest spots in the world. Also, shots taken with the Tracker in place at ranges of 35 yards or more have been known to slow, and therefore lower, a hunting arrow's flight due to line drag.

The Game Tracker is composed of three basic parts: the spool of 17-pound nylon line, a cone-like plastic spool holder in dull black finish, and a double eye-ring clip to attach line to arrow. The spool and its holder feature a threaded nipple on the rear surface, and most hunters insert this nipple into the threaded (female) stabilizer hole on the front surface of most modern compound bows. The manufacturer also makes an optional side-mount for use with bows offering no stabilizer-mount hole.

The line, which is colored white so it's easily seen in shadowed woodlands, comes with factory sizing as it lies on the spool. I've found it best to crush this sizing before installation by kneading the spool in my hand. This loosens the coils somewhat, enabling the line to pay out with a minimum of effort when the arrow is released off the string.

Once in place, the forward or working end of the line is threaded through a hole in the front of the cone-shaped plastic holder, and then attached to the arrow just to the rear of the broadhead. You can use Game Tracker's specially designed clip or, like me, simply pin the line under a wrap or two of electrical tape, making sure that all tape surfaces are lapped neatly down to aid arrow penetration and to assure a firm line anchor. The line should now be draped between the plastic holder and the arrow shaft, so you're ready for that big shot when a whitetail walks within bow range.

It's a good idea to do some practicing with the Game Tracker before the season opens, learning just how far you can shoot without experiencing drag on the arrow's flight. Get to know how the rig feels, what it will and won't do, and you'll be ready to put it to the acid test.

I want to emphasize right here that use of the Game Tracker does not eliminate the need for putting that arrow into a vital spot on your deer. A lightly wounded whitetail trailing a nylon line goes just as far as a poorly hit deer with no line attached, so accuracy remains paramount, Game Tracker or no.

OK, Mr. Big walked up, you hit him square behind the shoulder and he's galloped off, taking line from the spool so fast that it almost hums. Ninety seconds later the line starts to slow a bit, then continues to pay out at a slower but still steady pace. The line stops briefly, moves out another 20 feet or so, and then stops again. You remain on stand, eyes glued to the spool, waiting for line to begin moving out again. After 20 or 30 minutes without more line movement, you decide your deer is down and dead, and it's time to follow him up.

With the Game Tracker, *never cut that line until you find the deer*. If you cut

When you can come home with a nice big buck such as this, isn't extra effort while tracking worth the trouble? *TVA Photo*

the line, you could be in the process of following up when the deer decides to run some more, and you could have the revolting development of seeing the tag (cut) end of your line disappear forever into the cover behind a moving deer. Much better to remove the Tracker's holder from your bow and anchor it at your stand, pointing in the direction of the deer's flight. Most hunters use Trackers with 2500 feet of line, and it

would be a rare severely wounded deer that hauled all that line behind him before lying down to sleep.

When following that white line's path through cover, it's best to keep one hand on the line. This tells you instantly if and when that deer starts to move again. And if that happens, back off a good distance, sit down and have a smoke, anything to give the deer time to resettle and stop again. After a short while, take line in hand and follow once again. The little white line will lead you right to your trophy, regardless of where he goes.

And please, after you've dressed your deer, don't leave all that nylon string in the woods. Small wildlife can easily strangle and die in loose string, especially long lengths of strong nylon, and it only takes a few minutes to get all the line in hand for proper disposal back home. I don't imagine many landowners would enjoy having your long string fouled in his tractor's transmission or draped between fencewires, so pick it up and take it with you. If nothing else, before disposing of it you might want to measure the exact distance your deer ran from shot to drop, simply by putting a tape measure to the amount of nylon he hauled off the spool. Match this figure with first-hand knowledge of where your arrow hit and what internal damage was done; do this a few seasons in a row and you'll have a better idea of the best spots to aim for the next time a big whitetail comes within bow range.

The advantages of the Game Tracker are obvious when you're hunting in rainy weather and the wet threatens to wash out any blood trail your deer might leave.

The Tracker's nylon line isn't affected by moisture and its white color is easily followed no matter how stormy and overcast the day.

All in all, a lot of bowhunters think of tracking wounded deer in the same way they think about dental appointments, but I thoroughly believe that a positive attitude, following blood trails or a nylon line, will go a very long way toward recovering your deer, especially when the sign left for you to find, interpret and follow doesn't exactly jump up and shout, *Here I am!* It's a matter of responsibility for you to find the deer you've arrowed, no matter how long it takes, even if you have to beg or borrow a Coleman lantern and do the job after sundown. A Coleman lantern's quality of light is different than that of a flashlight beam, not to mention that it's a heckuva lot brighter, and blood spots on leaves and such show up much better (as a spot of solid black) when a Coleman is used. Successful shots taken just at dusk usually result in a nighttime tracking job, and the chore can be made easier if you'll use the lantern's glow. It also makes the eventual field-dressing easier in dark woods.

9

Be a Deer Watcher
All Year

If you're like most outdoorsmen, you just plain get a kick out of seeing wild deer, watching them interact with one another, or even just pause on the edge of a woodland road before disappearing into the brush. The whitetail is a beautiful and secretive animal, and seeing one or more by chance is a pretty rare—and very special—happening.

So it shouldn't take too much argument on my part to get you to go deer watching all year-round. If you enjoy seeing deer, how much work could it be?

But besides mere enjoyment, watching deer has important advantages for the hunting archer. Watch a small herd of whitetails (or even fallow deer, if that's all you can locate in your area) and after a while you begin to notice things you never saw before. Like the way a big old

doe takes the herd's safety under her care. Nobody appoints the old lady to that job—she just seems to assume it and the others follow along, perfectly happy to let the more experienced animal take the risks and make the judgments. They string out behind her when the deer move from place to place, most often single file if the movement is steady.

Notice how the lead doe moves slowly out into a clearing while her followers remain on the edge of cover. The doe walks halfway across the clearing, stops to look, listen and test the air, and then she continues, finally looking back over her shoulder to let the others know it's time for them to follow.

I once watched a herd of half a dozen deer feeding on the edge of a picked beanfield when a small farm dog walked

There is nothing like a trophy whitetail mount to dress up a home or office. This is the author's home office.

out of the woods, spotted the herd, and started walking toward them to investigate. Suddenly all of the herd's eyes and ears were on the dog's approach, but when the dog got within 50 feet of the deer, it was the old herd leader that began walking quickly toward the dog, her ears and eyes very alert, tail half raised, front feet prancing and ready for battle. The dog, finding itself confronted by such a determined defender, quickly turned tail and slinked off. The doe returned to her fellows and went back to feeding, another of her duties successfully carried out.

Of course, you can't just waltz out of the house some July evening and go watch deer, unless you know of a captive herd someplace nearby. You have to know where to find deer, and if you've been scouting year-round as you're supposed to, finding deer to watch shouldn't be overly difficult.

A friend of mine near Dayton, Ohio,

sits in his car just outside a fenceless nature preserve near his home several evenings a week. The local deer have a habit of coming into the preserve property to feed on specially planted vegetables, and my friend has seen the same buck so many times, along with a handful of does, that he's been able to watch the buck sprout, develop and finally shed three sets of antlers in as many years. The deer have become accustomed to seeing the parked car with one or two humans in it, and they feed unconcerned through it all.

The more you know about deer, the more complete deer hunter you will be. Even if the deer spot you watching them and react by running off, you've learned several things if you take a minute to consider. Where was the wind just before the deer reacted? How could you have approached the deer differently, given the same terrain and wind conditions, so they couldn't have scented you? If the deer not only scented but also saw you, how did that happen? Did you move when one animal raised its head from feeding? Did you draw its attention by moving, displaying your silhouette through the woods? Maybe you moved along the skyline of a nearby hill or ridge, drawing attention because of your movements.

If the deer you're watching are wild and not captive, noting when they do what they do is important, as well. If you've located a herd feeding in a cropfield, maybe on waste corn or soybeans or wheat, note the time of day they usually show up at that food source, the direction of their travel to and out of the field, and then note the wind at the same time. Had you been in the field when the deer approached, could they have

scented you, and how could you prevent it in a hunting situation?

Sometimes you'll see several does argue over a particular ear of corn or orchard apple. The does will kick at each other, sometimes even rearing up on their hind legs, ears laid back in anger, and kicking out at each other with their front hooves. I've seen summertime (antlerless) bucks drive other deer from some choice food morsel by butting them with their heads or kicking with a hind foot; bucks seldom rear up and fight with their front feet, although this will occur once in a while.

Watching deer get up from their day beds will tell you something about what to expect if you come upon bedded deer while hunting. Deer get to their feet in the same manner as cattle; first the hindquarters come up, then the front of the deer follows. Bucks often defecate and/or urinate immediately upon getting up, often right in the spot they were bedded a moment ago. A buck about to do this humps his back a little and raises his tail out of the way. Does and fawns, however, seem in need of some violent exercise upon leaving their beds and will race around in a game of you-chase-me-I'll-chase-you for a few minutes, then suddenly all participants settle down and maybe move off slowly to feed or go to water. I've seldom seen a buck race around in this manner; apparently it's beneath their dignity, or they don't feel stiff after bedding for a while.

When I lived in northern New Jersey, I spent many hours on the 6000-acre Great Swamp National Wildlife Refuge near Basking Ridge. The refuge is open to the public and I walked the miles of groomed trails wearing light boots and carrying a pair of quick-focusing 7 × 35 binoculars. Morning and evening, it was a good bet I'd find quite a few whitetails leaving the dense hardwood and cedar-woods to feed across the refuge's many small fields, and I'd plop down, my back to a comfortable tree trunk, put my elbows on my knees and glue my eyes to the glasses, watching what the deer did, how they moved, and what sorts of things drew their attention while other things were ignored.

These deer are accustomed to automobile traffic, and they largely ignore passing cars, even cars that slow down when a driver spots them. But if a car door opens, the deer are all alert and ready to bounce away to cover. For instance, that's why I once saw three deer enter and swim one of the refuge's small bodies of water. The trio moved quickly into the pond, waded in and immediately began swimming, heads held well above the water. On the far side they waded onto dry land (or what passes for dry land in the refuge's mucky interior), spread their legs all around and shook themselves violently, sending water droplets in every direction. The group then reformed, lead doe in front, and headed off for some secret destination.

I found that too much human foot travel in an area containing deer can and will drive deer to swim large or small bodies of water; the hollow hair covering them makes them bob around like corks and they don't seem to mind the water at all. Keep this in mind if your hunting area contains a wide river or lake with a wooded island in the middle. Deer have been known to abandon the mainland to escape hunter pressure while taking up temporary residence on islands reachable only by swimming.

I've seen woodland caribou in northern Manitoba do the same thing. In the middle of a shore lunch at a place called Coppermine, I suddenly heard hooves on rock and turned in time to see a fully antlered bull caribou staring at me as I chewed a sandwich. My fishing party was lunching on a lake island at least half a mile from the mainland, and my guide said the local caribou often swam out to the breezy island to escape the swarm of biting insects in the big woods ashore.

Of course, you can't watch deer if you can't find them, but there are ways around this, especially if all you're after for the moment is someplace where you can merely observe. Make it clear all you want to do is look and most landowners will admit you onto their place.

I'm twice blessed in this department. A friend of mine is the caretaker for a large sportsmen's club not far from my home, and one of his responsibilities is looking after a captive herd of whitetails in a 7½-acre fenced enclosure. The herd contains about 15 whitetails, twice that in late spring when all the fawns have been dropped, and it's a perfect place to observe the animals. Another local herd of fallow deer, on a private estate, consisting of half a dozen or so animals, is only a 15-minute drive from my house. Both of these herds are used to having people around, so they pretty much ignore observers and go about the business of being deer.

Deer watching can have very practical uses, too. Last fall was to be my wife Arlene's first season as a deer hunter, and I wanted to show her how to look for deer in dense cover, what to look for when a deer becomes aware of her presence, and where to hit deer in various positions. The best way I knew was to take her to these two captive deer herds and simply let her watch them. Occasionally I'd point out a particular animal and ask where she would hit it with her arrow, and what that arrow could be expected to do from that angle. The visits served to familiarize Arlene with the nature of whitetail behavior, and when the bow season rolled around she was no longer a novice; she knew what to look for, when to shoot and when to wait, and so on. Watching deer can do the same thing for you.

If you have no idea where to look for observable deer, call the state game protector or game warden in your area. Most such officers are assigned to counties or regions in all states and they have a working familiarity with which landowners report seeing numbers of deer, where the car-deer collisions take place and so on, and most are happy to pass this information along to interested sportsmen. Once you've discovered which farms, ranches, plantations or whatever contain deer, it's your next job to tap on the owner's door and ask permission to take a look at the deer on his place. Most farmers already know where the whitetails on their lands hang out, and they can point you in the right direction, thereby saving you time.

Just a few weeks before I wrote this chapter, I phoned the game protector in my home mostly-rural county and asked if he could point out a couple of nearby spots where I might inquire for bowhunting permission this fall. He obliged, suggesting the lands surrounding a small municipal airport, and a small tobacco farm overlooking the Ohio River not far away. Armed thusly, I drove over to the indicated areas. I stopped to chat with the airport manager and he agreed that the area contained a lot of deer. "I hope you get permission to hunt because sometimes we have a heck of a time with deer getting on our grass runways just when we want to use them," he said. I knocked on some neighborhood farm doors and lined up two places to hunt this fall, smack in the middle of a deer bonanza. The tobacco farmer was also friendly, saying his crop of tobacco plants were nibbled and stepped on by deer every year and he'd be happy to let me hunt all I wanted to. I'm now using both of these spots to not only observe deer during the offseason, but to do my preseason scouting as well. Come this fall, I expect to have three or four treestands in some real hotspots that have never been hunted before, and I'll have become familiar enough with the local herds to know when and how to get close to any trophy deer that might be around. Watching deer has all kinds of advantages.

I had an unusual experience last fall when I visited my friend's deer enclosure. All three of his bucks were in full antler at the time, although only one buck, a massive 6½-year-old who toted a 12-point rack, was fully in rut. He spent much of his time running the two smaller bucks, 8 and 6 points each, away from the ripe does. The caretaker and I were standing well inside the enclosure, just watching the deer and taking an occasional photograph, when one of the bucks decided we'd brought him a treat and he started walking toward us like a big friendly dog. When he got 20 feet away I stopped taking photos long enough to glance at the caretaker. When the buck got within 10 feet I stopped taking pictures altogether and began to look for a stick, or a tree to climb. Captive deer, especially bucks, can be very unpredictable during the rutting season, and I didn't want any argument with a mature, antlered buck. When the buck got three feet away, my companion took off his ballcap and waved it in the buck's face, yelling at him to get out of there. The buck, nonplussed, merely walked a small circle around us, sniffing all the while for the apples he was sure we carried. I was tempted to reach out to pat him between his handsome antlers, but that would have been pressing my luck. No telling what he might have done had I touched him.

If you do go among captive deer for observation purposes, be sure you have a quick escape route worked out because bottle-fed bucks can be dangerous. The late Kim Heller, a photographer for the Ohio Division of Wildlife, was lethally gored by a captive buck in eastern Ohio some years ago while trying to shoot some deer photos, and the supervisor of a Masonic home somehow got between a rutting captive buck and some of his ripe does and was severely gored. And I know of one instance where a bottle-raised buck, when mature and fully antlered, hung around a farm, chasing the farmer and his son, to the extent that a local wildlife officer had to shoot the buck to protect them. Remember, captive bucks have lost their fear of man and sometimes see the nearest human as a rival during the mating season, when competition between local bucks is fierce for available does. The former herd buck of a captive bunch of whitetails in Ohio got meaner as he matured and ended up chasing his owner right out of the pen every time he tried to feed the deer. Even a three-gallon

metal bucket bounced off his head failed to turn his charge, and the owner finally had to tranquilize the troublemaker with a dart gun, saw off his headgear and sell him to a horse breeder. Twenty-four hours later the breeder was on the phone, pleading to return the buck. "That damned deer is trouble," he shouted into the mouthpiece. "First he chased me out of the pen as soon as the drug wore off, and now he's in there beating up on my horses."

If you watch wild deer very often, sooner or later you will see a deer assume a certain position at the moment it sees and identifies you as a human. When that happens you'll have no trouble realizing that the whitetail has you made, boresighted, identified, and probably knows how much money you're carrying. First and foremost, the deer is looking directly at you; this can happen whether you're on the ground or in a treestand (deer *do* look up occasionally). The ears are fanned in your direction, the front legs are slightly spread, and the forequarters may appear to be slightly closer to the ground than the hindquarters. The deer's neck and rump hair may slowly rise on end, and the bannerlike white tail will also become erect and may even curl up over the lower back.

If the deer you've been watching (or waiting to arrow) assumes this behavior, you might as well tip your hat to the deer, lean back, light up a smoke and hum your favorite ditty because, buddy, you have been *made*. He knows where you are, what you are, and why you're there in the first place. A deer in this position is on the thin edge of being gone; you may even see the animal's back and shoulder muscles begin to bunch under his hide, in preparation for a fast exit. The next sound you'll hear is the *Huff!* of a deer breaking into a wild run, and the deer may snort shortly thereafter as it disappears from the scene. If the deer you're after shows this behavior, you will know one thing about the deer, and another thing about yourself: The deer is about to depart, and you sure screwed up someplace.

As you observe deer, try to notice whether they appear to react to different colors, because there is new evidence that whitetails *can* see colors, at least a few of them, at certain times of the day. University studies conducted in Ontario and Texas indicate that the deer's big, bulbous eyes contain both rods and cones, with the rods sensitive to black, white and gray and the cones sensitive to colors. Even with their excellent night vision, however, deer see color far better in bright daylight than at night, according to study results. There has been some discussion of whether white-tailed deer do in fact discern the bright orange safety clothing used by many gun hunters; some evidence suggests that they do. Of course, few—if any—bowhunters use bright orange. Bowhunters take great pains to blend into their surroundings and therefore shun any bright color, including blaze orange, but it's nonetheless interesting to learn that the game animal you've been after all these years has all along been able to determine certain colors in broad daylight. Just when I was certain that current information was correct and deer could see only black, white and shades of gray, along comes new information saying they see color as well. Next thing you know they'll tell us to brush our teeth side to side instead of up and down.

If you watch wild deer, you will eventually train your eyes to see (and your brain to recognize) deer in cover. If this sounds easy, try spotting a lone deer in heavy timber with the pattern of sun and shadow to complicate things. Sometimes you'll slowly scan the cover from one side to the other, and completely overlook a deer standing in a little opening but shrouded by shadow. There it is, standing broadside, and you overlook it. Don't feel badly. Every experienced hunter has done—and will occasionally continue to do—the very same thing. Deer in shadow appear very dark, almost black, as do the tree trunks and clumps of honeysuckle and everything else in a tall woods. It's a matter of knowing what to look for, then training your eye to see it almost automatically.

This doesn't come right away. It's sort of like deciding to train your hair to lie flat where it used to curl, or parting it on the other side all of a sudden. You have to comb your hair that way *a lot* before it gets the message, and it's the same with training your eyes and brain to see deer in cover.

Outdoor writer Byron Dalrymple made some pertinent suggestions in a magazine article he wrote some years ago in which he suggested that deer watchers use binoculars to look *into* cover instead of just *at* it. The idea was to penetrate the edges of the brush and trees and see what stood inside. The writer used the example of taking three pictures of the same deer from the same distance, using a 50mm lens, an 80mm lens and a 200mm telephoto lens; with every switch to a higher-power lens, the deer standing inside the cover became larger and more obvious. The point here is to look *beyond* the front edge of a woodlot, weedfield or patch of honeysuckle. It can pay off.

You've no doubt heard of hunts when a hunter walked into one end of a field just as a herd of deer ran out the other; seeing what was in that field, instead of just what was on this edge of it, could have put the archer within effective range. Observing deer in the offseason—be they wild deer or captive animals—will help train your eye to see what's there, even if it's not immediately apparent to the naked eye.

It follows that if your wanderings take you into good deer country, you can't help but run across sign left by those deer. Tracks, beds, rubs, droppings, even bits of hair left on wire fences—all will help you be a better woodsman and hunter by the time the fall season rolls around.

And if you like a bit of dark humor, as I do, you might want to do to your best hunting buddy what I did to mine a few summers back. We were scouting a large, brushy farm containing quite a few whitetails. I'd walked over this farm before and I knew it contained a heck of a lot of deer droppings, those small brown piles of one-inch feces that deer seem to leave all over the place. Well, I'd been eating a chocolate candy bar and had shaped the last bite into something of an oval. We came upon a very fresh pile of deer droppings and I went down on one knee next to it, remarking that it sure *looked* fresh. I reached down, palming the candy segment, and suddenly pretended to pick up one of the droppings, which was actually the candy segment. I sniffed it closely and reported that it sure *smelled* fresh. The fellow looking over my shoulder grimaced a little, and then I delivered the coup de grace: I lifted the candy to my mouth, sniffed it once more, popped it into my mouth, and remarked that, yes, it sure *tasted* fresh, too. The guy fainted dead away.

10

The Compound Bow

It's been said that eight out of every 10 bowhunters use compound bows. This sounds impressive, but even this 80 percent estimate may be a little low. The fact is, the compound has become less expensive to buy since manufacturers perfected two-wheel models. The compound also shoots a much faster arrow than either the longbow or the recurve, and this in turn allows the hunter to shoot heavier arrows for better penetration.

A complaint among old-timers and purists, however, is that modern compound bows are too "gadgety" and depart too far from what archery is supposed to be. There is some credit to this argument, and certainly to each his own when it comes to tackle preferences. But, it cannot be disputed that modern com-

pound bows help eliminate some of the errors bowhunters make.

One asset, as an example, is that compounds provide flatter trajectory for longer distances. When you take a shot at a deer at an unknown distance, the compound will deliver less of a rainbow trajectory, which means you can be accurate at greater distances with a compound than with a recurve.

I know this from my own experience. When I was new to compound shooting back in the 1960s and carried an Allen compound with four wheels, I had at least two shots at nice bucks, one at about 50 yards, the other somewhere between 55 and 60 yards. Let me say right here that both of these distances are beyond what I normally shoot, and certainly what I prefer, but both animals were standing broadside, had not detected my presence, and I just couldn't resist. In both cases I shot over the buck's back. I just couldn't get it through my head, having shot a fiberglass recurve for so long, that any bow would shoot so flat that I could hold dead on at these greater distances. I lifted my aim point a hair and that's where my arrow went—a hair high, for clean misses at both deer. One arrow buried itself in a tree trunk so deeply that I had to abandon the head, while the other went zinging away through a hardwoods and ended up Lord knows where.

It's a toss-up as to which of the two major advantages of the compound is more important to the bowhunter: draw weight let-off or flatter trajectory for the arrow. I suspect the former, however. Shooting a compound accurately is simply easier on the muscles because you're only holding a percentage of the total poundage. Compound bows offer let-offs of from 15 to 50 percent, which means if you're pulling a compound with a total draw weight of, say, 60 pounds, and the let-off is 50 percent, you're only required to hold 30 pounds of draw weight, which is a heck of a lot easier than holding a recurve's 60 pounds at full draw.

In addition, the modern compound usually offers you the option of changing the bow's draw length to fit your individual measurements. My two stepsons shoot Bear Whitetail compounds, and each of these bows is tailored to their individual draw lengths; a simple adjustment of the draw length with a small wrench is all that's needed. One of the boys is 6 feet 3 inches tall and uses a 30-inch draw, while his brother is 5 feet 10 inches tall and has a draw

The compound bow's adjustable draw weight and length makes it perfect for beginners and old-timers alike. Here, Arlene Bowring tries out a new draw length on her Proline bow.

length of 28½ inches. The adjustable compound bow is the ticket for both of them.

If you don't know your exact draw length, there are two ways to determine it. One is to stand with one fist closed and rest the front of it flat against a wall. Have a companion measure the distance from the wall to your lips. Another way is to come to full draw with an extra-long arrow on the bow, holding firmly when you reach your full draw length. Have someone put a tape measure on the arrow shaft, measuring from the bottom of the nock slot to the spot where the arrow shaft passes the front of the bow's arrow rest. Mark this spot and measure it; this is your correct draw length. It's important to know your exact draw length when you shop for a compound because some bows are adjustable and some are not. A bow is a very personal choice and it should fit you exactly.

Working out with weights is one way to build shooting muscles in the back, arms and wrists. Here, Dave Dornbach pumps a little iron.

A chap named Dr. C. J. Lapp designed the first compound bow way back in the 1930s, but it wasn't until the 1960s that H. W. Allen patented his first compound. But with archers being the conservative bunch that they are, it took quite a while for the newfangled compound to be accepted by either bowhunters or field tournament archers. Early development of a usable compound for hunters was developed by Tom Jennings, and his efforts were central to the compound's acceptance. This began a race between recurves and compounds that today has eight out of every ten bowhunters using wheeled bows with cables, let-offs and trajectories about as flat as a tabletop.

How popular are compounds? I recently had an old but fully serviceable 50-pound left-handed compound that I wanted to sell. I advertised it in a local newspaper's classified section, and had 18 calls from interested hunters the first day the ad appeared. I sold it that same evening for my asking price. Before I could kill the ad, it ran another two days and I had at least 30 more phone calls from prospective buyers. An old four-wheeled, left-handed compound, mind you, and with only marginal draw weight for big game at 50 pounds. Buyers, left-handed all, came out of the woodwork in response to the ad. Lovers of the compound bow must be all over the place.

Newcomers to archery and bowhunting, in particular, welcome the compound because the bow's requirements for the user progress along with the user's abilities. I bought my wife, Arlene, a Proline two-wheel compound a couple of years ago and have been able to slowly increase the draw weight from its lowest setting of 35 pounds, while she was still developing her shooting muscles, to its present and maximum setting of 50 pounds. The Proline offers a 50 percent let-off, which means Arlene pulled only about 18 pounds at full draw as a beginner, and today holds only about 25 pounds with the bow cranked up to full power. Yet even while using the same bow at increasing weight settings, the newcomer becomes used to the overall weight, balance and idiosyncrasies of the same bow throughout the development period. Perhaps because I'm an avid archer and bowhunter, or because Arlene has a natural ability with the bow, she really enjoys our shooting together and has developed into a fine archer on the range. I'm still introducing her to the fine points of bowhunting, but she approaches this with the same eagerness as target shooting, and it's just a matter of time before she sticks her first buck. Maybe it'll happen this fall.

I have a friend who is very involved in mastering the authentic English longbow he uses to hunt deer. He is determined to take a whitetail buck with this old-timer before moving on to the compound, and while I admire his tenacity and adherence to tradition, I also know he'll be delighted with how his arrow cast flattens out when he goes to a wheeled bow. The longbow he uses is some 70 inches long, and more than once his limb tips have ticked overhead branches just when he released an arrow at a deer, resulting in a miss of the animal. He'll also welcome the shorter length of most hunting compounds, which is much easier to thread through tight brush and to handle in a treestand.

Sometimes the efficiency of modern compounds smacks you in the face so hard you can't ignore it. A couple of Septembers ago I was in a party of five bowhunters in Idaho's Bitterroots, and it turned out that all five of us were using Browning compounds. All five of us got antlered bull elk in five days of hunting, and one fellow from Louisiana passed up a 4x4 bull for something better and ended up taking a 6x6 on the last day of the hunt. Could this incredible camp record have been set if some or all of us had been using recurve hunting bows? Maybe, maybe not, but I doubt it; at least one of the shots was at a range of nearly 62 paced yards shooting up-mountain, and the heavy hunting shaft and MA-3L head penetrated all of its length plus the fletching into the bull's boiler room, killing the animal within 75 yards. None of the five elk killed on that hunt traveled more than 100 yards after being hit, and only two of them required more than one arrow (two arrows in each case). How efficient is the modern compound bow? I know five hunters who are sold on it, dead certain.

Where does the compound get its tremendous power? The manufacturers will tell you it comes from the bow's ability to store energy for instantaneous release when the string is released and the eccentric wheels, or cams as they have come to be known, are allowed to roll back over into their original position. Add to this the terrific power built into modern laminated bowlimbs, which are designed to withstand repeated flexing and unflexing over a period of several years while remaining strung all the time, unlike a recurve which has its string relaxed when the action is over. Even the simplest compound bow contains as much engineering and development as half a dozen recurves, and this is certainly true of Bear Archery's Delta V bow, introduced in late 1981.

Gary Simonds is chief of research and development for Bear and says the Delta V, which was his baby while in development, may be the fastest bow on today's market. I don't know about that, but it certainly is the loudest; when the string is released, it smacks a pair of Power Bumpers so hard that the sound can be heard for quite some distance in a quiet woods. Consider these numbers when you think of the bow's speed:

A Delta V with a 30-inch draw length and a peak weight of 62 pounds will deliver 63.5 foot-pounds of energy using a 550-grain arrow. A standard two-wheel bow peaking at 70 pounds of draw weight with a 30-inch pull delivers only 51.5 foot-pounds of energy using that same 550-grain arrow. What all this engineering talk means to the bowhunter is that he can now use a heavier, thicker-walled arrow without sacrificing arrow speed.

For the deer hunter, a heavier arrow delivered faster means more penetration, often going all the way through the deer and leaving twin blood trails and faster bleedout. Simonds claims that a noisy release makes no difference even with wary whitetails because the arrow arrives too fast for the deer to jump the string or otherwise react.

"Assuming that animal reaction time is roughly half of human reaction time," said Simonds, "or about three-eighths of a second, an arrow from a bow shooting with a speed of 150 fps (feet per second) would travel about 21 yards in that time period.

"And a bow shooting an arrow at 200

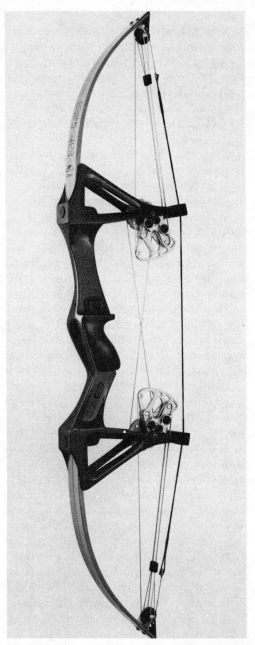

The Delta V compound from Bear Archery weighs nearly six pounds stripped, shoots a very fast arrow and makes a loud snap upon release.

fps would deliver that same arrow out to 30 yards in the same time period."

Simonds' point is that no deer can get out of the way of an arrow from the Delta V because the arrow arrives too quickly after the release and subsequent string slap. I've seen the Delta V in use, but because I shoot left-handed and the bow is produced in right-handed models only, I haven't been able to test the bow to date. The Delta V weighs a hefty 5 pounds 15 ounces stripped (without bow quiver, sights, and so on), which is about as much as the average hunting rifle without scope, and this may be a factor if light weight is important to bowhunters chafing for a new bow.

In fact, the majority of bowhunters that I interviewed for this book volunteered their preference for heavier bows, and all except one turned to the compound as their bow of choice quite some time ago. It's just plain easier to pull and hold a powerful compound, because of the let-off, than it is to use a recurve or longbow of similar power. This allows you to use a heavier, more efficient bow and heavier arrows offering improved penetration, and all this adds up to more deer on the ground in the long run.

It's a simple equation, really: The heavier the bow, the more energy will be available to cast the arrow faster in flight. And the heavier the bow, the heavier the arrow and broadhead that may be used efficiently. Instead of turning aside or even breaking when striking a rib, the tough cartilage between the ribs or other bones, the heavier broadhead can punch its way through and get into the vital area. I know hunters using 60-pound-pull bows whose arrows have gone right through a white-

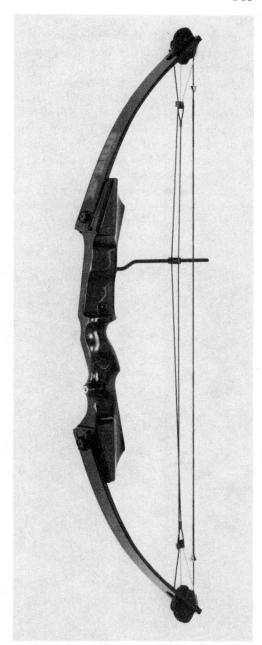

The XI 288 Graphite Plus bow is an example of how technology is providing better and better bows for the hunter.

tail's light bone structure, severed a path through the lungs and/or heart/liver, and exited the deer on the far side to imbed in a tree or the ground. This kind of power provides enough energy to shock any deer, and relates to what Doug Crabtree quoted as his bow's shocking power elsewhere in this book. It's the compound bow's terrific energy storage used to power the arrow in flight that provides this relatively newfound efficiency. The bowhunter still must get close to his deer (most hunters prefer the shot within 30 yards, much closer if possible), and still must be able to place the arrow into specific places on the deer for quick, humane kills, but today's compound bows have come a helluva long way from the old yew longbows that turned the tide of wars in Europe centuries ago.

Let's take a look at the archetypical compound bow's standard parts. It really isn't the pipefitter's nightmare it's been made out to be.

The handle section has three basic parts, or sections, each with its own job. The handle itself is usually pistol-

Left to right, these Deluxe Bushmaster, Hyper Cam and Drake compounds from Browning display the handsome and warm-to-the-touch wooden handle sections preferred by many hunters.

gripped, tailored to fit the palm and heel of the bow hand with comfort and stability. The areas immediately above and below the handle are known as risers, and just above the handle is the arrow plate or rest. Rests come in a wide variety of shapes, sizes and specific designs, and a few even have small holes to admit the small adjustable button used to "tune" the bow for precise release and arrow flight. If the shooter's arrows fly to the left or right, the tuning button can be adjusted in or out to correct the problem. The handle section is made of fancy, high-grained wood, such as hard rock maple with several laminated layers for shine and protection, or magnesium (heavier but more stable than wood).

Handle risers on modern compounds often come with threaded holes of standard diameters to accept a variety of accessories such as stabilizers, bow quivers, cable guards, bowsights and so on. Be sure to check that any bow you're considering for purchase is set up to accept the accessories you expect to use while hunting.

Above and below the handle risers are the limbs, and these handsome sections of most any compound require as much or more careful design than any other section of the entire bow. Consider what the compound's bowlimbs must do, over and over, season after season, all without cracking, splitting or losing their ability to flex in exactly the same manner time after time. Flex recovery must be predictable and repeated every time the bow is fired. It's flex recovery, and the improvements in same, that make your new graphite fishing rod so much better than its old fiberglass counterpart, by the way; the

This Mark-series compound from Golden Eagle shows the recurved limb design, the unique E-wheels and the laminated finish.

faster graphite returns to its unflexed (unbent) position after the cast, the faster it delivers energy to the flyline. The same principle applies to the compound bow.

The compound's adjustment bolt, used to adjust the draw weight peak, and therefore its let-off weight as well, is located at the base of both limbs where they attach to the end of each riser. The tighter the limbs are anchored into the riser sections, the greater will be the draw weight (pull) of the bow; the opposite will be true if the bolts are backed off somewhat, as would be the case when a new archer with undeveloped shooting muscles begins to break in a new bow. This is the beauty of the compound: It can be adjusted to match the abilities of anyone because its draw weight can be adjusted, as can its length of pull. As the shooter's abilities increase, so can the bow's power be pumped up by tightening the adjustment bolts at the base of each limb. A simple wrench for adjusting the bolts is provided with all new bows.

Although the more or less standard compound bow limb is made of a lamination of fiberglass and wood, some manufacturers have found that additional materials built into the limbs help performance and stability. Golden Eagle of Creswell, Oregon, for example, uses a total of five different layers in their limbs, each with its own specialty to add to flex recovery, smoothness and arrow cast. Golden Eagle uses wood from the yew found along the West Coast of the United States, a wood long known for its adaptability in archery. The English were using bows made of yew as far back as the Crusades.

The unique feature on any compound bow, however, is its wheels or cams, located at the tip of each bowlimb. As the bow is drawn, cables slotted into each wheel begin to move; slightly more than halfway through the drawing process, these wheels begin to roll over and the bow suddenly becomes much easier to finish drawing and then hold at full draw. A great deal of engineering has gone into these wheels, more recently called cams as the technology involved has become more complex. The use of eccentric cams, shaped more or less in oval shape and with two slots instead of one, is very popular today and has resulted in bows that are far smoother in operation, not to mention more en-

ergy-efficient, than ever before. Double-slotted cams transfer the cable automatically from one slot to the other in much the same way as the switch on a railroad track guides a train from one set of tracks to another. By changing the slots used on the bow cam, energy is stored even as the bow's weight at full draw is reduced by 50 percent, which is the standard let-off percentage for today's compounds.

The bowstring itself is attached to the steel cable system using a cable anchor made of steel. The anchor is held in place all the time because the bow remains strung all the time, except when repair or adjustments require a takedown best done by an experienced bowyer or repairman. No little engineering has gone into developing the right anchor design, because this item keeps the bow in operation and tuned shot after shot despite the terrific shocks it must absorb with every shot.

Quite a few of today's compounds come with the anchor point already pinpointed by means of a wrap-around brass band measured and placed by the bow maker. Most hunters are satisfied with this single anchor point arrangement, although a few prefer to add a second brass band just above the first, the idea being to anchor the arrow between the two fittings for precision in anchor placement.

The compound bow normally has a base weight (stripped of all accessories and add-ons) greater than that of a recurve bow offering the same draw weight. This is because of the added materials that go into modern compound bow construction, and apparently few archers mind this added weight since more than eight out of every 10

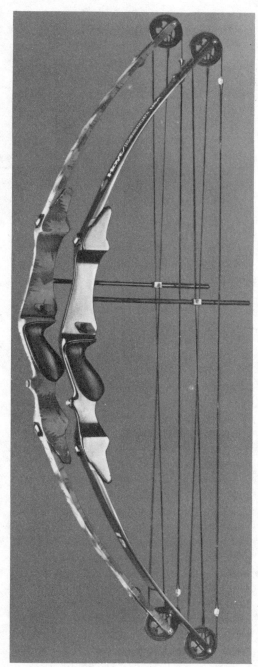

Both of these Hoyt/Easton Buck bows feature standard cable guards and snap-on handles.

bowhunters carry compounds. When you shop for a compound, keep in mind that the manufacturer's advertised bow weight is that of the bow alone, in most cases. It doesn't include such accepted add-ons as a bow quiver, half a dozen hunting arrows with heads, a bowsight, maybe a cable guard and stabilizer, or even the tiny added weight provided by a layer of camouflaging cloth, tape or spray paint. All of these must be figured into the bow's eventual total weight before you can decide if you want to tote the whole shebang into the woods come deer season.

I recently came across an example of how the compound bow can be greatly misunderstood by those unfamiliar with its abilities. I was flyfishing for brook trout in northern Ontario when a fellow angler told me that the provincial government was considering banning the use of compound crossbows for big-game hunting. The government believed, he said, that the combination of the crossbow's terrific accuracy and the compound's known power would result in an unfair advantage for any hunter carrying such a hunting weapon afield for moose, deer, caribou or other game. I tried to explain that a crossbow using a compound prod, or bow, would be no more powerful than a regular crossbow using the same weight prod. I pointed out that the only difference would be greater ease in cocking the crossbow with the compound attached, because of the let-off, and perhaps a lighter triggering system than was possible with the old style of crossbow. He wasn't having any of it, however. He'd gotten it into his head, and said the government had too, that any crossbow with a compound attached just *had* to be far more lethal, and that was that. I didn't argue with him—the brook trout were taking Muddlers that afternoon and we both found better things to do than sit and disagree—but the conversation nonetheless is typical of those who aren't familiar with the compound's capabilities.

I suppose this sort of response can't be unexpected from the uninitiated. The compound bow *does* provide quite a departure from the old longbow or even the modern recurve, and I guess it's natural for anyone confronting such a con-

The Bear Super Brown Bear compound features the clean lines and reduced weight of today's two-wheel compounds.

traption for the first time to believe that anything looking like *that* just has to be unfair, if not just a hair immoral. It is true, of course, that the compound is more efficient than other types of bows, but in the end this only means that the bowhunter is more efficient, likely to wound fewer deer, and is therefore in a better position to maintain the high standards all serious bowhunters set for themselves. It's fairer to the deer, too, because a better hunter will pass up marginal shots because he knows what he can and cannot do with his bow and therefore doesn't have to stretch its capabilities to have a successful hunt.

I recall the first time I saw a hunting compound in use. I was still-hunting my way along a grassy sidehill bordered by thick cedars when another bowhunter moved out of some thick brush and stood watching a thicket of trees that looked at least 55 yards away from his position. I couldn't see his bow at that distance, but when a doe appeared in the spot he was watching, I was amazed to see him raise his bow, draw and release. My first thought then was that he was attempting a shot that was far too long to be accurate, but suddenly the doe jumped, ran about 35 yards in my direction, and then fell.

When the hunter had reached his deer and drawn his dressing knife, I walked in his direction, determined to see what sort of hunter would—and could—take a shot and hit at such long range. He was just pulling his arrow free as I walked up; three-fourths of the shaft was blood-covered, indicating good penetration, and since it was the only used arrow to be seen, I had to believe it had been a one-shot kill. As he moved to roll the doe onto her back, I got a look at his bow resting on the weeds behind him, and it was a heavy-limbed compound, an Allen, I think he said. Four wheels, lots of cable, a handle with large diameter, and the whole thing covered with camo tape. With his permission I lifted the bow and was surprised by its weight compared to the little recurve I was using at the time. I looked the cables up and down, fingered the wheels, and for the life of me couldn't figure out how the darned thing worked. I asked the hunter and he said he really didn't know either. It just performed for him and that was all he needed to know. I walked away shaking my head and wondering what bowhunting was coming to when one-shot kills at 55 yards became everyday events.

Since that day in the late 1960s, of course, compound engineering has come a long, long way. The compound's overall bulkiness has been trimmed down into a slender, lethal-looking bow that's much simpler in appearance but much more complex in design. Trimming excess weight and mass didn't just happen, of course; it required lots of experimentation with new materials and combinations of materials and theories until the right answer was found. Each manufacturer prides himself on employing fine design engineers and craftsmen to bring the design to life; it's all very hi-tech and helps explain why compound bows cost more than modern recurves.

What does all this mean to the bowhunter after deer? It means he can choose from a large variety of compound bows averaging perhaps five pounds stripped weight that will cast a flat arrow for longer distances than has ever been possible before. It means he can tailor the bow, using accessories, to his particular needs and desires, and he can still go light, as bowhunting was meant to be, when compared with toting a rifle into the woods.

I've heard state fish and game officers insist that it takes a bow of at least 35-pound pull to effectively hunt whitetails, and maybe you've heard the same thing. I hope it sounded phony when you heard it, because it isn't true. It takes a bow powerful enough to punch your arrow into the vitals to take deer with any consistency and any amount of sportsmanship, and a 35-pound bow simply will not do that for you. This is why the modern compound is so popular: It's strong enough to do the job, yet gentle enough on us non-behemoth types to let everyone enjoy bowhunting with lethal tackle. I think it takes at least 50 pounds of bow power to seriously hunt deer; anything less isn't being fair to yourself or the game. Hunting with something less than enough bow isn't really hunting at all. It's fooling yourself. It also gives bowhunting a bad name because the bow in your hand is more likely to wound deer than kill cleanly. I know serious hunters who would hang a man by his own bowstring for using less than adequate tackle, and that includes a weak bow. My wife is a slender 5-feet 7-inches tall, yet she shoots a bow of 52 pounds at 29 inches, plenty strong enough to knock down the biggest whitetail around provided she hits her aimpoint. This is a two-wheel model compound that started out at 35 pounds and gradually was cranked up to 52 pounds as her strength and ability permitted. Only a compound bow has this flexibility.

Of course, the compound bow or any

The major advantage of the compound is its 50 percent let-off in draw weight. This allows a longer, steadier aim time. Some 80 percent of today's hunters use compound bows.

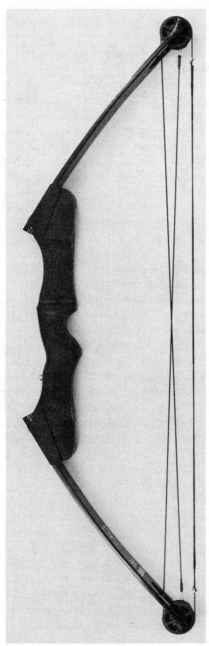

This sleek bow from Browning displays the beauty of simplicity, plus factory camouflaging.

other type of hunting bow requires that you be able to hit where you aim. No amount of let-off is going to put that arrow where you want it all by itself.

Whether you shoot instinctively or with a bowsight, your hold at full draw must be steady enough to allow a firm and consistent ability to aim accurately. This is where the compound shines, because you're required to hold only half of the bow's total peak draw weight. Even the strongest bowhunter around is going to wiggle a little when his muscles are working to hold the bow up and at full draw, and only hours on the practice range will tune those muscles so they'll perform without undue wiggle and wobble. The stronger your shooting muscles, I am convinced, the more accurate you will be on the range and in the woods. It just makes sense that once you're strong and smooth enough to hold that bow at full draw easily and with predictable steadiness, the more you can fine-tune your aim every time you shoot.

Many talented bowhunters I've spoken with claim that the faster you can come to your aimpoint and release, the better and more successful you'll be. This seems to make sense to me, based on my experience. I can recall moments when I struggled to put the sight pin just where I wanted it, failed, tried again and again, only to watch the unalerted buck get tired of hanging around and go wandering off while I fumed and swore at my own ineptitude. Part of this is buck fever, sure; but most of it is preventable by being prepared physically and mentally before that buck makes his appearance.

I've used the word *smooth* a number of times describing what I consider to

Two hunters using compounds took these nice Alabama whitetail bucks. The compound hunting bow has captured the American market nearly everywhere. *Westervelt Lodge Photo*

be the perfect draw, aim and release for me. This is because the smoother I perform the entire operation, the less chance there is that some flaw, some hitch, will appear to mess up the shot. You can actually see smoothness happen if you watch an accomplished shooter on the range. He looks downrange at the target butt, then brings his bow up to horizontal while starting the draw. By the time the draw is completed his shooting

eye has reached the target and he releases the shaft, his draw hand staying at the release point or perhaps drifting an inch or two to the rear. Everything you've just watched is smooth and without pauses or jerks. Although this sort of perfection is sometimes accomplished with the recurve bow, I believe it's an easier goal using the compound.

I recently had the chance to see a couple of professional bowyers put a pair of Golden Eagle compounds through their paces at a public demonstration. I wish I had filmed their performance and was able to provide a print of that film with every copy of this book, because they were as smooth as finely machined mechanisms. This can only come with repeated practice and attention to detail, as any accomplished archer would readily admit. Any pro athlete makes the routine plays look easy, and the exceptional plays look routine. It's the smooth, seemingly effortless transition from stationary to motion that fools our eyes into believing that the effort is routine when it really isn't, and this same thing can and should be a part of your shooting skills. Smoothness is built into the better compound bows; test-fire enough of them and you'll have little trouble determining which is for you and which isn't.

When I was a teenager, a carpenter friend made me a simple stave bow that tapered slightly along both limbs, had only a shallow notch in each end to hold the bowstring, and had no handle or arrow rest. I had to rest my shaft along the fist formed by my bow hand and was so new to archery that I rested my arrow on the same side of the bow that I drew on. I could hardly hit a thing with that bow (although I did manage to plunk a cottontail rabbit at five yards, much to my amazement), and with everything going against accuracy, it was no wonder. The bow probably pulled only 25 pounds or so, but to untrained young muscles even that was too much to hold for more than a second or two.

What a long way the compound bow has come from those days! Easy to draw and even easier to hold, forgiving for those who require an extra moment or two to aim, becoming lighter and lighter as new technology allows lighter materials to be used, the modern compound is truly the single most important factor in the explosion of bowhunting's popularity nationwide. Sure they cost more—it's a lot more bow that you're buying these days—but the benefits are worth every red cent.

A word of caution right here about retuning your bow after making adjustments in the length of draw or the draw poundage. Any adjustment that you make is likely to throw off the bow's tuning, which means it won't hit as it used to until you put all the parts back into sync with one another again. To do this, go ahead and adjust either the length of draw (from 28 to 29 inches, for example) and/or the draw poundage from, say, 54 to 62 pounds. Measure each new setting carefully to make sure it's what you want. If you don't have the proper measuring equipment, an experienced bowyer or tackle operator/pro can make the proper measurements for you.

Now that you have the new settings where you want them, put a dozen arrows through the bow at pre-determined ranges to get a starting point for fine-tuning the bow. The bow will feel

The draw weight adjustment on a Golden Eagle Mark compound. A simple twist adjusts the weight up or down.

different, of course, and this will be the first thing you'll notice. It's also likely that you will have to adjust the arrow rest, shooting button and so on to bring the compound's accuracy and smoothness back to where you want them. And if you're a new archer increasing your bow's power, it will take quite a few arrows to accustom your muscles and shooting eye to the new requirements of a heavier bow, even if the increase amounts to only a few pounds of pull.

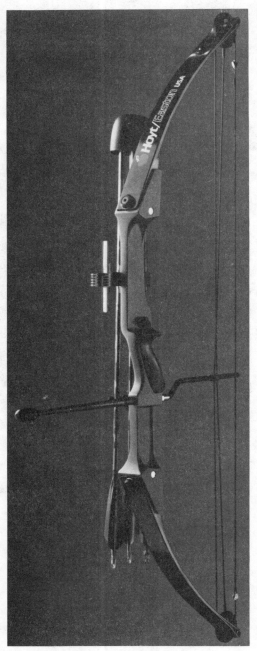

The Gamegetter compound shown here carries its own cable guard and stabilizer, plus a small bow quiver.

My wife bought a few dozen Easton Gamegetter arrows for her compound and they came about two inches too long. As an experiment, we had half the arrows cut down to her normal shooting length while the other half were left at their manufacturer's length and fitted with inserts and target points. At her old draw length, she was soon zeroing with her usual accuracy, but when we increased the length of draw on her old bow and she shot the new longer arrows, she found that she could group half a dozen shafts in a tighter group than had previously been the case. This took a bit of tuning and getting used to, of course, but Arlene is now shooting at nearly 30 inches and doing much better every time she shoots.

The adjustability of the compound, be it an old four-wheel bow or one of the new two-wheel bio-cam models, is perhaps the greatest factor in the compound's overall flexibility. Just keep in mind that this same ability to adjust requires some post-adjustment tuning if you're to hit every time you release an arrow with your bow at the new settings.

In setting up your compound for deer season, *listen* to your bow and it will tell you what's needed to make draw, hold and release perfectly silent. Shoot some arrows in a quiet spot with no background noises, as it is in the woods. Even the smallest sound can and will alert a whitetail, especially when the deer is only a few yards away. The scrape of an arrow across a plastic arrow rest, the noise made by two cables rubbing together, perhaps the little squeak made when you pull an arrow from your bow quiver's rubberized slots. All of these can alert the game just when you're preparing to shoot, and the only way to avoid it is to note and get rid of all extraneous sounds before you go afield.

A noisy arrow rest is easy to change; today's adhesive-backed rests make it a snap to switch to the one that will let your drawn arrow slide by with no sounds. Just be sure you install the rest at the right height and angle when the switch is made.

Cable noise can be silenced by adding cable servings available from Browning and other tackle makers. The serving is backed with adhesive and should wrap snugly around each cable, both above and below the point of contact. Quite a few hunting bows come equipped with a steel cable guard that prevents cable noise altogether.

It's unusual for the bow's wheels or cams to make noise when they roll over during the draw, but it can happen now and then. If your cams have a tendency to speak up when they move, add a bit of light machine oil to the cam axles to quiet them.

There is one noise common to drawing your bow on a big buck that can't be silenced with gimmicks, oils or any other add-ons that I know of, and that's the loud and persistent slamming of your heart against your chest wall when that big so-and-so walks out into the open, lowers his head to nuzzle the acorns, and you raise the bow and come up to full draw. The vibrations of this noise have been known to make arms and heads shake, eyes fill with tears, and your not-so-calm brain insist that anything *that* loud must be heard by the deer, too.

Well, I suppose lots of experience as a bowhunter might calm this noise

Practicing with your compound under actual hunting conditions is the secret to hitting when the season opens.

somewhat. Locate, approach and get a shot at enough big whitetails in your lifetime and maybe, just maybe, this condition will calm somewhat. But not completely, and maybe that's for the best. The most modern and expensive compound bow on the market is really nothing more than a product of technology, with no real connection to nerves and muscles and plain old buck fever. We get buck fever, you and I and 1000 other bowhunters, because we've worked so hard to bring the Big Moment about, and when it's here we find we're really only human after all. And if bowhunting for whitetails didn't make my hands shake a little and my heart do a Gene Krupa number in my ribcage, maybe I wouldn't be in the deer woods in the first place.

11

The Recurve Bow

The recurve bow is just what the name implies: recurved, or curved twice instead of just once, as is the longbow. The tips of the recurve's bowlimbs have a second curve opposing the bow's overall configuration, and this is where the bow gets its power.

The history of the recurve bow style is somewhat hazy, but it's generally believed that the style was developed in the Mideast and Far East many centuries ago. There are reports of recurve bows being made from the horns of sheep or wild goats, which in some animals take on the approximate shape of a recurve's smooth curves. Can you imagine an archer who could pull a bow made of horn? What a brute he must have been!

Unlike the much more popular compound bow, the recurve gets tougher to pull and hold the farther the bow is drawn; there is no let-off. Your muscles put as much energy into the bow on release as it is going to get. Also unlike the compound, most hunting recurves have no set draw length. The average archer draws to his personal measurements, say 28 inches, while another archer can pick up the same bow and draw it perhaps 29 or 30 inches, gaining more arrow speed because he has put more energy into the bow before shooting.

The recurve bow is generally much lighter than the compound, too. While the compound includes a handle and risers, special bowlimbs, wheels or cams, cables, counterweights and so on, the recurve is made up of only three basic parts: handle, upper limb and lower limb. The bow is simple, does not get out of adjustment as the compound can, and in my opinion much more closely resembles what bowhunting is all about in terms of overall experience.

I like to travel light when I bowhunt, and that includes the bow I carry. If I'm weighted down with gear, I might as well be gun hunting. The recurve bow lets me do that, yet I sacrifice relatively

The basic design of the recurve may be ancient, but modern materials make it excellent for the deer hunter. Here, Dave Fulmer pulls down on a buck.

little when I choose the recurve over the compound, considering the way I hunt.

It's true that the average compound shoots a flatter arrow at greater speed than a recurve will, and this must be taken into consideration when it's time to buy tht new bow you've been promising yourself. But a good-quality recurve costs less than a decent compound, too, so the pros and cons tend to buy that new bow you've been promsition to choose one style or another.

My first serious hunting bow was a Shakespeare Necedah X26 recurve with an average draw weight of 45 pounds. Very light, only 58 inches long unstrung, and capable of casting a hunting arrow with broadhead for a fair distance without undue drop, the bow served me well for several seasons. I killed three deer with it using Razorheads on cedarwood arrows, and in one case had my shaft pass completely through a standing whitetail at a distance of about 35 yards. The arrow then buried itself in a small tree 10 yards beyond the deer. The whitetail ran about 45 yards before lying down, and it was dead when I found it, shot through both lungs. With this sort of performance by a recurve pulling the relatively light weight of 45 pounds at about 29 inches, I can't knock what I was able to do with it.

A number of hardline bowhunters started with the recurve and have stuck with it despite all the furor over compound bows. Fred Bear, certainly one of the world's best and most successful bowhunters of big game, has for decades preferred to hunt with one of his own recurves, the Bear Kodiak, and his long, impressive list of big, heavy animals taken with the recurve is testimony

The limb tip of this old recurve, sometimes still used by the author, shows the recurved limb design and string slot. The brush button and string silencer are important for recurve hunting.

Fred Bear, the master among modern bowhunters, still shoots the Bear Kodiak TD made by his firm. Note the brush button just below the upper bowlimb tip.

enough about the recurve's effectiveness in the hands of a competent hunter.

Some years ago I was in a party of three archers hunting the rolling grasslands and brushy creekbottoms of southeastern Colorado for mule deer. I carried a two-wheel compound while one of my compadres, a local wildlife artist and avid bowhunter, toted a 60-pound recurve. This is big, wide-open country where any deer seen are likely to be on the dead run or so far away that a bowshot is likely to be chancy at best, but we managed to run a huge old velvet-antlered mulie buck out of some lowland brush and into a huge wheatfield. The buck knew he was safe in the open and had the audacity to bed down right out in the foot-high wheat stubble, where only his heavy-beamed antlers were visible.

My recurve-toting buddy sneaked as close as he could on two feet to that buck, then got down on his belly, infantry style, and began inching his way through the wheat. Using binoculars, I watched from half a mile away as the stalk began, and the closer the archer got, the more that buck turned his head this way and that, trying to discover the source of the faint sounds he was hearing. Finally the hunter bellied to within 20 yards of the big buck and slowly raised himself to one knee while bringing the bow up and drawing, all in the same motion. The deer spotted him immediately, scrambled to his feet and wheeled to run, but not before an aluminum shaft flashed in the afternoon sunlight and buried itself in the buck's shoulder. The buck had begun to run when the shot hit him, and was at a minimum 30 to 35 yards from the hunter and moving fast, yet the arrow lead had

been perfect and the buck went down, lung-shot.

Now, I have to agree that the successful ending to this account is mostly due to the skill and patience of the bowhunter who did the stalking and shooting, but it's nontheless true that the recurve he carried performed when he needed it. Don't kid yourself that recurve bows are child's toys. They are as lethal as any bow you can carry, provided your skills as a hunter and woodsman are honed sharp.

You will not get the flat arrow flight from a recurve that a compound of comparable weight will provide, plain and simple. The arrow from a recurve bow has a rainbow trajectory, but this isn't the handicap it may appear to be if you allow for it, and this means plenty of time on the practice range ahead of time. The arrow from a modern recurve hits with the power required to give good penetration, and this is the name of the game, after all.

Let's take a close look at the average recurve bow's parts and see how and where the bow develops its power without sacrificing light weight.

The handle riser contains the handle itself and generally is the heaviest single section of the entire bow. This riser is often made of handsome rock maple, rosewood or some other highly grained hardwood, and is finished in a high gloss. Because the riser is made of wood, the handle is warm to the touch and pleasant to shoot. Just above the handle is the arrow rest, and the sight window extends from the arrow shelf to the upper limit of the riser. For the purposes of bow strength and stability, the sight window on a recurve is usually not cut as deeply into the bow as is the case

Ohio hunter Bob Cramer shoots a 75-pound recurve and has taken quite a few whitetails with it. Notice the unusual camouflaged shirt.

The longbow may have been the forerunner of the recurve, and a few bowhunters still use these bows to hunt deer. Note the string silencers in the form of leather tassles.

with compound bows. Some of the newest recurve bows of good quality, however, are cut up to three-eighths of an inch past center to allow for the arrow's passage while maintaining the bowstring in the center of the riser.

Immediately above and below the riser are the bowlimbs. On a recurve bow, the lower limb is designed to be a bit stiffer than the upper limb. This is because most archers use the three-finger hold, with one finger above the nock and two fingers below. This in turn puts a bit more stress on the lower limb, which has to be a little stiffer so that both limbs catch up with each other on release and the arrow is propelled smoothly.

Some takedown recurve bows offer interchangeable limbs so the bow's power can be varied according to the shooter's needs. Bear's Custom Kodiak Take-Down, for example, offers limbs in 50, 55, 60 and 65 pounds; each limb fits into the acceptance key mechanism built into each end of the riser and locks into place. Take-down bows are a great answer if you do a lot of traveling: They fit into their own soft or hard cases, can be handled as checked baggage, and with the variety of limbs available on some models, you can hunt elk or deer, then switch off to grouse or rabbits for the pot. The Bear Kodiak TD, by the way, features a laminated hardwood handle riser in right- or left-handed grip with limbs of fiberglass-maplewood lamination. The overall bow length is 60 inches and the draw length is virtually unlimited.

Commercial air travel can be especially tough on the bowhunter. In one case, the pilot on a Republic Airlines flight happened to be an avid bowhunter and consented to carry my soft-cased bow in the cockpit with him; otherwise, I wouldn't have been permitted to take the bow on the flight enroute to a Kentucky deer hunt. The soft case meant I couldn't check the bow with my other luggage, and the FAA rules prohibited my carrying this "lethal weapon" with me as hand baggage. Thank the gods for a brotherhood of bowhunters at a time like this. A hard case would have avoided the situation entirely, and of course since then I've outfitted myself with a proper traveling case for my bow and other tackle.

The surface of the limbs turned away from the hunter while shooting is known as the back, while the side toward him is called the face. At the tip of each limb is a small groove designed to seat the loop on the end of the bowstring; this groove usually extends an inch or so down the near side of the tip to guide the string toward the far tip, and helps to stabilize the tips when the bow is fired. The distance from the bowstring to the handle is known as the fistmele or bracing height, and the string, if properly positioned, bisects the riser vertically; this is why the sight window on quality recurves extends past center a fraction of an inch.

The bowstring for a recurve bow has servings, or wrappings of monofilament or tough Dacron, at three points along its length: at each end of the string where the loop fits over the bow tips, and in the string midsection where the nock point is located. The serving protects the string in areas where it gets the most wear. The nocking point serving also acts as a cushion for the fingertips during draw and release, although serious shooters use a shooting glove or finger-tab to protect the fingertips.

The proper nock point on a recurve's bowstring is usually permanently pin-pointed with a small wrapping of brass or other metal on the nock point's lower edge. The nock is then rested firmly atop this wrapping, and the archer knows his arrow is seated correctly. Some nocks in use today have concave string grooves that snap firmly onto the bowstring and these, along with the metal wrap marking the correct nock point, make it a snap (no pun intended) to nock an arrow properly while your eyes are on that big deer that just walked out of the woods. Just be sure you keep your cock feather in the right position; nocks with tiny plastic ridges on them make this job possible without having to look at what you're doing. Arrows that are four-fletched don't present this problem, of course.

Camouflaging the recurve bow basically involves the same process, and uses the same materials, as does the compound. Here again I have to vote for the spray camo paint because I believe it allows the bow's flex recovery to operate at full speed, whereas cloth bow socks or even camo tape tend to slow the limbs somewhat. I know some hunt-ers, a few of them quite successful and dedicated whitetail hunters, who use no camo at all on their bows because they hunt from treestands and believe bow camo to be unnecessary when hunting from an elevated position. I'm torn in this situation: On the one hand, I know the importance of making sure that none of my gear catches the deer's eye in the woods. On the other hand, some of the finishes being used on today's recurve bows are so beautiful that it's a sin to

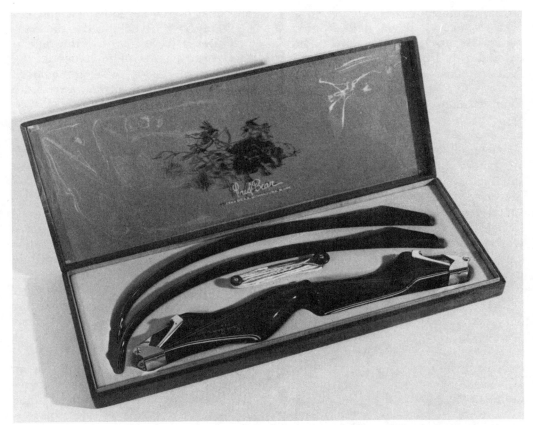

The beauty of a takedown recurve is its ease in transportation and interchangeable limb design. The Bear Custom Kodiak TD bow shown here has its own fitted carrying case.

cover them up with camouflaging. Turkey hunters face the same dilemma: Covering a handsome and expensive turkey shotgun with tape keeps the gun metal's flash from the gobbler's wary eye, but it can break a man's heart to see all the deep engraving and gun-metal bluing disappear under a roll of rubberized tape. A few guns and bows have been taped for so long that it's impossible to remove the tape without nearly destroying them. Maybe this is why so many bowhunters choose treestands; they can hunt effectively without covering all that beauty in their hands.

Most major bow manufacturers produce hunting bows that are already colored a dull black to avoid light reflections. One such is the Golden Eagle line of hunting bows. Maybe this is a trend of the future, and will henceforth avoid the hunter's dilemma of whether to camo the bow or not.

Because it casts a slower arrow than a compound, the recurve is much more subject to bowstring noise that can cause the deer to "jump the string" or leap ahead a yard or so when the string's twang is heard. For this reason, you'll want to add string silencers to the recurve's string to dampen the noise of your release. These silencers come in a wide variety of styles and sizes, from balls of bright or dull yarn to clusters of buckskin tassles and so on. The important thing is that the silencers you use do the job. When the string is released, the silencer is supposed to act as a miniature shock absorber, greatly reducing the noise of the string moving from a drawn position to the straight position again, and all in less than a second.

This undampened noise has cost more

than a few hunters their bucks, including yours truly. I was still-hunting through a rather dense hardwoods thicket in Alabama two seasons back when two bucks, a decent 6-point and a forkhorn yearling, ambled out of a copse of honeysuckle some yards away and looked in my direction. I stopped dead, one foot in the air, and managed to stay that way until the bucks decided I was part of the landscape and went back to browsing on the honeysuckle tips. I was carrying a new recurve takedown bow, and, since I hadn't really expected to see a good buck and because the bow still belonged to the manufacturer, I hadn't added silencers to the bowstring. As often happens, the sound of my release spooked the bucks and they both hopped forward at the sudden noise. My arrow passed just to the rear of the 6-pointer, which I was aiming at, and instead buried itself in the shoulder of the yearling. He ran about 35 yards before crumpling up, stone dead.

It isn't often that a mishap of a string-jumped buck results in the unintentional taking of another buck, and I certainly didn't mean to hit the smaller animal. However, the story does illustrate how important it is to silence that bowstring before you go into the woods. If you shoot a recurve, you must put some sort of silencer on that string, even if you come up with your own concoction.

Take a look at a recurve's upper or lower limb tip when the bow is strung and you'll see the need for yet another accessory, and this is the brush button. The recurve's double-curved limbs taper down to the tip in such a way that the string lies directly against the upper

The author's old recurve still spits a lethal arrow now and then. It pulls 45 pounds at 28 inches, but this is souped up to about 53 pounds with the author's longer draw length.

and lower limb tips when the bow is at rest. This invites snagging every small twig and branch between the limb tip and the string, which tend to pinch and hold anything inserted between the two. Brush buttons, really nothing more than half-dollar-sized rubber discs with a hole in the middle, slide down over the bowstring's end loops. When the bow is strung for use, the buttons are slipped toward each tip until they touch the inner facing of the limb, forming a little barrier against any twig that might otherwise lodge itself in the crevice. When the bow is drawn, the buttons are pulled slightly away from the bowlimbs and do not impair shooting or bow performance in any way.

Because the recurve bow is far simpler in design than even the least complex compound, the recurve is easier to maintain and therefore to own. The compound puts intense pressure on the bowstring, and this, added to the fact that the average compound remains strung virtually all of the time, means that string replacement is necessary every once in a while. For most of us, this means leaving your bow at the tackleshop for a few days while the pro replaces the string. Less often, a cam (wheel) may crack, the compound's snap-on handle may show undue wear, or even a cable itself may crimp or snap. Any of these means downtime for your bow, and if it happens during deer season, it can be like doing without your color TV during the Super Bowl.

The recurve, on the other hand, is not subject to the pressures and strains of the compound, so downtime is usually limited to how long it takes you, rather than an archery pro, to replace a bowstring, a worn or broken arrow rest for a new one, or maybe add some extra serving here and there. And if and when the day comes when you want to replace your bow, it costs less to buy a new recurve than a new compound, overall quality being the same for each bow.

With eight out of 10 bowhunters pulling compounds these days, I can hear some of you newcomers to the sport asking, *Why buy a recurve when I could have a compound?*

Good question, and one that can only be answered by you. It will be your bow, your shooting, your hunting experiences, and so it's your preference. But if I can put in my 2 cents' worth, don't disregard the recurve out of hand until you've tried it. Bowhunting, despite all the insistence to the contrary from some members of our fraternity, is not a power sport, it's a finesse sport, and the recurve performs very well when thought of in this light.

The idea, after all, is to get close enough to that deer to make your shot not overly long and not overly difficult. And when the big moment comes, the idea is to put your arrow into the vital area behind the shoulder deeply enough to cause heavy bleedout and a quick death. The recurve bow of proper poundage can and will do this for you, season after season, provided you learn how to use it well and consistently. This, of course, brings us back to practice.

If you've been shooting a compound and try a recurve bow for a change, you'll quickly notice how differently the two bows cast their arrows. The compound's arrow trajectory is flat and the shaft speed is great. Pick up a recurve of the same peak weight and shoot, however, and you'll quickly see how

Dave Borgeson of Lansing, Michigan, looks over the mature cow elk he downed using his modern recurve bow. Borgeson gets his buck every year with this bow.

much of a humpbacked trajectory the bow provides. That's the nature of the recurve bow's design. Hunters have been stalking and taking game with the recurve for many years, especially in Turkey where it's said the recurve may have originated centuries ago. This same bow design gave the Crusaders fits, don't forget, and it took the widespread use of the crossbow to equal the recurve's effectiveness.

Because the recurve's arrow cast does have a hump in the middle of it, this may limit the range at which you can expect to take shots. This isn't that big

of a deal, though, since a good bow-hunter normally gets within 30 yards of his deer, and many times inside the 10-yard range. Any decent recurve can handle these normal shots with ease, provided the hunter can handle them. Really long shots, such as the 55-yarder described in the chapter on compounds, are not advised for this or any other type of bow. These bow-stretchers remind me of those questionable types who sky-bust for geese; they know *before they shoot* that the birds are too far away for even their 30-inch mags to handle, but they bang away regardless,

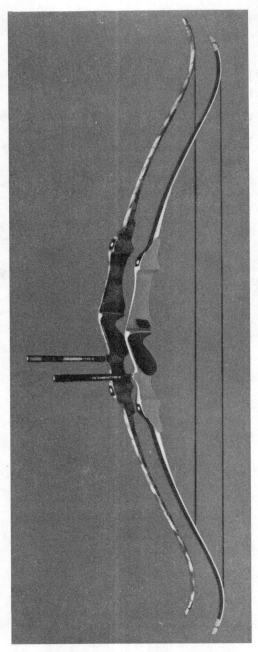

These Hoyt/Easton Reflex Hunter recurves have their own built-in stabilizers and separate riser-limb construction.

flaring the birds and maybe even wounding a few. Bowhunters who take ridiculously long shots are made from the same mold. May their bowlimbs break and may they sit on their broadheads all the way home.

Some seasons ago I was hunting whitetails in the Wayne National Forest in southeastern Ohio with a chap who'd bowhunted long enough to know better than to complain about a shot I *didn't* take. I was in a ground stand at the head of a tiny brush-filled hollow. Just as full darkness was falling, a nice big buck with good antlers paced slowly up the hollow, paused only 45 yards away, and then continued until he disappeared among the trees and the late-evening gloom. I never raised my bow because all I could see was his silhouette at a distance longer than I prefer, so I didn't shoot. I figured I'd come back the following morning and try for him then.

I told that story at camp that night and you'd have thought I'd committed some terrible sacrilege, judging by my companion's remarks. "You made a mistake not to shoot," he said flatly. "Hell, you wouldn't catch me passing up a shot at a good buck, I don't care how far away he was or how dark it got. You just blew it." I didn't say a whole lot in response to his remarks—you can't argue with ignorance—but there was no question in my mind that I had no shot at that buck at all, especially not with the rainbow-trajectory recurve I was using at the time. All I saw was a buck's silhouette, making it impossible for me to pick out the vitals area target that any arrow from any bow must hit to be effective. Maybe my companion would have taken the shot—judging by his remarks, I believe he would have—but the odds against doing much more than wounding that buck were too slim for me to chance. I'd rather come home empty than leave a stuck deer in the woods.

A friend of mine enjoys hunting several types of game with his recurve bow, deer included, but it's when he hunts gray squirrels that his ability with the double-bent bow is most apparent.

The gray squirrel is a tiny little thing compared to the boiler room on a whitetail, but this fellow can hit squirrels almost every time because he chooses only those shots he's sure he can make, like any smart hunter. He knows from long experience with the old 45-pound recurve he uses how to aim and how to allow for the arrow drop, yet he comes home with about 20 bushytails a season. I think that's exceptional for any archer regardless of his bow type. He uses old pistol brass for his blunt arrowheads, and he shoots only flu-flu arrows for safety reasons.

Because you must string the recurve every time you want to use it, rather than leaving it strung, it's important to know how to safely put string to bow. I like to use the step-through method. I take the upper bowlimb in my right hand and, placing the lower limb tip on the outside of my left foot, step between the bow and the string with my right foot. This provides the leverage needed to bend the bow, and I use my right hand to guide the string loop into its groove on the limb tip while keeping the bow flexed with the same hand. You can also use the method used for the longbow— gripping the bow at the handle with the left hand, bending the upper limb tip to meet the string while bracing the lower limb tip against your left instep—but

the step-through method is safer and more stable and I think the better choice. When stringing any bow, it's vital that you check both bow tips to make sure the strip loop is securely in place before letting the bow flex back into its strung position. It's quite a surprise to have the bow suddenly buck into a vertical posture, maybe causing injury and almost certainly breaking the bowstring. Avoid this with a bit of care while stringing.

A few recurves available today, such as the Mercury Hunter from Ben Pearson, offer built-in shock absorbers designed to take up some of the shock caused by shooting. The Mercury hunter has two mercury-filled steel capsules inside the handle riser to make for recoil-free shooting.

A friend of mine (and one who takes a decent buck season after season) in Michigan has a low-key campaign going for simplification in competitive archery. He isn't out to ban compound bows but rather to strip them of some of the add-ons that make competition compounds more science than art. Most of his hunting is done from treestands, although he will still-hunt when the woods are damp and quiet, and every bit of his hunting is done with a modern recurved bow. He shoots a 62-pounder, and although he isn't exactly a body builder in the muscles department, he has trained his muscles to handle the draw requirements of his pull weight with ease.

"It's easy to break in at a higher bow weight than you're used to," he told me. "I believe in a lot of practice, and of course this helps strengthen and tune my muscles, but I also pull my bow 10 times every morning and evening, holding at full draw for a few seconds each

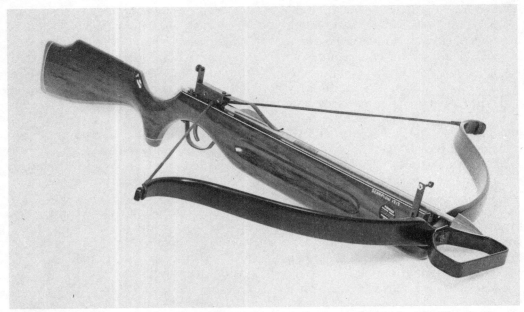

This crossbow from Scorpion utilizes the recurve design for its prod. Crossbow hunting for deer is slowly catching on as more and more states permit it.

time. I can break myself in on a new bow in a very short time using this method."

I bought a new recurve pulling 64 pounds at 29 inches last season and I tried this morning-evening workout method. Within only a few days I found I was able to pull and hold the powerful bow well enough to begin shooting small groups on my backyard range with it. And I killed a very nice 11-point buck with it later in the year, thanks to the luck of getting within 20 yards of the animal, but also thanks to a powerful enough bow that put the buck down after one arrow high in the shoulder and through both lungs.

You can get used to and master a heavy recurve bow if you're of average muscular build, and if you'll put the time into it. Keep in mind that power with the recurve bow comes entirely from you, not from a system of cables and eccentric cams. It's like anything else: A recurve bow will yield whatever you put into it, no more and no less. That's a pretty good exchange these days.

Military training provided many young men with their first in-depth experience with firearms, and this often led them to take up gun hunting after their discharges. It worked a little differently for me, however. I'd been mildly interested in archery and bowhunting since I was a child, so when my overseas Air Force outfit formed a sporting club for the purpose of buying sporting goods at reduced rates, I chose a recurve bow, arrows, armguard and back quiver along with a couple of rifles. Following the service, plinking and casual target shooting with my new bow came naturally, especially since I was fortunate enough to live quite near some woods. It took two years of this before I felt ready to go deer hunting with my archery tackle, and another two years before I put that first whitetail on the ground. Since then there have been more deer, newer and more complex bows, aluminum and then graphite arrows, newly designed broadheads, *ad infinitum*, but that doesn't change the fact that my first-ever whitetail fell to a recurve bow and cedarwood arrows—not to mention uncounted cottontails, a few squirrels, one hapless bobwhite quail and a couple dozen ringneck pheasants.

Even if the recurve hadn't produced those early successes for me, I'd still like the looks of today's double-bends. Lean an unflexed recurve in the corner and it beckons you to drop what you're doing to go shoot. Bend it until the string is tight and it sings to you in a soft, persistent voice: Let's go hunting. I attended a bowhunting school down south recently and only one student shot a recurve. Everyone else carried compounds. Yet it was this lone hunter who was always the last to leave the target range every evening and the first to start practice the following day. A short-sighted person might remark that a recurve shooter needs more practice than a compound shooter, but this isn't the case. If anything, it's the number of variables built into the compound that is tougher to master than the simple dynamics of a recurved bow. No, this long-practicing archer knew he had three mornings and evenings of prime deer bowhunting ahead of him at the close of the school and he was just fine-tuning his eye and shooting muscles to be ready to hunt when the time came. And you

know what? He killed the biggest buck among 12 students. Make of that what you will.

With its three curves, smooth, cornerless lines and trim overall shape, the recurve appears more handsome to quite a few bowhunters. And despite the extensive engineering that goes into limb design, riser materials and so on, the recurve is lighter and less cumbersome to carry than a compound. It recalls the days when archery wasn't just a way to collect your game or entertain you on the range, but was vitally important to protect your life and your home. Great armies have fought wars using the recurve bow; in fact, the recurved shape of the bowlimbs was adopted to give the arrow greater speed in leaving the string and in flight. This same principle remains today to make the modern recurve not only a thing of beauty, but a very practical hunting weapon as well.

About the craziest thing I've ever seen while bowhunting happened in northwestern Colorado's Flattops Wilderness, and it concerned a young lad no more than 15 years old who'd come along hunting mule deer with his father. The boy's father had already nailed his buck, a handsome 4x4, and was assisting the boy. I hunted with these two men for three solid days and not once did I see the boy pull his bow. Even during the midday break when his father and I kept in tune by shooting some practice arrows at an old rotten stump, the boy preferred not to shoot and just watched. Finally I asked the boy why he hadn't taken a shot at a nice little 2x3 buck I'd pushed past him, and with a grimace he said he couldn't pull the bow he was carrying, a brand new laminated recurve complete with bow quiver. "My father bought it for me just before we left for this hunt and I didn't have a chance to practice with it," he said. "I kept hoping I wouldn't see a deer so I wouldn't have to shoot."

I looked at the bow. It pulled 54 pounds at 28 inches, and the lad was slender and just could not get the bow back even close to full draw. To go on an expensive hunt with a bow you can't pull is inadvisable, to say the least, but I can understand the boy's reluctance to disappoint his father, even though it was the father who purchased a recurve that overbowed the lad to begin with. With only three days left to hunt, the lad had no real chance for a decent shot at any deer, considering he couldn't shoot the bow at all, much less with any accuracy, so he and I kept the situation a secret from his father and the boy said he'd work himself up to the new bow's requirements when he returned home.

If you've had your eye on a gleaming new recurve in the store but have been put off by the draw weight, by all means ask the store pro, if there is one, to advise you about the purchase of the bow. Tell him to watch closely as you draw the bow, tell him what experience you've had and the draw weight you're used to pulling, and so on. It could well be that you could increase your bow strength through a regimen of workouts with the new bow. The pat advice on bow choice is: Don't overbow yourself. At face value, I have to agree with this, but it's very possible that you can work your way into heavier bows, even in the recurve where all the power comes from you. A few archers I know work out with small barbells to strengthen the arm, wrist and back muscles needed for a steady draw and solid hold with the bow. Done regularly and in the right way, pumping a

little iron can give you the strength to use a bow of the increased power you desire.

The trend toward heavier bows, as related elsewhere in this book, came about because bowhunters realized that heavier bows are more efficient and result in quicker, cleaner and more predictable deer kills than the lightweights can provide. This same thing holds true with the recurve; the difference is that you must do all the grunt-and-groan work with a recurved bow.

While fishing for arctic char along Canada's northern coastline some years ago, I came across an Inuit (Eskimo) in our party of guides who carried an old, round-limbed fiberglass recurve. The bow was so old it must have been among the first recurves marketed in North America, as even the maker's name had been worn off the tiny riser section. I asked the Inuit what he used the bow for, and his answer surprised me. He said he used the bow to kill seals, thereby saving himself the cost of a box of expensive rifle shells at the Hudson Bay trading post. And then he said he hoped one day to kill a polar bear using his bow and the cedarwood arrows he'd ordered by mail. I pulled that bow and it couldn't have provided more than 50 pounds at my draw length (a bit over 30 inches), so I sure didn't envy this fellow's ambition to go after 1500 pounds of white bruin armed with only this diminutive weapon and a handful of mail order arrows. Still, the father of this same Eskimo regularly takes full-grown polars using an old and battered .222 rifle. His method is to take a dog along on his bear hunts—other than those pulling his sled—and when a bear is sighted he releases the dog. The animal chases the bear and keeps it occupied while the hunter stalks up close and shoots the bear in the head with the taped-up .222.

If the older Inuit could kill polars using a very light varmint-caliber rifle, maybe there's no real reason his son can't do the same thing with his old recurve. And for that matter, maybe too much is made of the power of the bow instead of the skill of the hunter. As somebody once said, it ain't the dog in the fight, it's the fight in the dog.

Get close enough and you can kill almost any big game animal with a recurve bow, even a bow of only moderate power. Howard Hill did himself proud in Africa, as has Fred Bear, and both of these gentlemen used recurve bows to take about everything from bull elephant to black-maned lion; and in North America, everything from Alaskan grizzly to trophy elk and moose. As the Marines say, you don't have to be big and tough to pull a strong recurve bow; you can be little and tough.

A friend of mine, an avid hunter who lives in West Germany, was surprised to see me show up for a black bear hunt in Canada not long ago toting a 52-pound recurve bow.

"I would not go after these bears with only a bow," he said, fingering the bow and running his fingers over its triple curves. I asked if he'd ever had any experience in bowhunting and he shook his head. "Hunting with the bow and arrow is *verboten* in Germany," he said.

I thought that a real shame, especially in view of this particular chap's love for hunting. He was genuinely interested in my archery tackle and its ability to take big game, but the only way he's likely to get to try it would be to make another very expensive hunting trip to North America. By the end of our bear hunt the German had put several dozen arrows through my bow and could shoot a 12-inch group at 20 yards, which I thought exceptional since his experience with archery had been nil a week before. I wouldn't be surprised if he wrote to say he'd booked a deer or elk hunt in the mountains of the American West one of these days. German laws say you can't hunt in that republic with the bow and arrow, but nothing in the rules say you can't practice with 'em. This same fellow killed a 275-pound blackie three days into our hunt using his 7mm Mag rifle, then toted the entire animal on his back for 200 yards to a forest road. I don't think he'd have any trouble pulling a 65-pound recurve bow, do you?

It's reasonable to expect the recurve to continue to improve as new materials and designs come into use. A few of today's bows are being made with magnesium risers and handles, for example; this makes for a somewhat stiffer bow that weighs a bit more than wood handle bows, but the use of a metal for the riser section opens up all sorts of possibilities for new handle designs, deeper-cut sight windows, and so on. At least one manufacturer is producing a takedown recurve with a magnesium handle section.

Some bowhunters stick with the recurve over the compound because they like it and because the style has produced well for them over the years. It is for this faithful minority that the new recurve bow developments will be big news. And who knows? It just may be that the recurve may win back some of the compound hunters willing to put a bit more muscle into their sport come autumn.

12

The Hunting Broadhead

There was a time when I was positive I'd found the only *right* broadhead for deer. The head contained four razor inserts sharp enough to shave with, and it screwed onto the end of my hunting shafts for a tight fit. But it wasn't anything technical that convinced me I was using the right head. Instead, it was a missed shot at 60 yards.

I was sitting on a weedy sidehill when a big-bodied spike buck came walking up a dry creekbed and across a small field in front of me. The buck, which carried very long spike antlers, at least 12 inches long to the side, came to a stop, broadside to me, about 60 yards away. The shot was a little longer than I preferred, but I couldn't pass it up, so I drew, took aim and released.

Oh, but that shot looked good in flight. The shaft glinted once in the afternoon sunlight, heading directly toward the unalerted buck, and I was certain the deer was as good as tagged and field-dressed—until the arrow arrived, that is. The arrow did a little maneuver in the air and flew a few inches high, thunking solidly into the trunk of a beech tree two inches above the deer's withers. At the sound of the arrow's arrival—a loud *thwack!*—the buck bolted back the way he had come. I walked to the spot and found that the broadhead had completely buried itself into the tough beech wood, and I had to unscrew the shaft to retrieve it, leaving the broadhead out of sight in the tree. Any broadhead with that kind of penetration must be terrific, I reasoned, and I stuck with that brand for another full season, much to my later regret. It didn't occur to me until later that the reason I missed was that the deep-penetrating broadhead also had a tendency to sail in flight when the breezes blew just so. I missed two more deer that season, and another pair of easy shots the following autumn, before the problem dawned on me. Talk about tunnel vision . . .

Sailing is only one of the considerations a bowhunter must confront when choosing a broadhead for deer or any other game. It is especially important for us venison seekers, however, because we need a rather hefty head to do the job correctly, and the wider the head, the more tendency it has to take wing

on its own and veer off course. Some hunters have used the same brand of head for many years. They often hit on it as the result of a friend's advice or experience, or perhaps an archery dealer sold them half a dozen when they were first starting out, and, since the head seemed to work, they never had reason to switch styles or brands.

But for many other hunters, especially the most adventurous, the choice of broadheads can change right along with the seasons. One chap I know not only changes heads every fall, but bows as well. That's OK for him, but not for

The overall appearance of the whitetail buck, covered with its supple hide, is soft, yet beneath that hide rests bone, cartilage and gristle, all work for the properly designed and placed broadhead.

me. I don't want the added chore of getting used to an all-new system of bow mechanics, muscle mechanics and such, plus the discovery of how yet another style of arrowhead is going to perform, when all I want to do is get myself tuned up when the deer season is close. I have enough trouble conquering my own body to extend that combat to new terminal gear.

Discovering the one right broadhead for you can be made simpler if you'll keep in mind what a deer hunter's arrowhead must do. Unlike a bullet, shotgun slug or muzzleloader's miniball, all of which kill mainly by shock resulting from a terrific amount of impact, a hunting arrow kills by internal hemorrhaging. The cleaner the cut and the better placed the shot, the quicker and more sure the kill. So the head must penetrate a deer's thin skin, slide between (or in some cases, smash through) the ribs, and get into the cavity containing the deer's heart, liver, lungs and other vitals. The optimum hunter's target is the broadside shot just to the rear of the shoulder. And once the broadhead arrives inside the ribcage, the shot must have enough velocity remaining to cut its way into those vital organs to start the heavy bleeding required for a quick kill. If the broadhead's blades are so thin and brittle that contact with the ribs or other bones breaks them off on penetration, it stands to reason that the head will include too few cutting edges once the vitals are reached.

If the head is so loaded down with extra cutting edges, weight-forward gadgets and other extraneous junk, it's likely that all that extra baggage will impair good penetration, and if the head doesn't get into the vitals, all those add-ons won't mean a thing. Heads that rattle (I've seen a few that do) can defeat your efforts to get close, and if a head is loose enough to rattle, it's loose enough to come apart on contact with the target. This of course serves nothing except perhaps leaving a lightly wounded deer in the woods, something every bowhunter should disdain.

Fortunately, most commercially manufactured heads available today are made to tolerances too small to rattle, come apart or otherwise fail to function well, provided you install them right to begin with. Furthermore, most of today's heads fly well, do a reasonably good job of penetration, and seem to get into the vital areas pretty consistently. Today's broadheads average a bit more than an inch maximum width, contain from two to four cutting edges, and, for the most part, relieve the hunter of the head-sharpening chore by providing factor-edged cutting blades that attach by one of several methods to a central bullet-shaped core with the pointed head to aid penetration. These heads usually can be revamped with replacement blades should one or more of the original blades become chipped, broken or dulled. That old standby, the Razorhead from Bear Archery, still offers two stationary blades of rather heavy steel requiring sharpening by the hunter, plus a set of two cutting edges that fit into a slot near the base of the head. The Razorhead has remained popular all these years because it's reliable, can be sharpened to whatever edge the hunter prefers, and is tough enough to chop through ribs without falling apart. I expect this head will be in wide use for many years to come.

Unlike most other broadheads on the

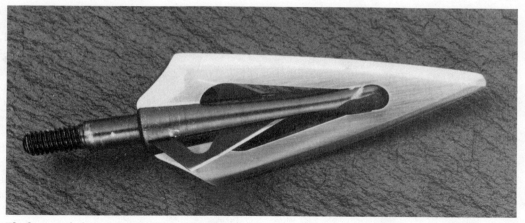

The best made better, Bear's Super Razorhead with two permanent blades and two replaceables. Note the chisel point for punching through small bones and cartilage.

market, the Razorhead features a permanent central twin blade made of stainless spring steel, thicker than most others available today. And instead of being only .015 inches or so thick, the blade is much sturdier than replaceable blades and offers a chisel-like edge. This includes the Razorhead's point, a fast-tapered edge that is squared off in front. This type of edge both cuts and punches its way through hide, flesh and smaller bones. A D-shaped seating arrangement is said to withstand up to 300 pounds of force. This is important if you, like me, sometimes put an arrow into a tree instead of a deer.

Whatever broadhead you end up using, be sure to ask the dealer if the heads you select fly well with both plastic vanes and feather fletching on the arrows. A hunting buddy of mine switched heads in midseason last fall and missed the buck of the year because the new heads veered off course at downrange distances. He finally discovered that such erratic flight was due to the vanes-broadhead combination, so he re-fletched all his hunting shafts with feathers and finally achieved the accuracy he was used to. He ended the season on a successful note, sticking a nice little buck that weighed about 120 pounds dressed and carried 6-point antlers. But the 12-pointer he'd seen and missed in midseason is still remembered and lamented, and at least he'll still be there this fall when the maple leaves turn golden.

As mentioned, most of today's commercial broadheads feature replaceable cutting blades, all of which attach in some manner to the central ferrule. Some of these heads seem to be designed as dexterity tests for the archer: Slide the blade into the slot in the ferrule, then hold it firmly against the ferrule while anchoring the blade's slotted rear edge by the adjustment of a ring or a notched bit of steel or . . . It could drive you nuts, not to mention cut your fingers to ribbons on the cutting edges, just trying to assemble your broadheads and get them installed on the arrows. I've started several bow seasons with one or more fingertips wrapped in Bandaids after cutting them during the assembly process, and sliced fingertips don't lend themselves to smooth draws and releases, I can assure you. Broadhead wrenches help a little. Normally made of plastic and designed to fit over the head's business end while keeping the fingers away from the edges during the threading and tightening process, the wrenches are helpful to a certain point, *but you still have to handle the blades with your fingers during assembly.*

The simpler the better, somebody wise once uttered, and this is certainly true with broadheads. Not only are simpler heads easier (and less dangerous) to assemble and install, they have fewer of those annoying little parts to come loose at exactly the wrong moment. One archer who hunts Kentucky extensively got tired of cut fingers so he started to build his own broadheads with tough, thick steel and a few welds here and there. He came up with a one-piece three-bladed broadhead that he screws onto the shaft and then sharpens with a small file and then a fine-grain stone. He never has to handle sharp edges with his fingers, and claims it's easy to touch up a dulled edge in the field with just a few strokes of his stone. He'd killed three bucks with his heads, the last I heard.

And this, I think, proves a point: There are so many broadhead styles on the market because there are so many differing tastes among bowhunters, who are renowned "fiddlers" with tackle, trying this and rejecting that. All a broadhead has to do is punch into a deer's boiler room and then make a few smooth, clean cuts through which the deer bleeds heavily enough to bring death. If it were any more complex than

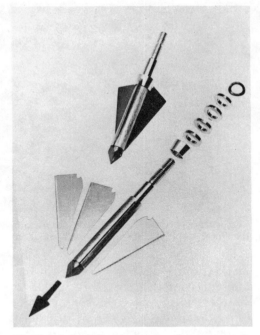

The Kolpin broadhead, showing the components separated and assembled.

this, the chipped-flint arrowhead used for centuries by the American Indian on everything from rabbits to bison wouldn't have put meat in the lodge. In view of this, it's easy to smile at all the new-and-improved broadhead models that come and go every year. Most of them work, and some of them are easy to use, but the job at hand just isn't that complex, advertising claims to the contrary.

Let's take a closer look at some representative broadhead styles currently available, pointing up what makes them different and maybe giving apprentice bowhunters a head start toward tackle selection.

Wasp

The Wasp broadhead has been around for a while and is available in three-bladed and four-bladed styles. It's one of the family of heads employing replaceable blades, and, to be honest, is not among the easiest of heads to assemble while keeping your fingertips unsliced.

The Wasp features what its manufac-

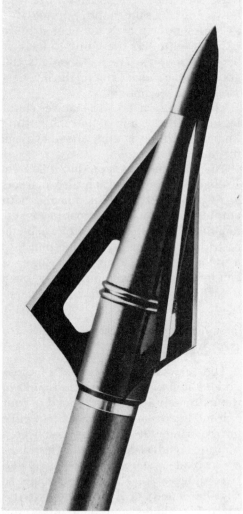

The three-bladed Wasp broadhead displays the standard design for replaceable-blade hunting heads. A pair of wires (center) hold the blades firmly in place.

turer calls a Cam-Lok system of assuring that the blades, if properly installed in the slotted cylindrical body, will stay firmly in place. The blades are slipped into the individual slots in the body and slid forward until the notch in each blade locks into a matching spot in the rear of the pointed tip of the body. The blades are vented (open in the middle), and the base of each blade is secured to the body by means of a pair of tensile steel retainer rings. What makes installation a challenge is that each blade must be held in place, usually by finger pressure on the unsharpened rear edge, while the rings are twirled to fit the slot in the rings around the base of the blade; this must be repeated for each blade to complete installation.

The three-bladed Wasp weighs 130 grains total, while the four-bladed model weighs 140 grains. A package of Wasp heads contains six complete broadheads, and replacement kits of extra blades, tips and rings are also available.

I have hunted with Wasp heads for several seasons in the past and have been pretty much satisfied with their performance with both feathered and vaned shafts, and I've noted no tendency for these heads to sail or veer in flight. They do an adequate job of penetration, and of course the extremely sharp blades (either three or four) do cause internal bleeding if you hit the deer in the right spot. I like the looks of the Wasp: It just plain *looks* lean and mean, and for anyone sharing this opinion, use of the head would probably be a confidence builder.

Satellite

The Satellite is another head that's been in use for some years, and a number of hunters I know have been using it, with good success, for as long as I've known them.

This head also employs replaceable blades, and comes with three or four blades per head. The three-bladed model, thanks to a long shear line of 15 degrees built into all models, offers a bit more than 4½ inches of cutting edge, while the four-bladed model increases the cutting edge to a total of more than six inches, plenty to start adequate bleeding if you put it into the boiler room. Hunters have the choice of using carbon-steel blades .010 of an inch thick, or stainless-steel blades that go a bit heavier at .015 thickness.

The four-bladed Wasp using cutout design to reduce wind planing. These blade edges are truly razor-sharp.

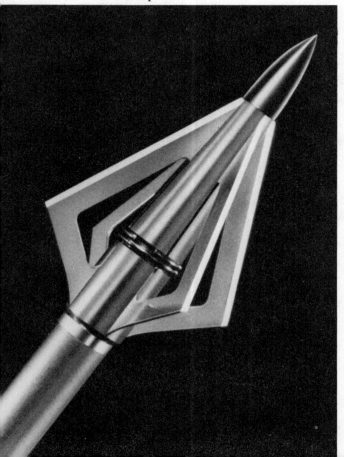

The Satellite is not vented and employs a front-and-back system of locking blades to body. The cylindrical point is made of swaged and pressed steel.

Thunderhead

This head's claim to fame is a heavier design specifically intended for use with bows drawing 60 or more pounds, due to the manufacturer's belief that more and more hunters are going to heavier bows these days. The head weighs 180 grains and is indeed among the heaviest models on the market.

The Thunderhead also features stainless-steel blades and a 1.4-inch cutting diameter, which is a bit above average for heads of its type.

The Thunderhead is produced by New Archery Products, which also markets Razorbak 4 and Razorbak 5 heads, both employing a modular broadhead system that allows the user to change blade cartridges. The blades are molded into a nylon cartridge so that replacements can be installed easily and safely, even though the overall design is called fixed-blade.

Redd Head

The Redd Head is another of those vicious-looking head designs, thanks to the extremely long point ahead of four rear-mounted blades. The head looks like an experimental rocket as much as a hunting broadhead. The Redd Head uses a four-blade system, two permanent and two replaceable. The head is made of case-hardened steel and the two replaceable blades are made of aluminum. The overall head weighs 125 grains, and the cutting diameter is 1³⁄₁₆ inch.

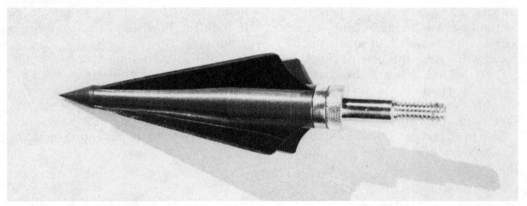

The Satellite broadhead has been popular for many years and remains one of the best-designed heads on the market. The head weighs 125 grains.

PSE Brute 3 and Brute 4

These heads from Precision Sporting Equipment offer the hunter the chance to interchange his broadhead configuration by swapping one type of blade for another, all of which fit on the PSE body. You can, therefore, fiddle with various blade combinations until you hit on the one that performs the way you want it to. Head weights range from 126 to 140 grains, and the usual stainless steel/aluminum combination is also used here. The cutting diameter is 1½ inches, and the larger blades are vented to reduce wind-planing.

Maxi-Head

This is another head that departs somewhat from the standard designs. The head features greater length than most others and weighs a hefty 172 grains. It's popular among longbow hunters and has a one-inch cutting diameter. This head's two fixed blades are serrated on the rear third of their cutting edges. I haven't used the Maxi-Head, but I shy away from anything that might lessen good penetration and plenty of bleeding. It's been my experience that the smoother and finer the incision, the greater the bleeding that results. This is why all bowhunters should use only razor-sharp broadheads.

Magnum I and II

For archers looking for a really wide cutting diameter, the Magnums may be the answer. Each head features two regular and two bleeder edges, all of which are fixed and non-replaceable. The maker says the blades are hard enough to be tough, yet soft enough so a bit of sharpening puts a good edge on dulled blades. The cutting diameter is 1⁹⁄₁₆ inches on the Mag I (weight is 140 grains) and 1⅜ inches on the 120-grain Mag II.

Catclaw R-Z

This head is vented so widely that its overall appearance is that of a finely honed frame rather than that of a head with vents. Major cutting is performed by the large single blade, and you can insert either two or four much smaller razorblades near the rear of the main blade if desired, or use the head without inserts. The main blade can be removed from its ferrule for ease or sharpening, such as on a flat surface.

This head comes in 1¼-inch and 1½-inch widths, and weights are 145 and 160 grains respectively.

Anderson 245 Magnum

Magnum, indeed: This head has a 1½-inch cutting diameter but produces a four-inch-square hide stretch-out for increased blood trails. The 245's replaceable blades are mostly vent, somewhat like the Catclaw R-Z's, and the head can be used with two or four blades. The head weighs 100 grains with two blades and 125 grains with four blades.

The tip of the 245 is unique in that it includes three ridges leading to the front of the blades and is designed to split bones in the same manner that a log splitter works on firewood. Penetration is said to be excellent despite the head's width, and the deep venting reduces sailing.

Black Diamond

This is a fixed-blade head available in two- and four-blade models. The front of each model is made of heavier steel while the rear trailing (cutting) edges thin out for sleeker cutting performance. The two-blade weighs 115 grains with a 1⅛-inch diameter, while the four-blader weighs about 125 grains and has a 1⅜-inch cutting diameter. The Black Diamond has been on the market for

more than 44 years and is said to be the oldest broadhead in continuous production.

I have used this head and been impressed with its overall strength. It's not the kind of broadhead that is likely to become nicked or bent under normal field conditions. It penetrates very well and is easily sharpened either afield or in the shop at home.

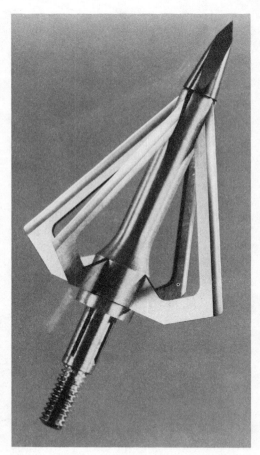

Anderson's 245 Magnum head uses four blades and a chiseled point for cutting through soft bones and organs. The head is designed to create a hide stretch and a four-inch cut through soft tissue.

Viper

The Viper broadhead, relatively new on the archery market, uses four blades designed to "open up" upon impact through the use of an arrangement of rings at the rear of the blades. All four blades snap from their position parallel to the shaft into an erect position to inflict a wound nearly four inches in diameter for increased bleeding and quicker kills.

The Viper can be touchy if it isn't installed just right, however. Friends who have used this head say they must be careful not to screw the ferrule's threaded portion down tight into the end of the shaft; doing so, they report, impairs the proper opening of the blades on impact. It's also necessary to use a full, left-handed (counterclockwise) helical fletch to prevent the arrow's drag from tightening the head too much in flight.

Although most Viper users claim it's most effective at ranges up to only 20 yards or so, one experienced bowhunter I know killed an 8-point whitetail at 42 yards using Viper's broadhead and said his arrow achieved excellent penetration, with the stuck deer running only a few yards before lying down. Quite a few hunters go to the Viper when they intend to hunt small game such as squirrels or wild turkeys.

Scissors Head

This is another self-opening head. The two-bladed Scissors Head employs two hinged blades that, when in position to fire, lie nearly flat along the shaft. Two curls snaking up from the rear of each blade pull the blades erect upon impact, increasing the cutting diameter to more than four inches total. I know a hunter who arrowed a Pennsylvania whitetail buck with the Scissors at a range of 15 yards from a treestand, and the wound looked as though the entry hole had been caused by a heavy axe or had perhaps been doctored with a knife, the wound was so wide and bloody.

A Personal Choice

The first broadhead I ever used was permanently attached to a cedar shaft, which was four-fletched. The heads contained three fixed blades welded in place, and the entire head appeared to have been brass coated with exposed steel edges. Fixed-blade heads require sharpening by the archer and I filed and honed and whetted and honed until I could shave the hair off my forearm with only light pressure on the edges. When I finally went afield, it was only after quite a lot of practice with the actual heads I would use to hunt. I shot at half a dozen stacked hay bales with the usual paper silhouette of a deer painted on the front. Got pretty good, too, but I never got to find out what those three-bladed heads would do when they hit a deer.

The only shot I got that first day was ridiculously short, something under 10 yards. The buck eased out from behind an oak trunk, busily nuzzling the leafy carpet for acorns, and he had a few does in tow. But I was a greenhorn at this treestand business and neglected to allow for the angle of my shot from 15 feet up in my beech platform, and my shot just grazed his back, trimming half a handful of hair off his hide and scaring the bejeebers out of him. He bucked like a goosed mule and went trotting into some nearby saplings where I could see him but not get a second clear shot at him. He finally got over his fright and eased back near the base of my tree, reached out his Roman-like nose and sniffed the shaft of my arrow sticking out of the ground. Before I could shoot again he detected my scent on the arrow, snorted and took off, ladies in full gallop behind. The only thing I learned about my first hunting broadhead was that I'd sharpened it well enough to chop hair off a deer, and when I pulled it from the ground I had to do it all over again because the steel was soft and the edge was gone. That broadhead and cedar shaft would have killed the buck, I have no doubt. I just couldn't hit the thing to begin with.

Not everyone has this problem, obviously, and Bob Cramer is one of them. Cramer lives in southwestern Ohio and has been an avid bowhunter for many years. He even hunts wild turkeys with the bow, not to mention pheasants in flight, running cottontails, you name it. But the white-tailed deer remains Cramer's ultimate quarry every fall and winter.

Like many bowhunters before him, Cramer did some initial swapping between broadheads early in his hunting career, but 12 years ago he settled on the MA-3L fixed-blade head and he's been with it ever since. This head's blades are made of relatively soft steel which, according to Cramer, "don't hold an edge worth a darn but are easy to sharpen in the field, and that's one reason I've stuck with them so long." The MA-3 features three fixed blades, and, in the large size Cramer uses, weighs a total of 125 grains. He says the head flies

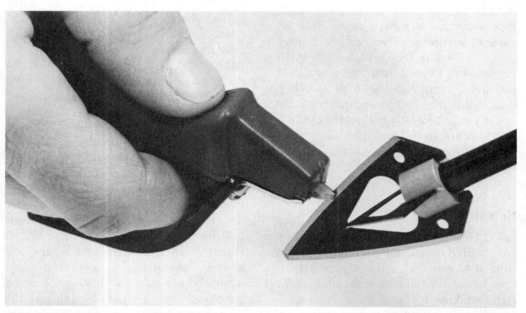

Sharpening a modern broadhead with two permanent blades and two replaceable blades. It's best to sharpen while the removable blades are not installed. *B. Townsley*

right for him, and he has confidence in the head's ability to penetrate well. It should be added that Cramer has always chosen a rather heavy hunting bow, compounds pulling in excess of 60-plus pounds, mostly, not to mention one Herculean monstrosity he used for a couple of seasons that required a hefty 72 pounds of pull at his normal draw length of 31 inches. Even with a 50 percent let-off, this compound required something more than a nudge of the muscles to pull correctly, much less doing so smoothly for a careful aim and release.

Cramer's use of a heavy hunting bow, plus his utter dedication to razor-sharp MA-3L broadheads, has enabled him to compile an enviable record. Cramer has taken quite a few whitetails with this lethal combination, and reports with some pride that every arrow that felled a whitetail for him passed completely through the animal. This not only created maximum wounds within the deer's vital areas every time he hit, but it also left two blood trails, one from each hole in the deer made by entry and exit of the broadhead. Few of Cramer's trophies went far after the shot.

I recall one October afternoon in Kentucky. I'd positioned myself against the base of a low hill while Cramer, using his portable treestand, was 18 feet up in a large hickory about 200 yards downwind from me. As it happened, a nice 7-point buck came galloping down the hill at my back, paused only long enough to stare at a hunter just as amazed to see him as he was to see me, and then leaped out of sight, my parting bowshot going a yard off the mark to thud into a fallen log. The deer continued to run directly toward Cramer's treestand, and

he passed directly under Cramer, who'd seen him coming and had prepared himself. Using a careful, nearly vertical aim (and no small amount of just plain luck), Cramer released his MA-3L-tipped Easton shaft and drove it just to the left of the whitetail's spine and between the ribs, catching the deer's left lung and heart before the arrow exited the deer's body at the brisket. The buck piled up, dead or nearly so, only 10 feet beyond the arrow's point of impact, its body cavity full of blood.

This was a good, average Midwestern buck. It field-dressed at about 135 pounds and carried a 7-point rack. It had been at full gallop when the arrow went home, and certainly its system was pumped full of adrenaline since it had already been spooked twice when it ran under Bob's stand (by whatever had pushed it into a run past my position near the hill, and then by the sight of me at close range, not to mention my errant bowshot as it departed), and yet the buck dropped nearly in his tracks when Bob's heavy arrow and broadhead sliced through its vitals.

Bob gives a lot of credit to his choice of broadhead and heavy bow for this particular kill, but the fact remains that he could have used identical gear, failed to hit the deer in a lethal manner, and it's possible (or even likely) that the animal would have run on out of sight, perhaps severely wounded. Cramer and I have hunted together for a long time and I know beyond doubt that he credits accurate aim for a great part of his success over the years. Site selection, attention to wind direction, keeping alert, even proper camouflage are all important, and so is the selection of the right broadhead for his particular manner and habits of bow use, but none of the above will put deer on the ground if that arrow isn't placed where it will do the most good, and that means draining as much blood as possible, through internal and external bleeding. That's why more and more hunters, Cramer included, are going to more powerful bows: These heavier weapons easily handle heavier, more damage-causing shafts and broadheads, and they do more damage by increasing penetration on impact.

Blood loss is the only thing hunting arrows have going for them. If a shaft-broadhead combination fails to bring

Enoch Pratt, president of Autumn Archery, tries his Shear Advantage head in a Delta V compound bow. *B. Towsley*

about sufficient blood loss when the vital areas are penetrated, you might as well have shot a twig off your backyard maple with a hairpin glued to the tip, for all the good it will do.

But how much blood does a deer have to lose before it can be expected to suffer shock leading to eventual death? Studies have shown than the average 100-pound deer contains approximately eight pints of blood, and that the deer must lose up to 2½ pints of blood to suffer severe shock and death. That's a lot of blood, relatively speaking, more than 25 percent of all the blood in its body. Good arrow hits behind the shoulder and into the lung-liver-heart area should cut one or more of these blood-filled organs, resulting in quick blood loss if the broadhead is razor-sharp and the cut(s) are smooth and clean. In such a case, blood loss is too rapid for normal coagulation to slow the flow, and the deer's body cavity quickly develops a pool of "free" blood sloshing about just inside the cavity wall. Notice that most of the blood loss described in this typical situation took place *inside* the deer; even the most solid of ideal hits isn't going to result in a blood trail a foot wide and unbroken from start to finish. Even those broadheads offering 1½-inch cutting diameters create relatively small passageways in and out of a deer's body.

The broadhead must get inside the deer's ribcage and sometimes between its shoulders for hemorrhaging to be severe, so pick your hunting head with this in mind. Heads featuring long, thin points seldom do a good job of getting through even light bones, as the thin metal tip usually rolls up or bends off to one side, preventing any more penetration. Heads with chisel points, however, can and will chop their way through soft ribs, provided they carry enough force/velocity from the bow. If the head you're used to has a long, slender point, you can use a file, hone or stone to change the business end of the head to a chisel point. This is seldom feasible if you're using a replaceable-blade head with a cylindrical central ferrule, however. If this is the case, you may want to change the type of broadhead you're using, in order to achieve the chisel-type point. Generally speaking, fixed-bladed heads are built from thicker steel, and therefore punch through bone better, than the replaceable-blade models on the market. True, a fixed-bladed model means you'll have to use a file or hone

to put an edge on the blades and keep it there, but quite a few hunters appreciate this extra element of control. It's also less expensive to expend a little elbow grease with a file than it is to buy new razor inserts in order to put a hunting shaft back into operation following a missed shot.

There is currently a unique Easton arrow shaft on the market, finished for the public by Shear Advantage of Poultney, Vermont, that promises to greatly enhance bleedout after a solid hit, and I think it's worthy of mention here.

The system is composed of a specially constructed Easton aluminum shaft which is, of course, hollow front to back. The broadhead is attached to

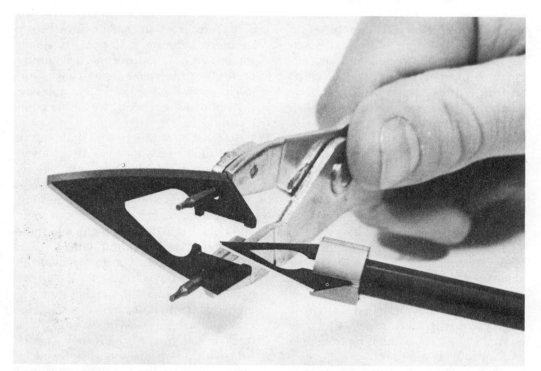

A Shear Advantage broadhead can be easily disassembled by using a special tool. This head features a hollow tube from mid-broadhead to nock, allowing quick bleedout. *B. Townsley*

the shaft just to the rear of the open end of the shaft; that is, the head contains no central ferrule, leaving the hollow shaft to convey blood from the wound to a series of three small holes in the rear of the shaft, near the fletching. The hollow shaft, open on each end, allows air to flow deep inside the wound from the outside, facilitating a quicker bleed-out and lung collapse.

In addition, the special shaft used in the Shear Advantage system contains a series of shallow grooves at regular intervals for its entire length. These grooves are designed to allow the shaft to break off when transverse (side-to-side) pressure is applied, such as when a wounded deer runs through dense cover, brush or whatever. When the shaft breaks off just outside the body cavity, the shortened hollow shaft further facilitates bleedout by avoiding the protruding shaft's acting like a plug. By finding and measuring the broken end of the shaft after the hit, the hunter can determine exactly how much penetration his shot achieved.

This new system offers a choice of three Easton shafts graded according to spine; heaviest is the XX75 with 96,000 psi tensile strength, followed by the Game Getter at 86,000 psi, and finally the American Eagle shaft with approximately three-fourths of the Game Getter's bend resistance. The Shear Advantage broadhead is composed of four blades, two fixed and two inserted. The blades are made of high carbon spring steel that are best sharpened by removing all burrs and rolled edges with a drag-type sharpener (crock sticks or honing stone), then finishing the edges on a strop or leather belt.

When I look at a deer broadside to me, all I see is brownish-gray hide. It's easy to forget that not far under that handsome pelt lies a skeletal system that, for the bowhunter, presents a sort of barrier through which the head and shaft must pass in order to do its job. I think a lot of other hunters tend to forget bone structure, too. All we see is nice, smooth hide, and all a broadhead has to be is sharp enough and pointed enough, and that's all we need be worried about.

But continuing to think this way is asking for trouble. Choose a broadhead that's too thin, too fragile, and those ribs, shoulder bones and other tough parts of the deer's anatomy will shear off those dainty little razor inserts, leaving you with only the pointed ferrule to get inside the ribcage where the hunting arrow's real work begins. Oh, you'll get plenty of penetration, provided the tip of the ferrule doesn't smack into a heavy shoulder bone or an especially tough rib, but with no cutting edge remaining on the head to cause hemorrhage, you might as well have used a suction cup instead of a broadhead, for all the good it'll do.

So what does this mean when you're shopping for broadheads? Aren't all of the dozens available pretty much alike, *really*?

Nope. Some are sturdier, some will absorb more knocks and abrasions, some don't plane or whistle in flight, and some get inside the ribs without falling apart.

The best way for you to discover the right head to buy and stay with is to ask experienced bowhunters what they use and why. If you know a truly successful bowhunter, a guy or woman who gets a buck every year with the bow, batter him with questions about the head he uses, how it performs, how easy is is to keep in hunting sharpness, its cost per

Broadheads should be safely covered by a hood while in the bow quiver. This Gamegetter quiver safely carries eight arrows within easy reach.

more before finally deciding what head to go with, unless you're satisfied to keep switching around from model to model until you hit on one that works well for you. That's the long way, though, and getting next to an experienced and successful bowhunter cuts the decision time in half or more.

And what happens when the decision's made and you go to buy those carefully selected broadheads? If you're smart, you'll spend a few more shekels

When your arrow is cut to the correct length for your draw, the broadhead will clear your bow hand at full draw.

dozen versus similar heads, and so on. Do the sharpened edges cut his hands during installation, and if not, why not? What is the average distance a stuck deer travels after being hit with one of these broadheads, and what is the draw poundage of the bow from which the heads are shot? Do most shots taken with this broadhead result in the arrow passing completely through the deer? How does it perform when the head strikes a bone? You need to know all this and

and pick up a dozen target or field tips with the same grain weight as your new heads. These matching field points should fly in much the same manner as the hunting heads, and you'll have to become proficient at hitting with first the practice heads and then a few target-designated broadheads before you're ready to take them into the deer woods. Example: I recently acquired some new hunting arrows, one dozen for practice and another dozen for hunting. These shafts are as identical to one another as the manufacturer can make them, so one arrow from the bunch should fly just the same as all the others, right? Not really. I like to screw a practice broadhead on *each* of the shafts, take two dozen or more shots at a broadhead target with each, and then either designate the shaft for hunting or for practice. Some shaft-broadhead combinations simply fly better for me than others—maybe it's the slight difference in fletchings, I don't know for sure—but I want only the best shafts in my quiver when all my efforts have brought me within bow range of a good buck whitetail. This is no time to discover that one shaft or broadhead flies just a bit wobbly, whistles in flight or whatever.

How complex bowhunting has become since the first Indian lashed a chipped piece of flint on the end of a wooden shaft with fletching and went looking for a deer for dinner. I doubt that native hunter thought very much about what his arrowhead was supposed to do, although he probably kept the head as sharp as possible. More likely he was most concerned with getting as close to that deer as possible, to reduce chances of failure, and then to put the arrow where it would surely kill the deer, and that's always been behind the shoulder. If the head was sharp and the bow strong, the hunter only needed to worry about finding an unwary deer and then creeping close enough for a shot. He had infinite patience and was willing to wait all morning, if need be, until things were right for a shot to be taken. That Indian hunter usually went home without a deer, and he had to settle for grouse or rabbit for the pot.

Things were simpler then, but far more serious. The hunter had to kill to live, and few modern bowhunters are in this situation. Bowhunting tackle has vastly improved, but along with this has come a wider variety of broadheads from which to choose, most of which will kill a deer under ideal circumstances. But, clearly, some heads perform better than others, and these few are the ones you want on the business end of a hunting arrow when the October woods turn red and golden and an antlered buck comes tiptoeing up a hollow and your heartbeat triples and you find yourself hyperventilating and thinking one more step, you beautiful son of a gun, one more step and you're mine. Nobody thinks about broadhead performance at a time like this, and no one should have to. Do all your homework ahead of time and *know* you'll kill that buck when the big moment arrives.

13

Accessories for Deer Hunters

There are countless accessories for the deer hunting archer. All claim an ability to help the hunter, make his efforts easier and more productive, and a great many of the gadgets on the market accomplish this to one degree or another. As with all sports, some of the add-ons do exactly what the manufacturer claims, while others fall short and end up actually making the effort more bother than help. It's up to you to think through how you hunt, and then look over the available add-ons to find only those that will solve definite problems. Using too many add-ons can force you to pay more attention to your tackle than to the sport's basics, and this ends up being counterproductive.

Add-ons sometimes can get downright ridiculous. A friend and hunting buddy of mine rigged his English long-

bow with a peepsight woven into the bowstring a few inches above his nocking point; attached to the string at this point was a length of surgical tubing, and the other end of the tubing was attached to a jerry-rigged, flip-up peepsight attached to the facing of the bowhandle. The idea was that every time the string came to full draw, the little front peep would jump into the archer's line of vision, giving him a third point of reference when a shot was to be made. Well, the front sight was forever sticking and failing to move into position, and when it did work it didn't, sad to say, add to the hunter's accuracy. Many a slip twixt the shot and the hit, so to say.

My advice is to choose only those extras that will solve a specific problem you've encountered, disdaining all the rest. Bowhunting is supposed to be a simple sport, but the more you clog things up with the superfluous, the more complex it becomes. Stick to the basics.

Let's look at some of the basic accessories on today's market, and see what might be of real use come this autumn.

Arrow Points

It goes without saying that you will need more than broadheads if you're going to do much practice shooting, and this calls for a small variety of threaded heads matching the diameter of your arrow inserts.

There are two basic types of practice heads available: target points and field points. The standard target point features an abrupt taper to a rather blunt point. This design should imbed itself in all target materials, yet not penetrate so far as to make arrow removal a tug-of-war. A field point, on the other hand,

Blending in with the surroundings is the name of the game for the successful bowhunter. Here's a camouflaged Browning bow, three tubes of face camo cream and a few camo-finish items.

Belt quivers keep target arrows close at hand yet out of the archer's way while shooting. Here, Steve Maslowski draws a shaft for a shot on the practice range.

has a much longer taper and is designed to stick into dead logs, packed soil, the sort of things a roving bowhunter might plink at on an afternoon of roaming the woods or countryside.

Whatever your choices among the many brands of target and field points, it is important that each point's weight match that of the broadhead you plan to hunt with. This will let you approximate the arrow flight of the hunting shaft with the target shaft you use in practice. It's true, of course, that target and field points are basically cylindrical in shape, while all broadheads have flat surfaces, so you can't expect to completely imitate broadhead flight with round points, but sticking to the right weight head will help you shoot about the same with both types of heads. Remember, consistency is all-important, even when you shoot just for fun.

If you use your hunting gear for species other than deer, you may want to add a few other specialty heads. Bowfishermen, for example, use points with round centerparts that are attached to stiff wire barbs designed to penetrate into roughfish such as carp and suckers and hold them until they can be hauled in hand-over-hand by means of a running line from head to bowhandle. Some of these fishing heads have fixed barbs while others have barbs that fold flat before the shot. Dedicated bowfishermen also favor plastic vanes rather than feather fletching because the vanes are impervious to water.

Archers who pot sitting or running rabbits and jacks favor flat-surfaced heads designed to stun the game. Upland bird hunters use flat heads, small broadheads and a sort of snagging head complete with little wire loops. All such heads are designed to bring down flying gamebirds, although, as is recounted elsewhere in this book, heads used on strong birds such as ringneck pheasants don't always stop the birds immediately. Flu-flu arrows feature very wide fletchings designed to grab the air and stop the arrow in flight after a normal shot of perhaps 30 yards; the arrow's velocity drops to nothing and the shaft drops nearly straight down to earth where retrieval is easy, even in weedfields.

Broadhead Wrench

This plastic device is designed to allow easy attachment or removal of supersharp broadheads while protecting your fingers from those inadvertent little cuts that always seem to happen the night before opening day. The wrench is roughly cup-shaped and designed to fit down over a three- or four-bladed broadhead so the entire head can be threaded firmly into place in the female part of the arrow insert. These little wrenches weigh next to nothing, are very inexpensive, are available at almost all tackleshops, and when you have to remove or install a sharp broadhead, they are worth their weight in gold.

Fletching Equipment

Quite a few archers like to fletch their own arrows because it's less expensive and allows a bit of tailoring. If you switch to a heavier broadhead, for example, you would want more of a helical twist on your fletching for more shaft stability in flight. An arrow jig or fletching jig not only holds the shaft tightly in place, but offers a disc that shows you exactly

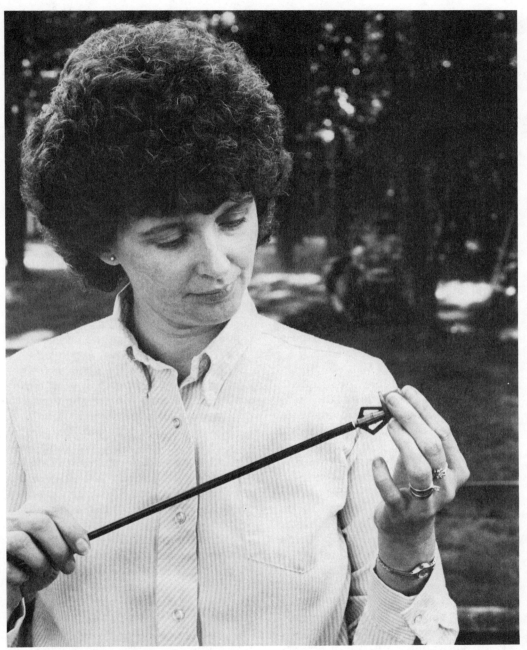

The broadhead wrench keeps your fingers intact while installing or removing sharp-edged broadheads. The wrench is made of plastic, weighs little and costs even less.

where each of the three or four fletches should be positioned. Home fletching also requires certain other supplies, such as feathers used to fletch in lengths from four to perhaps six inches, epoxy to adhere feathers to shaft, and perhaps an electrical wand or needle to shape feathers as you desire.

Bowstring Add-ons

I've seen some bowstrings in the field that might as well have been clotheslines, considering all the stuff their owners had hanging from them. It seems to me that there are three basic jobs any bowstring must do, and only three. It must propel the arrow straight; it must provide a rearmost reference for the archer's aim; and it must do both of the aforementioned tasks silently or nearly so. Anything that aids the string in these jobs is fine; all else is not needed.

No add-on I know of will effectively help the string propel the arrow straight, so I don't use any accessory claiming to do this job for me. When it comes to shoving the arrow into flight, the string is on its own.

Of course, maintaining the bowstring in top condition is your responsibility. Bowstring wax goes a long way toward keeping the string in good condition, both in helping the string repel water that might otherwise be absorbed into the string's fibers, and in making those little fuzzy ravelings lie down flat. Saunder's Bow String Wax, for example, is easy to use and comes in a push-out tube for easy application. There are several other good brands on the market.

Peepsights come in handy if you insist on using the precise same spot for aiming each time you shoot. These come in two basic types having to do with installation and use. One type is inserted into the string's fibers and requires you to rotate the string slightly with each shot in order to look through the peep's aiming hole. The other type fits on the string, rather than in it, and because of its several aiming holes, is always in position for use and does not have to be rotated.

Do it right, and do it the same way every time. This rule is applicable to where and how you anchor your draw hand each time you shoot, and I believe that any add-on that helps you gain consistency in anchoring is worth a look. The so-called string kisser, little more than a supple disc of soft rubber, is slid down the string to the exact spot on the string where the draw hand meets your lips (for those using the lips as an anchor point). The kisser is then glued in place with a drop or two of epoxy. Along with the bowstring, the kisser is drawn to a point touching your lips, and you can then be sure you are anchoring to the precise same spot every time.

Bowstring and cable servings (wrappings) for compound bows help quiet the otherwise noise-causing friction between bow cables that rub together when the bow is drawn. These servings are waterproof, long-lasting and come in a variety of color combinations for camouflage. Some of the servings have peel-off backing, revealing an adhesive underneath, while others simply wrap around the cables and are then pinned in place with small copper or brass C-clamps installed with pliers. I placed some clamp-type servings on my Browning X-Cellerator's cables two years ago and they continue to silence the cables and remain just where I installed

EASTON ALUMINUM HUNTING SHAFT SELECTION CHART

(Most popular size selection is shown in the unshaded area of each box)

ACTUAL BOW WEIGHT (At Your Draw Length)	CORRECT HUNTING ARROW LENGTH — 26½-27½ (27") Shaft Size	Arrow Weight	27½-28½ (28") Shaft Size	Arrow Weight	28½-29½ (29") Shaft Size	Arrow Weight	29½-30½ (30") Shaft Size	Arrow Weight	30½-31½ (31") Shaft Size	Arrow Weight	31½-32½ (32") Shaft Size	Arrow Weight	32½-33½ (33") Shaft Size	Arrow Weight	33½-34½ (34") Shaft Size	Arrow Weight	COMPOUND BOW PEAK WEIGHT 30% Let-off	50% Let-off
35-39	1913* 1815□ 1816	415 424 440	1913* 1915□ 1916 1818	426 447 471 490	2013* 1916 1917□	451 481 501	2114 2016 8.4^M 1917□ 1918	486 507 508 511 537	2114 2016 2115□ 1918 8.5^M	496 517 524 549 565	2213* 2115□ 2018 8.6^M	505 535 583 619	2213* 2117	514 587			41-46	47-52
40-44	1913* 1915□ 1916 1818	415 438 461 478	2013* 1916 1917□ 1820**	442 471 490 530	2114 2016 8.4^M 1917□ 1918	476 496 497 501 526	2114 2016 2115□ 1918 8.5^M	486 507 513 537 553	2213* 2115□ 2018 8.6^M	495 524 571 612	2213* 2117 2018 8.7^M	505 575 583 675	2117 2216	587 587			47-52	53-59
45-49	2013* 2016 1917□ 1820**	433 461 479 517	2114 2016 8.4^M 1917□ 1918	466 486 487 490 514	2114 2016 2115□ 8.5^M 1920**	476 496 502 541 559	2213* 2115□ 2018 8.6^M	485 513 558 598	2213* 2117 2018 2020 8.7^M	495 563 571 609 660	2117 2216 2020 8.7^M	575 575 622 675	2216 2217□	587 609	2219	658	53-58	60-66
50-54	2114 2016 1917□ 1918	456 475 479 503	2114 2016 8.4^M 2115□	466 486 487 492	2213* 2115□ 8.5^M 2018 1920**	475 502 541 546 559	2213* 2117 2018 2020 8.6^M	485 551 558 595 598	2117 2216 2020 8.7^M	563 563 609 660	2216 2217□ 8.7^M	575 596 675	2216 2217□ 2219	587 609 644	2219	658	59-64	67-72
55-59	2114 2016 8.4^M 2115□ 1920**	456 475 477 481 534	2213* 2115□ 8.5^M 2018 1920**	465 492 529 534 546	2213* 2117 2018 2020 8.6^M	475 539 546 582 585	2117 2216 2020 8.7^M	551 551 595 645	2216 2217□ 8.7^M	563 584 660	2216 2217□ 2219	575 596 631	2217□ 2219	609 644	2317 2219	648 658	65-70	73-79
60-64	2213* 8.4^M 2115□ 2018 1920**	455 477 481 522 534	2213* 2117 8.5^M 2018 2020	465 527 529 534 568	2117 2216 2020 8.6^M	539 539 582 585	2216 2217□ 8.7^M	551 571 645	2216 2217□ 2219 8.7^M	563 584 617 660	2217□ 2219	596 631	2317 2219	634 644	2317	648	71-76	80-86
65-69	2213* 2117 2018 2020	455 515 522 555	2117 2216 2020 8.6^M	527 527 568 571	2216 2217□ 8.7^M	539 558 629	2216 2217□ 2219 8.7^M	551 571 603 645	2217□ 2219	584 617	2317 2219	621 631	2317	634	2317	648	77-82	87-93
70-74	2117 2216 2020	515 515 555	2216 2217□	527 546	2216 2217□ 2219	539 558 589	2217□ 2219	571 603	2317 2219	607 617	2317	621	2317	634	2419	685	83-88	94-100
75-79	2216 2217□	515 533	2216 2217□ 2219	527 546 575	2217□ 2219	558 589	2317 2219	594 603	2317	607	2317	621	2419	670	2419	685	89-94	101-107
80-84	2216 2217□ 2219	515 533 562	2217□ 2219	546 575	2317 2219	580 589	2317	594	2317	607	2419	656	2419	670	2419	685	95-100	108-114
85-89	2217□ 2219	533 562	2317 2219	567 575	2317	580	2317	594	2419	641	2419	656	2419	670			101-106	115-121
90-94	2317 2219	553 562	2317	567	2317	580	2419	627	2419	641	2419	656					107-112	122-128
95-99	2317	553	2317	567	2419	612	2419	627	2419	641							113-118	129-135
100-109	2317	553	2419	597	2419	612	2419	627									119-129	136-149
110-119	2419	583	2419	597	2419	612											130-142	150-163

Matching your bow with the correct arrows is all-important. Easton Aluminum, makers of the most popular arrows in the United States, provides this selection chart.

The tube mill at Easton Aluminum, where shafts are drawn after they've gone through the anneal operation.

them. I can't ask for better performance than that.

Recurve bows, in particular, and compound bows to a lesser extent can be made to shoot more quietly with the addition of string silencers, all of which are designed to deaden the shock of a released string through the absorption of some of the motion. As stated elsewhere in this book, I use the yarn-type

Puffballs midway on the string between the limb tips and the nocking point. Other worthwhile silencer types use small bundles of leather thongs three inches long, a dozen or so bits of yarn and so on. The idea is to provide bulk without weight to absorb the shock.

Nocking your arrow in the same spot every time is part of consistent shooting, and the way to accomplish this is

The Flipper arrow rest from Bear Archery replaces worn rests and installs easily thanks to adhesive backing.

to put a permanent nocking point on your string and use it every time. The most common way to do this is to clamp one or two C-clamps on the string's nock point after measuring to determine that point. Compound bow users also use the bow square, a lightweight, T-shaped tool used to determine the correct nocking point and bracing height. Such squares are usually made of non-corrosive aluminum or wood.

Serving thread, whether made of twisted nylon or monofilament, is used to dress up the bowstring while thickening the nocking point a bit. This is a popular add-on for those not satisfied with how the bowstring comes from the manufacturer, and as a way to tailor the string to the hunter's requirements. Sold with the serving material is a small plastic or steel server that holds the spool of serving material firmly in place.

Bow Accessories

Arrow rests offer perhaps the widest variety of types and models of all the accessories the bowhunter can choose from. There are simple rests, complex rests, adjustable rests, expensive rests and inexpensive rests, not to mention rests for hunting bows, for target bows, those designed for fine tuning, and even some that grip the arrow in place until the draw and release. Which is for you? Keep in mind that it's best to go with the rest (or any other accessory) if and only if it solves a problem for you. And the simpler the better.

Most arrow rests are adhesive-backed and simply adhere to the proper spot above your arrow shelf, sticking directly to the bow finish or camo covering. The trick is to determine exactly where the rest should be positioned; this

By adding small weights to the riser section of your compound, you can smooth out the release and gain accuracy.

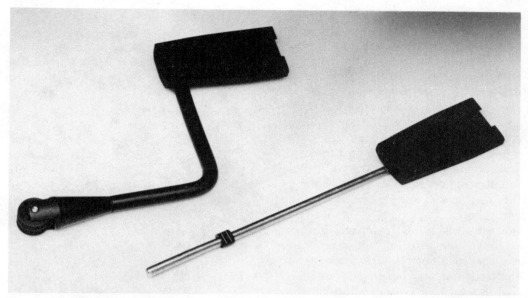

These cable guards offer both straight-line and dropped-arm choices; both attach directly to the bow.

can be easily determined by you or your local tackleshop pro.

Simply put, a rest is a sort of shelf, of one shape or another, on which your arrow lies while you draw and aim. A good rest doesn't interfere with the draw, and it doesn't make much noise on the draw or release. Most bowhunters use

Stabilizer bars can be screwed right into the threaded holes designed to accept them on most compound bows and some recurves.

care in positioning the rest, and they don't mess with it thereafter unless repair or adjustment is needed. The exception would be adjustable rests, those with buttons used to fine-tune the arrow's right or left flight pattern. Whatever rest model you choose, it should shoot well for you with your shooting style; it should be weatherproof, capable of easy installation and removal; and above all it should allow your tackle the utmost accuracy. Anything short of this can spoil your season by ruining your shots.

Most rests used by serious hunters employ some sort of soft cushioning material to silence the friction of arrow shaft against rest backing. Sometimes this is simply a type of short-sheared fur with the fur grain facing the front of the bow, a bit of thick and soft cloth, or some sort of synthetic cushion along which the arrow is drawn. This, too, must be weather-resistant to do the hunter much lasting good.

For the fine-tuning archer, bow stabilizers can balance a heavy bow, add little weight and enable the precision shooter to put his arrow into the bull consistently. Modern compound bows come with stabilizer threading holes already drilled and tapped, and they use standard diameters. The stabilizer itself is usually made of solid steel and should feature a non-glare, dark finish so it doesn't reflect sunlight in the woods. Stabilizers can be ordered through all complete tackleshops. Consult your local archery pro for tips on which type and weight stabilizers to use.

As mentioned elsewhere in this book, which type of camouflaging material you use is pretty much left to your personal preference. You have the choice of camo

This Bear bow quiver uses a dull finish available from the factory.

tape, camo bow socks and camo spray paint in a variety of earth-tone colors. Any of the three can be easily put on modern hunting bows, and all will cut sun glare and help keep you and your tackle out of sight in a dark deer woods. The benefit of spray paint extends beyond just camouflaging the bow itself, however. The paint can also be used on such items as glaring white wood in new treestands, stand ladders, backpacks, bright arrow shafts and so on. The cans of paint are available at tackleshops and cost very little. Be sure to ask whether the brand you buy is removable after application.

Tubes of face and hand cream in camo colors help keep exposed skin from giv-

ing away your position, which is especially important if you still-hunt or use a ground stand positioned at deer level. You may opt for a gauze facemask, of course, although these have a way of getting snagged on twigs and limbs.

Bowsights have become quite common among shooters using compound equipment. The sights extend slightly beyond the bow facing and have several vertical slots in the steel housing; shooting pins are fitted into these slots and can be adjusted up or down by sliding them up or down the slot. The pins can also be adjusted to move arrow impact right or left by adjusting the pin within its own brass housing. If your arrow is

This face cream camo kit from Bear Archery can be carried in the field or applied back in camp. The cream washes off easily following the hunt.

consistently striking to the right of your aimpoint, move the pin slightly to the left, forcing you to move your bow hand slightly toward the intended point of impact.

Most shooters use four-pin sights, with the pins' intended distances ranging from perhaps 15 yards out to 40 yards or so, in approximately 10-yard increments. Each pin's tip has a different color for quick reference. Adjustment is made by first loosening the pin's holding ring, screwing the pin to the left or right, then tightening the holding ring and clamping the pin in place. If you're a beginning archer or bowhunter, I'd suggest

starting off with a simple bowsight until you achieve accuracy, and then, if you prefer barebow (instinctive) shooting, remove the bowsight once your shooting eye has been developed. If you're a novice, starting off with no sight at all can cause you to shoot arrows all over the place with no reference point to use as a steadying factor. Better to start with a sight—and lots of practice on the archery range.

Lighted sights with their own batteries have become popular in recent years, more and more as hunters became tired of having to pass up otherwise decent shots at deer showing up just at first light or at marginal evening shooting

This bowsight includes a protective C-bar to avoid knocking the fragile pinheads out of alignment.

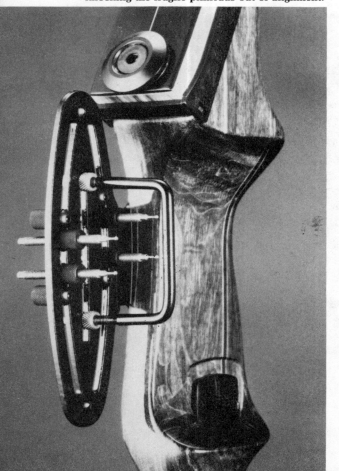

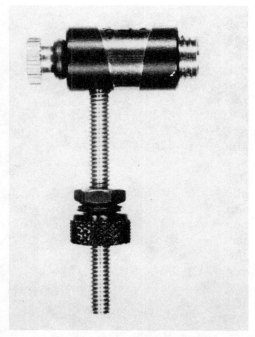

The Li'l Red bowsight light allows for those early dawn and late-dusk shots where the ambient light level is very low. The light is battery-powered and screws right to the bowsight.

light. In short, lighted sights include a tiny red light powered by alkaline or silver-oxide battery units. The light fits right into the bowsight's steel housing, with the red glow directed downward to illuminate the head of each shooting pin.

There was a time when I would have traded my left leg for a lighted sight. I was hunting in northeastern Alabama and was on my way to the cabin at full dark when a big buck trotted across the dirt road 25 yards ahead of me and paused just inside a dark woodsline. The buck stood and looked at me in the late-evening gloom, and all I could do was look back because the sight pins on my bow disappeared in the dark, rendering the sight useless and any chance for a shot even poorer. I didn't take a shot and the deer finally wandered away. Since then I've used a bowsight light on occasion, and it's accounted for shots I couldn't otherwise have attempted.

By the way, bowsight lights are colored red because few animals can sharply define red light after dark. I know this to be true because I have spent long winter nights calling foxes into the glare of red lanterns, and the otherwise wily animals come galloping right into the red glare as if the light weren't there.

Once you get that bowsight and its delicate pins sighted-in for certain shooting distances, it stands to reason you'd like to keep them that way, and this means avoiding hard knocks that ruin your alignment. Pin guards do this job and consist of nothing more complex than a squared-off C-shaped steel bar that fits, like the sight light, right into the slots in your bowsight. The bar keeps the pins protected in much the same manner as a rollbar on a racing

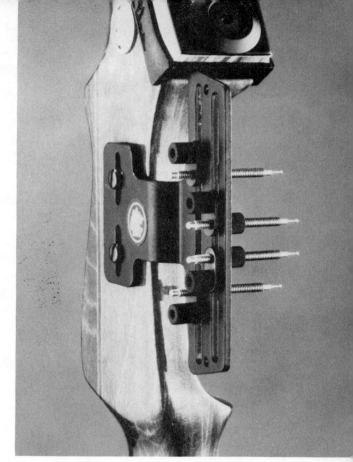

The standard bowsight attaches to the side of the handle riser, placing the pintips in the hunter's line of sight in the sight window. Individual pins can be adjusted up and down and back and forth until precise positioning is achieved. This is a Bear Shur-Hit sight.

car; the bar takes the knocks instead of the pins.

Bow quivers are all the rage now. They keep half a dozen or more hunting shafts within quick reach of your draw hand, keep the unused shafts rigidly in place, and the good quivers also include some sort of hard hood to protect the fragile broadheads and the hands that use them.

A few bow quivers snap onto the bow and come with flexible armatures meant

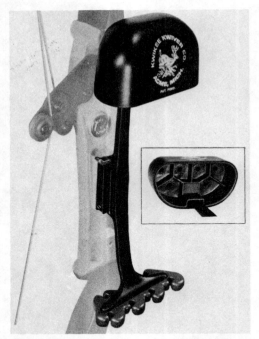

The Kwikee Kwiver for use with compound bows snaps on and off through the use of a small base screwed to the riser section of the bow.

for this purpose. However, the better models are designed to match specially tapped drill holes manufactured into the bow handle or riser; a seating add-on is screwed into the bow and the quiver slips in and out of this add-on easily by means of a spring-loaded clip on top. The quiver I use has a dull-black finish and includes a handy built-in scent pad inside the hood in case I want to use a bit of masking scent while hunting. Treestand hunters often remove the quiver once they are settled in the tree, which allows them to use a light, fast-handling bow. The quiver is hung or fastened close at hand in case a followup shot is offered.

One type of bow quiver designed for use with either compound or recurve bows is the Sagittarius's Orion, which comes in right- or left-handed models. The quiver has a large thumb screw for easy removal and is made of aluminum. The hood or cup is lined with foam for broadhead protection and safety.

Many states require bowhunters to carry their hunting bows in cases while moving to and from the site, and quite a few hunters use soft cloth cases with zippered closures to meet this requirement and keep their expensive gear protected. These cases, available in a wide variety of styles and sizes, usually come in either basic tan, brown or camouflage finish. Cloth or leather handles are included.

Mechanical releases are also popular, both for archers who like extra smoothness when releasing the arrow and for those hunters who suffer from arthritis or some condition that makes holding a powerful hunting bow impossible with the bare hand. Most such releases have plastic housing and steel internal triggering systems. These quality release mechanisms also allow older hunters to make quick, sure shots, and their operation is silent. Be sure to check state laws because mechanical releases are not legal everywhere.

Other Extras

If you don't shoot with gloves on your hands, you'll probably want some sort of cushioning add-on to protect the fingertips on your draw hand, and you have a nice choice from which to choose.

Shooting tabs are very popular. Shaped like miniature mittens and made of reinforced soft leather, the tabs include a rubberized finger separator that fits be-

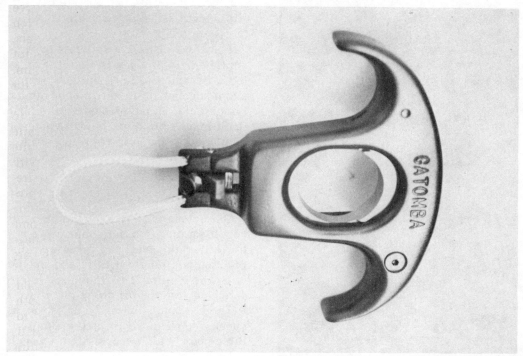

The mechanical release is popular, especially among those bowhunters whose arthritis requires assistance in a smooth release.

tween the shooter's index and second finger for a firm, sure fit. Shooting tabs weigh almost nothing, stay on the shooting hand when you're active, and cost little. They do a good job of protecting the shooting hand, and of course come in left- and right-handed models.

Shooting gloves are little more than three strips of soft leather with glove-like tips that fit over the three shooting fingertips. The entire glove fastens around the wrist by means of Velcro strips or elastic straps and clasps. Gloves remain popular, but are slowly losing out to shooting tabs.

Shooting arm guards come in varying lengths, from those only eight inches long to those protecting the inner sur-

face of the entire bow arm. All guards are made of soft sewn leather with reinforcing steel bands inside. Most use Velcro fastening straps, although a few of the older models still employ elastic and clasps. Their main function for the deer bowhunter is keeping bulky coat or jacket sleeves from interfering with the bowstring movement when a shot is taken. This in turn allows the shot to be smoother, and dampens the noisy slapping sound of a bowstring striking cloth. Generally speaking, full-length arm guards are most often used in practice when the archer is wearing short sleeves and needs the protection a long guard provides. Shorter arm guards are popular in actual hunting when arm

With compound bow, arm guard and shooting glove, this lad needs only arrows to practice on the shooting range.

the bow is drawn. The better slings are installed by means of an adaptor bracket, and length is adjusted using built-in buckle or snaps.

The bow holster is an attempt to reinvent the nail. Made of leather, the holster is designed to hold the bow firmly and in an erect position while the hunter is on stand, and is designed to adjust its fit to all compound bows. Whatever happened to hanging your bow from a handy nail or twig?

Making Practice Palatable

OK, not many of us enjoy practice and yes, it's a dirty job but somebody's got to do it, right? You can dress up your practice equipment a little and maybe you won't mind it so much. Here are some suggestions for doing just that.

Targets come in many faces, so to speak. You can shoot at the standard three-color bull's-eye, assigning each color a different number score, and make a game of hitting the most bulls with a given number of shots. Or you can use a two-colored bull with only the central ring in white and all else blue. Or you can do away with boring bull's-eyes altogether and go to animal figures to spice things up.

There are almost as many different animal target faces as there are animals. Javelina, whitetail buck, ringneck pheasant, mountain ram, coyote and moose are just a few. These faces are usually made of some tough material designed to take quite a lot of puncturing by target points and even broadheads without falling apart. Some even come with small bulls done in black for the purists among us.

Target matts and butts are a must re-

protection isn't needed, but uninterrupted shots are a must.

The bow sling is simply a leather or rope lanyard attached immediately below the bow handle. The lanyard's loop fits loosely around the archer's bow wrist and allows the shooter to loosen his grip on the bow as much as he likes while drawing and releasing. The sling prevents the bow from being dropped, and may provide the archer with uniformity of draw and release. The sling also helps brace the wrist and hand correctly when

This arm guard has Velcro fasteners and covers all parts of the inner arm from wrist to above the elbow.

A good practice target is a must if you're to sharpen your skills during the offseason. This target in the author's side yard handles target heads only.

gardless of where you practice, in backyard or rural bow range. This is because you don't want to damage valuable arrows by shooting repeatedly into anything else, including the ground. The larger circular target butts can be mounted on target easels for easy moving and built-in erection for shooting. My backyard practice range has a few bales of hay with a soft wood backing and a target face out front, and I've been quite happy with the arrangement.

Once you get your practice eye down pat on targets, you may want to go with a target that allows hunting broadheads to be used. Highly compressed polyurethane is the answer. This material will effectively stop all broadheads shot into it, yet will allow easy arrow re-

moval following the shot. Some shops and mail-order catalogs offer broadhead targets cut into life-sized deer silhouettes. One such is Ole Norm's Archery Supplies of Clemson, South Carolina, phone 803/654-1652.

Gear You Can Count On

You'd be surprised how a small, light pair of binoculars comes in handy when you're trying to spot deer standing in distant cover. The extra magnification and brightening qualities of the glasses have a way of popping deer figures into our vision much better than the naked eye. I carry a small pair of binocs on all my hunts and scouting trips. It's one thing to find fresh sign, but actually

This liquid soap, featuring the squeeze bottle and squirt cap, claims to remove human odor from hands and clothing, making it easier to approach deer.

With any type of optics, of course, it's important to avoid flashing sunlight with the front lens surfaces. This can be accomplished by gripping the glasses so that your palms shade the front glass from sunlight. If you're prone to dropping things from your treestand, you may want to go with one of the rubber-armored binoculars which bounce instead of breaking.

What type of knife do you carry while bowhunting? A chap from Italy I ran across in Ontario had an honest-to-Gawd bayonet strapped to his hip. The 15-inch blade on that sucker was honed razor-

The Catquiver totes four spare arrows in the middle of the back while its camouflaged pouches carry other small items in backpack fashion.

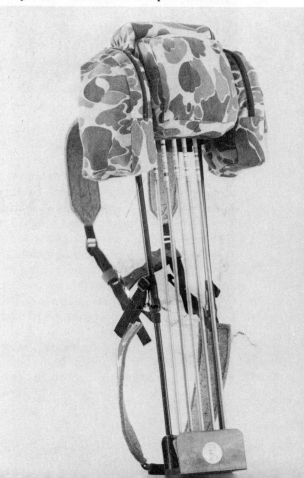

seeing deer when scouting helps the confidence to no end. There are quite a variety of available binoculars that fit this need; all are relatively small and light, quick-focusing, rugged and easily packed. A few models come in camouflage finish, but I'd prefer to stay with the standard black and have even added a few strips of blaze orange tape so I don't lose them if I put the glass down in the woods somewhere. A camo finish would make finding them a lot tougher.

Need a knife for deer hunting, or a small hatchet for punching through the loin area? This selection from Buck provides quite a choice.

sharp and it was about as suited to dressing or skinning game as the tongue of your boot. I like a lock-back folding knife with a grip shaped to fit my hand. The blade itself is six inches long (four inches of sharp blade will dress the biggest deer around), wide enough so I can apply a bit of pressure when coring the apple, so to speak, and heavy enough to take a sharp rap or two when needed. I've added a strip of bright tape to each side of the knife handle to help me find it after I've put it on the nearest rock. The knife fits into a nylon belt sheath with a Velcro-fastening top, weighs only

a very few ounces, and is available from Buck Knives.

If you prefer non-folding belt knives, you have a wide selection to choose from. Just be sure that the blade isn't so long that the knife is unsafe to use when you reach up inside the deer's body cavity to trim away membrane, and that the handle doesn't become so slippery when field-dressing that you could seriously cut yourself should the knife slip. Any belt knife should be carried in a quality sheath made of either tough leather or pre-fitted nylon.

It's not a bad idea to carry a small,

The new Bucklite lock-back knife from Buck Knives features a hand-molded grip of light synthetic Valox and a three-inch blade of typical Buck quality.

fine-grain stone in your hunting jacket if you plan to skin your deer on the spot. Nothing's better than working with a good, sharp knife, and nothing's worse than using a dull blade. A few deft strokes with the stone puts a working edge back on the knife, and the stone is so light you won't know you're toting it until it's needed. A few belt-knife models have stone pockets sewn right into the sheath.

Have you ever tried to hack or pound your way through the pelvis area of a deer, down through the hams, without the use of a small folding meat saw or a light hatchet? It's like wading through mud. Folding saws are available at most discount department stores (K-Mart, for example) and do a fine, quick job of splitting the hams down to the anus for a complete dressing job. Belt hatchets (the lightweight models with all-steel construction are fine) do a similar job and can move through the deer's small bones with ease. The same tool can help put your tree or ground stand in fine fettle, too.

Can you read a compass? If not, you'd better learn if you plan to hunt in any

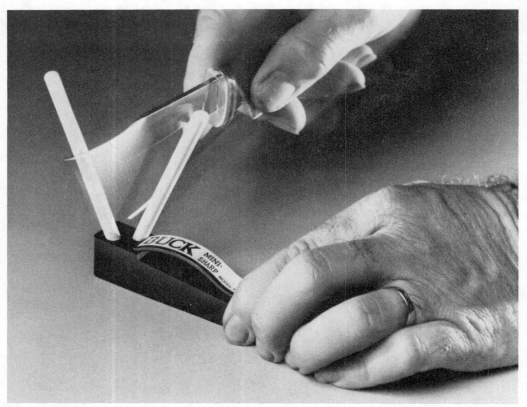

The Mini-Sharp is designed to put a cutting edge on any knife, in the field or at home, in just a few seconds. The two rods are made of ceramic material.

woods larger than 20 acres, because we all get lost sooner or later—or think we do, which is really the same thing. A compass helps keep you oriented in the woods and costs and weighs so little that there's no real reason to leave it behind. And when you become really proficient with a compass, you can make a lot more sense out of topographical maps and aerial photos. It's a great help when you want to return to a certain spot in an unmarked woods, such as returning to a good-looking spot you found just at dusk last night. Another

tip for navigating in the woods, a method that timber cruisers use to relocate specific spots in tall timber, is this: When you walk out of the woods and away from a spot you want to return to later, count every time your left boot strikes the ground, taking a heading on your compass at the same time. When you reach the road or your truck or whatever destination, you'll know that to return to that spot you must count, say, 264 steps on your left foot on a heading of the reverse, or reciprocal, compass reading you used on the way out last evening. For example, you're leaving this hotspot of yours at dusk and head along a compass reading course of 90 degrees for a distance of 264 steps. Tomorrow morning, you'll repeat those 264 counts of your left footsteps but along the re-verse compass heading, or 270 degrees. Doing this correctly should put you within arm's reach of the spot you want to relocate. Try it the next time you scout or take a short hike. It works every time and saves a lot of thrashing about.

If your state game laws permit it, try using a fake doe deer the next time you rattle for bucks (detailed elsewhere). The model can be slightly smaller or larger than life size, and the legs should have small pointed pins on the bottom so the doe can be placed wherever you want it by sticking the pins into the ground. The trick is to put some drops of doe-in-heat scent on the model's hindquart-ers, then back off and hide in a tree or some dense ground brush within bow

The camouflage facemask helps hide the hunter but can get snagged on brush. It remains popular with wild-turkey hunters, however.

range. The buck attracted by the rattling comes looking for other deer and spots the model in a little clearing. He walks right up to her, sniffing all that gorgeous doe scent, and stays put while you swallow the lump in your throat and take a nice, relaxed shot at a buck out in the open. Again, *make sure deer models are permitted in your state* before going ahead with this bit of animal subterfuge. You can construct your own model from a wire frame and plaster of paris, and the deer likeness doesn't have to be perfect to fool a buck.

Every serious bowhunter I know carries some sort of artificial light while hunting. You should too. You'll have to climb into your treestand before dawn

Easton's new Camo-Hunter shafts come in camouflage finish, which should make it interesting to try to find the next arrow you miss with.

and down again after dark, and you'll want a reliable flashlight to make the job easier. Most discount stores offer a variety of pocket-sized, battery-operated flashlights: some have replaceable batteries, some are rechargeable, and some are throwaways after their charge has been depleted. Personally, I like the rechargeable models. Even though they cost more to purchase, I save money in the long run by not having to buy batteries. Also, by recharging often, I make sure I have the brightest possible light when I need help in the dark. A good flashlight can save your life by attracting others' attention if you're injured, it can help you get in and out of the woods safely and is a definite comfort when it's 9:30 p.m. and two miles to your car.

When blood-trailing wounded deer after dark, however, I'll take a Coleman lantern every time. There's something about the glow thrown by a Coleman that makes even tiny spots of blood pop out in vivid black against foliage. The lantern's wide glow also lets you track a wide swath through heavy cover, something the thin shaft of a flashlight doesn't permit. I keep a Coleman in the back of my car during bow season, and make sure it has a full fuel tank before every hunt. You never know when you'll need it.

My feet often get cold during the latter part of bow season, especially when I've been on stand so long my mustache has begun to frost over. To combat this, I bought a pair of battery-powered electric socks. The socks are knee-high and operate on a pair of regular flashlight batteries that fit into snap-closure plastic pockets, one on the top of each sock. The socks are thick, on the order of athletic socks, and comfortable inside boots,

Screw-in tree steps are a handy way to gain access to that treestand, but keep in mind that such steps do penetrate the tree and can cause damage. *Michigan DNR*

and the heating feature can be switched on or off by putting the batteries in or taking them out of the plastic pockets. Electric socks don't cost much, they last a long time, and the thickness of the fabric keeps my feet comfortable in moderate weather when the batteries aren't needed. You can obtain electric socks from better sporting-goods outlets or from several mail-order houses.

If you run across a bowhunter who doesn't carry a length of rope, you've met a man who has no way to pull his bow up into a treestand, lash a buck's legs out of the way during field-dressing, or comfortably drag a deer out of the woods. Rope is that useful to the deer bowhunter.

I used to carry 25 feet of small-diameter nylon line. It was strong enough, with a breaking point of about 250 pounds, but the small diameter creased my palms and fingers when I put pressure on the rope. Consequently I went to a half-inch-diameter cotton rope of the same length that is only slightly bulkier, weighs no more than nylon, and does all I want rope to do but with more

This archer uses a nylon safety belt in case he should lose his balance. The belt allows him to hang until he can release himself and shinny down the trunk. *TVA Photo*

hand comfort. You can buy cotton or nylon rope from any good hardware store in whatever length you need, with the cost depending on how much rope you buy in certain diameters. I also like to singe both ends of a new rope until it turns brown; this prevents the fibers from unraveling. You can accomplish the same thing by wrapping each end of the rope, to a length of about six inches, with serving thread or monofilament fishing line. A length of 25 feet does all jobs well.

Something called the Compound Caddy from Ole Norm is just the ticket for traveling bowhunters, especially those who use public transportation where all tackle must be checked as baggage. The protective case comes with a tough outer construction and an inner foam layering accommodating 18 arrows, a strung compound and all small accessories. The green case weighs six pounds and has lockable clasps.

I think a small pocket camera is a must, too. Bowhunting is the sort of thing you talk about, brag about and dream about in the off-season, so why not have a few color photos for just this purpose? I use one of the Kodak disc cameras; the camera has a long range of focus, a built-in flash and film advance, and takes passable color snaps in any light. The camera is about twice the size of a pack of cigarettes and weighs just a few ounces. The disc film presently available is a bit grainy, but for the type of snapshots we're talking about, the film is fully suitable. Disc film comes in 15-shot capacity and is flat, so you can easily carry extra films in your shirt pocket.

If you use a broadhead with permanently installed blades, the chore of putting a cutting edge on those blades falls to you. Sometimes you'll have to do this afield, like when you've taken a shot and missed, maybe tried to collect a grouse for dinner, or maybe just smacked one of the heads against a hard surface, dulling one or more blades. For this, Bear Archery makes a pocket blade sharpener that's smaller than a pencil and has two cutting/sharpening edges fitted into a shallow V in one end of the sharpener. The sharpener is simply drawn along the blade to be sharpened, front to rear, until a cutting edge is obtained. The idea is to remove all burrs and crimped edges, and this little tool does the job.

A small stuff pack, which can hold everything from a lunchbag to a flashlight, extra bottles of scent, rope, saw and so on, is almost a must if you want to remain in the woods all day. I even carry a thermos of hot soup in my stuff bag, and it's mighty welcome after I've been on stand for several hours.

Stuff bags come in lightweight and waterproof nylon, in either camouflage or solid colors, and with Velcro or snap closures. Backpacks are handy and can be removed while you're on stand, as can the fanny packs that are now popular. The important thing is to have the pack and its contents there when you need 'em.

A twist on this theme is Catquiver's bow quiver bag. The compartmentalized camo bag fits right on the top of the Catquiver and has zippered closures for easy access. The Catquiver comes with backstraps for carrying.

And from the same company (Rancho Safari, Box 691, Ramona, CA 92065) comes Catlegs, leggings covered on their outer surfaces with real or synthetic fur to help you stalk through dense cover without scraping your pant legs against noisy brush. Catlegs come with zipper

Everything better work at a time like this: compound bow, arm guard, mechanical release and, of course, the broadhead. *TVA Photo*

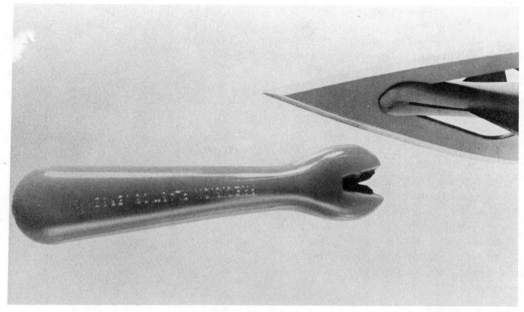

This pocket sharpener for nonreplaceable-bladed broadheads can be used in the field for hurry-up jobs between shots.

closures and elastic at the upper and lower eges.

This is a good a place as any to include the names and addresses of national archery organizations you may wish to contact for more information about the specialties they have to offer. While not bowhunting accessories in the strictest sense of the words, they nonetheless are worthwhile.

American Archery Council
200 Castlewood Rd.
North Palm Beach, FL 33408

Bowhunters Silhouettes Int.
P.O. Box 6470
Orange, CA 92667

Bowhunters Who Care
P.O. Box 269
Columbus, NE 68601

Fred Bear Sports Club
4600 S.W. 41st Blvd.
Gainesville, FL 32601

National Archery Assn.
1750 East Boulder St.
Colorado Springs, CO 80909

National Field Archery Assn.
Route 2, Box 514
Redland, CA 92373

Professional Archers Assn.
731 N. Cliff
Sioux Falls, SD 57103

Professional Bowhunters Society
25233 TR 192
Coshocton, OH 43812

Bowhunting accessories are useful when they solve particular problems or make a day afield easier. On the other hand, adding accessories in an attempt to bypass the basics, such as regular practice with your bow on a target range, merely lessens your ability to hit when the moment arrives.

Buying one of the new and exciting overdraw bows may seem appealing to you, for example, but if bow season rolls around and you still can't hit consistently with the newfangled bow, it's doing more harm than good to your enjoyment of the sport and your ability to hit that deer you've worked so hard to shoot. Don't sell yourself short, or buy yourself short. Have definite goals in mind when you take your checkbook to the tackleshop. And if you see someone shooting at an indoor range with an add-on you haven't tried, take the time to ask him about the accessory, what it will and won't do, and why he uses it. Maybe it's for you and maybe it isn't. Only you can answer that question.

The bottom line is, don't bog yourself down with shortcut hardware when what you really need above all else is to practice and practice some more. As this is written I'm still honing my shooting for this fall's season, and I'll keep honing it until I've got it right. I use eight or 10 rounds of practice as a getaway from this typewriter, and I imagine you could come up with a similar reason to go shoot a couple dozen arrows a few times a week. That's the best accessory of all.

14

Scents and How to Use Them

There are three types of scents used by bowhunters after deer: masking scents, attractor scents and the *wrong scents*. Keep this in mind. It's important.

If you hunt in the South where pines, cedars and other evergreens are prevalent, the natural scent to use as a mask for your human odor is pine scent. But suppose you choose another popular masking scent, that made from concentrated apple juice. The deer in your southern hunting area have probably never encountered an apple tree or its fruit in their entire lives. So what's the result? You end up spooking the deer with that alien odor instead of soothing them into accepting it and the hunter wearing it.

In short, the *wrong scent* is any scent not native to the area. In an area where pines are populous, the common acorn scent would similarly be out of place and counterproductive. Scents are very beneficial aids for the bowhunter trying to get close to unspooked whitetails, but only if used intelligently. Used incorrectly, scents can and will work against your success—as will the incorrect camouflage, ignoring the wind direction and so on. Let's look at the major types of scents used by deer bowhunters, and say a little about the proper use of each type.

Masking Scents

These are supposed to do exactly what the name implies: mask your scent so you can move about in deer country without your human odor alerting the game that a man is in the woods. Human odor flakes off into the air, and onto any

A small selection of commercial scents. Just be sure the scent you use is appropriate for the location you're hunting.

brush you might lightly touch as you go in and out of the woods; in short, it follows you everywhere. Deer react to scent in a variety of ways, depending on the individual scent and whether the deer are used to encountering it. Human scent is perhaps the most distasteful scent to any deer, simply because we are a major predator, from the deer's viewpoint. A deer can spot you in the woods and may or may not dash off. But let the same deer get a whiff of your human odor, whether he has spotted you or not, and he is gone. Deer seem to trust their sense of smell more than their eyesight—probably because they know their nose is sharper than their eyes—and this seems reason enough for you to employ a little chemistry to allay that defense mechanism called smell.

So what type of scent do you use? It

depends on where you are and what you plan to do.

Most commercial scents come in liquid form. The usual marketed amount is a few ounces of liquid in small glass or plastic bottles with screw-on caps. The idea is to use enough of the stuff to cover your odor, but not so much that the sheer volume of the stink drives all game out of the area.

That's a good rule of thumb: don't use too much scent. But there is an exception for every rule, and here it is. A husband and wife, friends of mine, like to bowhunt together, and last season was the lady's first ever for bowhunting whitetails. Her husband gave her a bottle of some type of doe whitetail estrus scent, told her to put some around her stand, and await developments. But he didn't tell her *how much* scent to use, so she scattered some here, some there, some on the tree trunk, some on her clothes. She emptied a full bottle of the odorous stuff, then climbed into her stand before first light. And that's when things started to happen. "I could hear them coming up the ravine and from all over the place," she said later. "By the sounds of them, there must have been a dozen or more deer right around my stand. And when it got light, there were two deer bedded down not five feet from my tree. I think all that doe scent made them a little crazy." Don't use too much scent, but how much is *too much?* All I can say is, experiment with different amounts and see what happens.

Masking scents would include just about all of them, with the exception of those designed to imitate the scent given off by a doe in her estrus cycle and ready to accept a buck for sex. These would include acorn, apple and pine scent, so-called natural scent, and those made from extract of fox urine (phew!) and skunk oil.

A very good hunter I know, the former holder of a state whitetail record, told me he uses Old Spice after-shave lotion, of all things, just before he goes out to hunt. If Old Spice works on women, maybe it works on deer as well. And another bowhunter, an instructor in a fine bowhunting school held at Alabama's Westervelt Lodge, told me he uses inexpensive but effective Pine Sol on the edges of his boot soles just before hunting. He says the cleanser's scent effectively masks the scent normally left in his tracks in the woods. Deer notice the pine scent (or any other scent used as a mask), of course, but they usually don't spook out of the neighborhood upon detecting it.

I've had many opportunities to watch deer react to the scent left in my tracks. One such chance came when I'd put a few drops of doe scent on my boots before still-hunting my way along a wooded creekbed in Pennsylvania. Not many minutes later a mature doe with twin yearling fawns came by the stump where I sat, in plain view but immobile, and the big doe immediately detected the scent trail of fake doe scent, stopping dead in her tracks without crossing my scentline. She dropped her head to sniff the scent, moving a step or two right or left to inhale more of the odor, and then she raised her head and looked in all directions. She still didn't spot me, and she stomped her foot in what looked like annoyance. The two fawns remained obediently behind her. Again she dropped her head and sniffed the scentline, and again she looked around as if trying to spot the odorous doe that left such a strong scent across her path. After 10 minutes of indecision, the doe turned and led her youngsters back the way they'd come. She was plainly unwilling to cross that scentline without more information about what lay ahead, and she was unwilling to risk her own welfare, and that of her fawns, in that situation.

Bucks are, if anything, even more adamantly unwilling to step across a human scentline. They simply will not do it. A good masking scent on the boot soles may put the buck's fears at ease, however, especially if it is a scent the buck is used to.

There are several methods of applying masking scent to your person, both for the still-hunter who moves around a lot, and for the stander who wants to keep his presence unannounced while

A drop or two of scent dribbled on boot soles will help mask human odor. You can also place the scent on a tuft of grass, then scrape each boot sole over it for adequate coverage.

traveling to and from his stand. The easiest way is to apply a few drops of the scent either directly to the bottom of your soles, or to place a few drops on a tuft of grass and then scrape your boots over the tuft a few times. Several hunters I know just smear a bit of the liquid scent on the sides of their boot soles, and this seems to work well, too. The idea is to get the masking scent on the ground to mask the smell left in your tracks. Either of the above methods will work.

My wife doesn't like the method, namely because it makes my camo clothing smell like the lion house at the zoo, but I usually place a couple drops of masking scent on the narrow bill of my cloth hunting cap, a few more drops across my back, and one or two more drops on the outside of my knee area on the pant legs. With this distribution, I reason that my human scent is masked downwind from me as well as along the path I take in the woods. I also have a few two-inch-square scent pads, which are made of rubber-backed lamb's wool and equipped with safety pins for attachment to my hunting clothes. I could add scent to these pads before each hunt, pinning them where I think best, and then remove them when I arrive home again. I could do that, but I usually don't, preferring to simply apply scent to my hunting garb. My wife wishes I'd switch.

Several modern bow quivers come equipped with built-in scent pads, usually up around the hood covering the

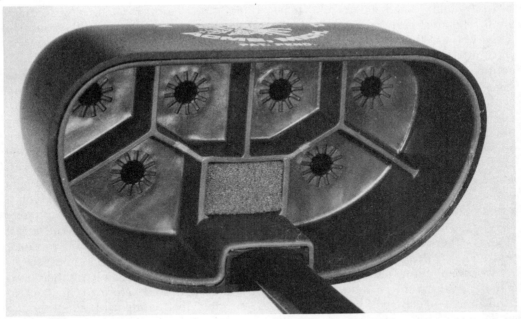

The built-in scent pad made of foam in this bow quiver hood holds a few drops of scent to cover human odor.

broadheads. Scent can be dribbled onto this pad and the masking odor will drift downwind in the desired manner.

Once on stand, you can put a drop or two here and there in a circle around your stand, but this patterning of scent where you hunt is best left to attractor scents. Remember, you want to bring the deer within easy bow range, not give them reason to steer clear of the area.

Attractor Scents

These smells are designed to attract buck deer, and since they are almost all derivatives of the doe deer's estrus (menstrual) juices, attractors are most effective when used during rutting season. Sometimes a curious doe will follow up on these scents, probably driven by a curiosity to find which new lady in the neighborhood smells like that, but for the most part you'll see the buck when you use the attractor scent.

An attractor is often used in combination with a masking scent. The masking scent is used to get you in and out of the woods by covering your human odor, and the attractor scent is used at the hunting spot to, hopefully, bring a horny buck close enough for a shot. Attractors are applied right around the stand, often in the circular pattern mentioned above. Some hunters like to use a single scent post, hanging a bit of cloth or even the bagged lint from the family's clothes dryer near the stand and then putting a few drops of doe scent on it.

I've known young and naive bucks to actually walk up and sniff the scent post itself, and I once saw a forkhorn first sniff, then take the bag into his mouth and tear it down from the sapling where it was hanging from a string. The little

buck bit, butted and then pawed the bag, as if completely taken by its delicious smell. He wouldn't leave the bag alone until yours truly, sitting amused practically over the little fellow's head, shooed the youngster away and climbed down to put the scent post back where it belonged.

An application method I've used with occasional success calls for locating a line of buck scrapes, then adding a few drops of doe scent to each scrape. Sometimes I'll scent just one scrape—the freshest and largest—and then find a place within bow range where I can conceal myself. I find this to be very effective when the bucks are deep in the rutting mood and making daily—or sometimes twice-daily—rounds of their scrapes in an attempt to locate does ready to mate. This scenting method has several things going for it, too. For openers, you already know that you'll be hunting in a spot frequented by an actively rutting buck. It's likely to be a good buck, too, because the biggest buck in an area will try to prevent lesser rivals from rutting. Wait long enough, conceal yourself intelligently with a clear shooting lane from stand to scrape, and sooner or later Mr. Big will come along. A few drops of doe scent on the scrape will give the buck something to investigate when he arrives, and this gives you a little extra time to wait for him to move into just the right position, come to full draw, take aim and release. In some cases, a miss won't even spook scent-held bucks. They'll merely lift their head and look around before getting back to sniffing that wonderful smell before adding their own urine to the mix. I once had as many as three shots at the same buck in this type of situation, although I'll admit that I should have stuck him on the first try. Nobody's perfect.

Application methods are important, especially if you want to keep hunting buddies for any length of time.

Two buddies of mine were driving to a deer woods, and when they got close the guy not driving hauled out a spray bottle of fox urine and began spraying it all over what, in the pre-dawn dark, he thought were his boots. What he actually did was miss most of his boots and instead spray nearly everything in the front seat of the car. It reportedly took about two weeks of open-window driving to make that car livable again. There are several accepted methods of applying fox urine to hunting clothes, but the above is *not* one of them.

Hunting boots can have an effect on how much scent you leave behind you. Rubber soles don't become permeated with human scent as do leather or composition soles, and if you keep your hunting boots outside and away from frequent human handling, they'll keep your scent off the ground come bow season.

Another way to keep your scent at a minimum is to shower or bathe just before hunting, keeping your camo clothes hanging outdoors, washing the clothes in unscented soap powders, and cleaning your hands and face with unscented hand soap. I use something called Hunter's Choice Camo Soap. This liquid contains bicarbonate of soda and chlorophyll, both of which eliminate existing

This sole pad from Tink's allows the hunter to use whatever scent he wants by adding a drop at a time on the padded section inside the round opening.

odors and suppress the creation of new odors for a period of time. Hunter's Choice comes in an 18-ounce plastic bottle and is suitable for washing clothing in electric washers as well as cleansing hands and face.

All of this attention is called for because the white-tailed deer, buck or doe, is driven right out of its gourd by human smell. Deer simply will not tolerate it for any length of time. Not long ago I was hunting an area of the South and decided to still-hunt along a sort of natural trail between a pinewoods on my

Don't think for a minute that deer don't depend on scent every day. This buck takes a whiff of human scent just before fleeing.

right and a thickly overgrown and thorny old clear-cut on my left. I pussyfooted down the narrow strip as quietly as I could; recent rains had dampened the underfoot debris and I made little sound as I eased along, arrow on the string, alert to anything that moved. I was just approaching a fallen log inside the thick stuff on my left when, suddenly, there was a snort loud enough to wake the dead and three whitetails leaped across the trail ahead of me and disappeared into the pines. Moments later a fourth deer, apparently hoping that I'd pass by and miss seeing it, could stand my scent no longer; snorting loudly, it bolted right through all those brier bushes, thick saplings and overgrown bushes. He made his own trail, probably losing some hide in the process, in getting the hell away from whatever it was that smelled so bad. How much do deer hate human scent? With every fiber in their sensitive olfactory systems.

In sum, it would be foolish for you to ignore this most sensitive of the whitetail's senses while in the woods.

Scents in General

It's been said that human scent is so repulsive to deer because we are meat eaters, which affects the nature of the odor we emit. To deer, we probably smell like predators, which of course we are during the annual hunting seasons. And this in turn might explain why a deer snorts at the moment it decides to bolt from close proximity with humans. The snort, as the name implies, is made when the animal exhales through its nostrils a blast of air from its lungs. Who's to say this isn't the deer's way of ridding its nose of that fearful odor of ours, in addition to warning other deer in the area that something is amiss? Until we can accurately read the minds of deer (assuming they have minds as well as instincts), we'll never know the answer to that one.

Sometimes hunters intentionally let their scent reach the game's sensitive nostrils, but only under special circumstances. Bowhunters seldom drive deer, but more than once I've been in a group of bowhunters who posted archers along the heads of little wooded hollows and valleys, then sent another hunter or two to the far end of the covers in hopes that their scent, reaching any deer in the hollows, would push the deer to within bow range of the standers. This is all right for those who like to bowhunt that way, I suppose, but most of us would rather stick to the axiom that the lone bowhunter is the most effective hunter, and leave the deer drives to the orange-coated rifle crowd.

In fact, bowhunters take the opposite tack and make every effort to keep their scent away from the game being hunted. Let's say your treestand is on the edge of a soybean field where you've seen deer come to feed in the morning and evening. If you're a smart hunter, you wouldn't walk right across that field enroute to or from your stand, because the soft earth in the field would retain your human scent long enough to spook deer coming out to feed. Much better to take the longer route around the edge of the field, making sure that even this circuitous route doesn't approach the trail that deer use to enter or leave the field.

Rabbit hunters using hounds are certain that some days are better for hound use than other days, and this has to do with the amount of moisture in the soil

surface and on the foliage. Moisture retains scent. Frozen soil is a poor retainer of scent, because the moisture is locked up in ice crystals. The more moisture, the better the scenting conditions—and this is as true for scent-sensitive animals like deer as it is for rabbit hounds. Human tracks left in soft soil hold their scent longer than tracks made in powdery dust or sand, so watch how you move around in the area you plan to hunt, or you'll give yourself away and probably never realize it. Deer don't point out what you're doing wrong. They just leave.

It's entirely possible that deer depend on their olfactory senses far more extensively than we imagine. Perhaps deer locate food sources from half a mile away when the scent of that food is carried on the wind, much as a bird dog homes in on gamebirds whose scent is carried on an incoming breeze. It could be that deer use or avoid certain travel routes through their home woods on the basis of one or more scents they detect along those routes. I've seen small deer herds go hundreds of yards out of their way to use paths leading through hardwoods to avoid more direct routes through evergreens and vice versa. Was there something in the evergreen thickets that spooked the deer, or was it merely the aroma of pine sap? Or perhaps something about the hardwood trees attracted the deer while the evergreens held no interest for them. Until we discover a talking deer, we'll never know all there is to know about how whitetails use scent, or the lack of it, in their daily lives.

If you hunt the rut, you've probably seen a buck as he approaches a doe for the first time. He comes with his head and neck outstretched, perhaps with his head cranked over to one side. His upper lip curls up toward his nostrils, and I've even seen a few buck doing this with their eyes closed. Based on observation, the buck is so close to the doe that he can easily detect the fact that she is in heat and ready to accept him sexually. The buck comes at a steady walk, perhaps aware that a ripe doe isn't going to run off and make him chase her. She is as ready to mate as he is, although it's always the buck that does the pursuing, not the doe. She is quite content to let her ripe estrus scents trail along behind her, attracting any rutting buck who will then drop whatever he's doing and follow that delicious scent wherever it leads. I've seen several bucks jump wire fences, run right in front of cars moving along a highway, even wade streams right under the amazed noses of fall steelhead fishermen.

As mentioned, the doe is the passive one in this little woodland romance. She stands and watches the buck leave the woods and saunter toward her, neck all swollen, lip curled back. The doe usually stops eating when the buck approaches, standing there and just watching him walk toward her. When he arrives he usually sniffs her hindquarters thoroughly, as if to make certain she is actually ready to mate. And still the doe stands there, as if to say, "Well, are you gonna do it, or are you gonna keep fooling around?" The two will remain together for as long as the doe remains in the mood to accept the buck, which may be for as long as several days. When the doe is successfully impregnated with semen from the buck, her estrus cycle enters another phase

and she no longer emits the scent so attractive to bucks. However, if for some reason a mature doe in her estrus cycle fails to be impregnated by a buck, the cycle ends for a time. She will then re-enter the cycle a few days later for another try at reproduction.

It is scent that makes it possible for buck and doe to come together during the fall rutting season, because if the doe didn't emit an involuntary odor announcing her readiness to mate, it's doubtful the buck could find her. Moose and elk use calls to locate one another for mating purposes, but whitetails rely almost entirely on scent detection. No wonder these animals have such keen noses: without them, the species would have a tough time even surviving.

It's been said that deer *always* travel into the wind in order to scent what lies ahead of them. This sounds nice and pat, but I don't think deer *always* do anything, and this includes moving into the wind. I've seen far too many deer, undisturbed and relaxed, moving in the direction they want to go in order to reach a goal. This has often been nearly directly downwind, or in some cases crosswind. I do believe that whitetails will, when conditions permit, move into the wind when something has recently occurred to make them wary and expectant of danger, such as when they detect a nearby hunter, encounter something that's out of place along the edge of a farm (old rusted tractor body, for example) and the like, but these are occasions that come and go quickly in the normal day of a deer and don't describe their overall behavior. Seeing deer only in these circumstances can lead us to make gross inaccuracies in how we think deer live. It also tends to make us over-estimate the degree to which deer rely on their sense of smell. Example: We humans have eyes that can see colors, but we don't usually study colors unless something calls our attention to them, such as the passing of a bright-red convertible or the like. It's the same with a whitetail and its olfactory senses. Deer normally breathe through their noses (unless they've been running hard for some distance and are winded, in which case they open their mouths and breathe through them), so it stands to reason that they would almost immediately detect a notable scent on the wind as soon as it comes within reach of their noses. You've probably seen deer feeding quietly in a harvested cropfield; all of them have their heads down clipping off edible plant tops when suddenly every deer's neck and head snap to attention, and every pair of ears is fanned across the field in the same direction. It's possible that those feeding deer all heard a slight sound at the same moment, but it's more likely that the tiniest breeze brought an alien scent to the nose of each deer, and before all those heads came to attention, every deer in the herd knew from which direction the scent was coming, simply because scent can't move against the wind, but is carried *with* the breeze like the white fuzz from a dandelion.

A friend and I were bowhunting a little wooded valley in Arkansas a few seasons ago, and we split up to still-hunt our way back to the truck. A natural field near the truck contained deer sign and I decided to edge my way along the field's border while my buddy chose to pussyfoot along the spine of an open

ridge. Sure enough, I found several deer in the field. The wind was blowing directly in my face, so I was safe in that department, but before I got within 150 yards of the herd every animal came alert and soon bounced into the woods. Only then did I realize that my companion on the ridge was directly upwind from the herd. Even though he was a good 500 yards from the field, the deer must have detected his scent, and it drove them into the cover of the trees. I once had a bowhunting school instructor tell me to forget seeing deer downwind from my location, whether from a treestand or on the ground, because deer simply will not approach an area where they detect human scent. We smell like trouble to deer, and they've long since learned to give human smell a wide berth—even at 500 yards under ideal scenting conditions.

As in locating the opposite sex for mating, deer of course use scent for reasons other than avoiding hunters. A herd that scatters for some reason often contains one or more half-grown fawns still dependent on their doe for lessons and protection. If doe and fawn become separated, the doe will sometimes bleat to attract the fawn, or the fawn will bleat to call its mother, but I've also seen does track their fawns by scent in much the same manner as rutting bucks follow a ripe doe's scentline through the woods.

This habit of bleating among fawns can be pretty funny sometimes. Some years ago I was bowhunting Kentucky's Blue Grass Army Depot when some hunters well off to my right spooked a pair of mature does, and the deer came thundering past my stand on the edge of a small woods. The does galloped on out of sight and all was quiet for about two minutes until a half-grown fawn showed up, bleating as though the biggest mountain lion in the woods was about to eat him. The fawn turned in my direction and came bleating up to within two feet of my immobile form among the trees, and when it finally spotted me it stopped dead, quieted down and, eyes as wide as they would open, stuck out his neck and sniffed me. He was so close I could see the little wrinkles in his nose as he sniffed. Surely he had a good whiff of my scent at a range of 24 inches, but man-scent wasn't something he'd learned to fear yet and besides, he was in dire need of his mommy along about then and didn't have time to worry about this odd-looking thing with paint on its face hidden in some brush. After 30 seconds or so, the fawn turned back into the little field and started bleating again, and soon here came its doe. She stopped on the edge of some trees and bleated just once; the fawn downshifted and headed for her side at a gallop. I often wish I'd slowly reached out my hand and tried to pat the little fellow between the ears, just where his antler bumps pushed little tufts of hair an inch off his scalp. I had a pair of mule deer twins come within a yard of me in Colorado once, and that time I *did* manage to pat one of them on the head before they bounced off. I don't think deer are born with a natural fear of man-scent. Like so many other lessons they learn at their mother's side, a fear of man has to be taught by example, and that includes a complete revulsion to the way we smell.

In Michigan, where it's legal as I write this to put out a few apples or other deer treats to attract game during bow season, I've seen deer discover a new cache of fruit within two hours. A hunter in my camp took half a peck of apples and dumped them onto the ground within 20 yards of his ground stand. The apples were dumped about noon on the day before opening day, and my companion reasoned that this would give the local bucks plenty of time to discover the apples and start feeding on them by the next morning, when he planned to be secreted in his ground stand, arrow nocked and ready. Well, the deer beat him to it. When he arrived at the stand the next morning, he spent over 45 minutes waiting for shooting light. Then, when the sun came up, all he could find of his apple bait were two lousy and well-chewed cores and a 10-foot-square area of disturbed leaves on the ground. He put out more apples, planning to come back that afternoon, and again the deer got there first. He put out the second load of apples at 1:00 p.m., and by 3:00 p.m., when he arrived to begin hunting, the fruit had been devoured again. He said he'd be damned if he was going to feed a bunch of deer that refused to show up when he did, so he went and sat in a tree over a picked beanfield for the rest of the week, and ended up sticking a nice 8-point buck when it came to scrounge for waste beans.

How did those deer discover the newly-placed apples so quickly? The local deer had already picked several local apple orchards clean of grounded fruit, so when the scent of more apples, a real deer treat, came wafting through the woods, I think every deer within scenting distance headed for the banquet and gobbled them up. Apples are a common tree crop over much of Michigan, and the deer there are used to smelling this delicious scent every fall, and feeding on them when they can, so it's no wonder they cleaned up the bait so quickly. In a case such as this, the archer might have used a few drops of commercial apple scent around his stand, once he'd established the spot as a source of fruit among the local herd. Apple scent is a lot cheaper than half a peck of fresh fruit, and it's also a lot easier to carry into the woods.

Personally, I'd be more confident using some sort of natural animal extract scent to mask my scent than one of the fruit-imitating scents on the market. I leave scent behind me when I still-hunt or move to my stand for the day, and it seems to me that any deer happening across that scentline in the woods has got to wonder how and why an acorn or an apple went on a hike past this spot earlier this morning. Animals move through the woods, plants do not, so I'll stick with fox or skunk scent, or perhaps the smell of a doe in heat, on my boots to mask my scent. Once on stand, I'll use doe scent on a scent pad provided the rut is deep enough for bucks to be actively looking for ripe does.

Safariland Hunting Corp., more commonly known as Tink's, has come up with a scent pad designed for wear on the bottom of your boot sole. The idea is to use the pad's built-in elastic lanyard to hold the pad in place so it contacts the ground every time the boot takes a step. The bottom of the pad, which is leather-bound, has a small portal through which you place a few drops of scent onto the pad's inner absorbable surface.

With such a device, you'll leave scent with every step you take through the woods. This sounds like a handy item, but hunters can accomplish pretty much the same thing by placing that scent directly onto the soles of their boots. I like to freshen the scent on my boots in the afternoon if I plan to use the same scent placed there earlier that morning. It makes it easier for the deer to detect the scent and gives them a clear scentline to follow if they are so inclined.

There are about a zillion gadgets designed for today's bowhunter, and this book contains a full chapter about them. Plentiful among this zillion are commercial scents, urine derivatives, masking and attractor scents, about anything your heart (or nose) desires in the way of so-called shortcuts to get you close to unalerted deer, horny bucks, curious does, pussyfooting forkhorns and so on, if you believe all the advertising claims. If you like to tinker with gadgets, scent-oriented items are a good place to start. Who knows? Like that lady bowhunter mentioned earlier who didn't know how much scent to use so she used a whole bottle, you never know what might work. And while the use of scents, or avoidance of them, is strictly a personal choice for the individual archer, there are some flexible axioms concerning scents and their use. Here is a sort of easygoing checklist. It may not be the alpha and omega of deer hunting, but at least it's easily read.

Common Sense with Scents

• There are three basic types of scents: masking scent, attractor scent and the wrong scent.

• The wrong scent can be defined as any added scent not found naturally in a deer hunting area. The scent is wrong if it's likely to spook more deer than it attracts or puts at ease.

• Human scent is distasteful to deer because we smell like predators.

• A deer's ability to smell is better than its ability to see, although smell and sight are often combined to confirm the presence of food, danger, other deer and so on.

• A doe will sometimes, but not always, cross a scentline left by a human. A buck will *never* cross such a line, and its presence may well spook the buck from his normal haunts for 12 hours or more.

• The right masking scent placed on soles or clothing can effectively mask your human smell enough to allow you to move about a deer woods without spooking game. Scent should be placed on the hunter's boot soles (or on a scent pad on the bottom of the soles), and on cap, elbows and knees, which are areas usually touching trailside foliage.

• It's a good idea to keep your hunting clothing—cap, camo suit, boots and so on—outdoors before and during bow season to minimize the amount of human odor, smoke smell and such that you carry into the woods on your person. Unscented, chlorophyll-treated soaps can help keep the clothing's human smell to a minimum. You can use the same soap on hands, face and hair.

• An attractor scent is usually imitative of the estrus scent naturally emitted by a doe ready to mate. It's usually most effective during the deepest part of the rut, which varies according to the region of the country where you live. In the Midwest the rut normally occurs in late November and early December, while in the South the rut may occur as late as January or February.

• Using a doe scent in and around a fresh buck scrape takes advantage of two facts: The buck will be back to check his scrape, and he may linger longer to check out the doe scent dribbled on his scrape.

• Bucks deposit their own urine and glandular scent on the scrape to identify it for passing does.

• Besides warning other nearby deer, a whitetail's snort serves to clear its nostrils of unwanted smells.

• Days after a rain, or days when high humidity has moved in, are better for scenting than are drier conditions. This is because moist soil holds scent longer than dry soil.

• Testing scent is a normal activity for deer because they breathe through their nostrils, plus use scenting ability to locate other deer, find trails and food, and locate mates in the autumn. Deer do not always travel into the wind, except when spooked.

• Once a ripe doe is impregnated, changes within her body eliminate her "ripe" odor and she is no longer attractive to bucks. A doe not mated during her first estrus of the autumn will go out of heat, then come back in a few days later.

• A doe will often follow the scent trail left by a fawn from which she's become separated. A bleating call is also used by both animals to get back together.

• Do not spray fox urine in your hunting buddy's vehicle cab, or he will stop being your hunting buddy.

15

Tips on Getting Close

It was one of those chilly October mornings in eastern Michigan that make you glad you're wearing plenty of warm clothes. The edges of the little river, where the water was quiet in the little bays, wore thin fringes of ice formed during the cold night just passed. Jeff Redman and I slipped silently downstream in a 15-foot canoe, hoping to ambush a sleep-dulled buck before he could stampede from his riverside bed among the tall grasses bordering a cedar swamp.

Jeff has a way of propelling the canoe without lifting the blade from the water, so we moved at current speed slowly past deadfalls and cedar sweepers, abandoned deer beds from other nights, and the occasional tiny tributary brook that carried heavy doses of cedar acid that gave the river its amber color. The clear morning's sunrise tipped the tree-

tops with orange and yellow, promising a warmer hunt once the sun rose in the sky.

"This is really a good way to get close to deer," Jeff had told me when we eased his canoe into the river below an upstream bridge half an hour earlier. "The deer don't seem to expect trouble to come floating down the river, and they just stare at a canoe instead of running from it. You'll see what I mean before too long."

He was right. We hadn't been on the river 20 minutes when the first two deer appeared. A pair of does, with only their heads and long necks showing above the grasses of their bedding area, looked solemnly at us as the canoe slid by within 15 yards of them. They just cocked their big ears in our direction and remained bedded. I could have taken either with

The use of a small canoe in deer country allows the hunter to silently get very close to bedded and unwary whitetails. *Steve Griffin*

an easy bow shot, but I wanted a buck this morning.

He showed himself not long after the does. We'd just eased the little craft around a sharp bend when a deer stood up in its bed less than 20 yards away, shook itself and walked into the cedars bordering the grassy riverbank. Then two more deer stood up, one of them a handsome 8-pointer, and all that was required of me was to draw the bow, settle the sight pin behind his shoulder, and send the shaft flickering across the river's misty width to bury half its length into the buck's flank. He ran about 55 yards into the cedars before piling up dead; after dragging him to the river, I was more than a little glad we were in a canoe large enough to carry two hunters and a dead whitetail to the pickup point a mile downstream.

How do you get close to deer?

Any way you can, nearly. Deer always seem to suspect that they are being watched, stalked or about to be attacked, and any critter this wary is tough to get close to. Because of this, almost anything that works is fair play.

How close is close? This nice 8-point buck knows you're there (note ear position) but hasn't spooked yet. Better take that shot quickly.

And you do have to get close. Tournament archers may be able to hit what they aim for at 100 meters in a stiff wind, but most of the bowhunters I know would refuse a shot much beyond 40 yards, and they'd like to cut that in half if at all possible. Thus the need for getting close.

A big benefit to getting what an old deer guide called "spittin' close" is making as little noise in the woods as possible. This means paying attention to everything from the type of footwear you choose, to the way you put your feet on the ground, to doing what you can to silence the sound of an arrow shaft sliding across the shelf on the way to full draw. It's paying attention to the entire experience of the bowhunter in the woods: noise, scent and how to minimize the chances of being seen by deer. Everything. It's the careful hunter who gets close enough to put his arrow where he wants it.

Let's take a close look at some of the things you can do to get near deer, and see if there's a thing or two you might adopt.

The Bow

Whether you carry a modern compound, a recurve or even a modern version of the old English longbow, it's likely that the weapon came from the dealer wearing a bright and shiny coat of lamination. You know what I mean: all fancied up with a glossy finish that reflects every bit of light in an otherwise dark woods. More than a few deer have spotted reflections off such glossy bow finish while still well out of range of the

Camouflaged all over, this hunter was able to sneak within range of his deer without being seen. *Ohio DNR-Christman*

hunter's eye. The hunter turns to check behind him on stand and inadvertently moves his bowhand an inch, and the flat surface of the risers catch sunlight.

The best way to avoid this is to cover that lovely bow with camouflage coloration, and there are a number of ways to do this. Some hunters use bow socks, which are really just camo-finish cloth sewn to the rough contours of the bow risers and limbs, complete with elastic sewn in each end of both socks. Bow socks do cover the entire bow (except the handle) with proper camouflage, and keep the sunlight from reflecting, but the socks themselves can alert nearby deer because they have a way of scraping and catching on tree bark, arrow nocks and about anything else that contacts them. I also happen to think that bow socks slow the reflexive action of the bow somewhat, because they bulge out from the bow unevenly and catch the air when the bow is released.

You can also use camouflage tape to cover the bow. This tape is partially elastic and can be installed so that it covers every inch of the bow with camo finish; in this, it's a good answer to avoiding reflections. However, it does add a bit of weight to any bow, and covering all the edges and built-in contours of the bow makes it a bit less usable, especially when that big deer saunters down the trail and you have to draw, anchor and release the bow while keeping your eyes glued to your target.

In my opinion, camouflaging your bow with spray paint made especially for this purpose is the best way to avoid reflection. The paint comes in brown, black and dull green and can be patterned by the user to approximate a camo finish that no deer alive could see under normal circumstances. And besides being an effective camo finish, bow paint doesn't snag on anything, and contours itself to the bow which in turn allows for maximum limb speed when the arrow is released. I realize that you may hate to cover all that pretty shine with paint, but it's the best way I know of to help you get close to white-tailed deer.

The draw and release of a compound bow includes some interaction on the part of the bowstring and the cables, and the best way I know to silence this is to serve, or cover, the cable with felt-backed elastic tape made just for this purpose. I use Browning cable tape, and there are other brands on the market as well. The tape I use is green, adheres very well to the stiff surface of my bow's cables, and stays in place regardless of the weather.

Arrow rests are another way to tailor your bow for silent running. There are dozens of shelf/rest types on the market, some of them with clamps, some of them with push buttons, others offering nothing fancier than a flat platform of turkey fletching on which the arrow shaft is rested before drawing. Without playing favorites with those rests available, I'd suggest two things: Select a rest that keeps the arrow in place regardless of the tilt of the bow when you shoot, and make sure it includes an inch or so of fur backing that adheres to the side of the shooting window of your bow. This cushion keeps the arrow from making that ever-so-slight (but important) scrape while being drawn.

There is only so much you can do to alter the noise your bow makes when the arrow is released, and this is especially true if you shoot a compound. But regardless of the bow type you carry, you can help silence the *twang* of the release by adding string silencers to the string a few inches below the end of each bowlimb. These silencers act as shock absorbers, deadening the natural reaction of the string as the released limbs yank the string taut again following the release. Some archers use little bits of buckskin fringe tied in a two-inch bundle halfway between limb and nocking point. I like the ball of fluff type that uses a brightly-colored ball of yarn. The fluff does a good job of silencing the release noise, and I think the ball of yarn on each end of the string adds to the bow's appearance. Suit yourself on this one, but do use some type of silencers.

Of course, some bows just refuse to be silenced. As this is written, there's one on the market that is said to be about the fastest around. It is also one of the loudest. The string strikes the rubber bumpers so hard that the bow makes a loud *whack* every time it's shot. I spoke with one of the bow's designers and he admitted that the bow is loud, but countered by saying that the terrific arrow speed produced by this powerful weapon made bow noise considerations obsolete. I'm not so sure about that. A friend of mine said this bow was both loud and heavy, adding that it reminded him of his first wife, and anything that threatens to involve me in family squabbling is best avoided. Don't buy a bow that defeats the purpose of bowhunting: silent hunting with a light weapon.

Most compound bowstrings are guaranteed for several hundred releases; the stronger the bow, the fewer releases you can expect to obtain from its bowstring.

This archer's partial beard does a pretty good job of darkening his features for a successful ground stalk.

Check your string frequently, especially if you shoot a lot. Breaking a string in practice or, far worse, when you finally get a shot at that big buck, is enough to ruin the entire afternoon. String wax, available at all good tackleshops, keeps the string free from ravelings and can prolong the life of the string. If you don't know how or aren't equipped to change bowstrings yourself, your tackle dealer can do it for you quickly, safely and inexpensively. The manufacturer of the bow you carry will be able to sell you a replacement string if the tackleshop owner can't.

Camouflage Clothing

There is camo clothing and there is camo clothing. Some of the stuff does a nice job of letting you blend into your surroundings, and some of it isn't worth the wooden match needed to burn it.

Camo outer gear must be matched to the type and color hues of the place you'll be hunting. Using green-brown camo in

Today's hunters even have their own deodorant to keep the human odor masked or reduced for deer hunting.

late fall after all the leaves have changed will make you stick out like a pair of overalls in church. Conversely, using brown-tinged camo while the foliage is still green won't do the job, either.

The tree-bark type of camo finish is a nice compromise for those who'd rather invest in just one set of camo for the entire bow season. The tree-bark finish uses both green and gray colorations that do a nice job of blending into the woods regardless of the season (except when there is snow). Users of this camo report that it also blends well into most western color patterns, should you be bow-hunting deer, elk or pronghorn in that part of the country.

The older your camo outerwear gets, the greater the chance that it will give you away to wary deer. This is because oft-repeated machine laundering of camo slowly washes away the color intensity of the cloth, and you end up with a washed-out pattern and hue that is many shades lighter than the average deer woods—which in some cases is worse than no camo at all.

A friend of mine used to think that he could wear a loose-fitting outer camo shirt and a pair of jeans, insisting that if he stood still no deer would notice his legs anyway. Well, he wore jeans all right, jeans that had been through the washing cycle so many times that the blue had turned into a sort of bluish-silver color that showed up like a light-house at all times of day. The darker the woods, the more those no-longer-blue jeans were apparent. I finally proved to this chap that his pants needed replacement by wearing a faded pair of jeans and letting him see me along about dusk. Now he wears camo pants that match

his overshirt and he can fade into the deer woods with the best of 'em.

I like to tuck the cuffs of my camo pants into the toops of my boots. This helps avoid rustling when I pussyfoot through dense, low cover, and it keeps my pant legs from snagging on thorns, twigs and the like during stalks and while I move to and from my stand. Cotton fabric will wash quite soft, which is very important because stiff-finished fabrics have a way of scraping against both themselves and the stuff in the woods. Cotton is also fairly warm, although I may switch to something heavier, such as wool, for late-season hunting when the weather is downright cold. A coverall type of camo gear is good because it covers you from neck to ankles, and because it doesn't part at the belt line as a shirt-pants combination always does at the wrong time. Coveralls are a bit bulkier than other camo clothing types, but I think they more than make up for it with coverage and warmth.

Nearly every bowhunter I know wears a camouflage hat or cap of some kind in which to hunt. It goes with the rest of the clothing and helps the hunter to blend into his environment. But there is no rule that I know of denying us a warm hunting hat, and for cold weather this means earflaps and enough of a bill forward and rear to keep rain or snow off us. They can impair your ability to hear those soft sounds of a deer's steps, and the bill shouldn't extend so far from your head that it bumps into your bowstring or anything else around your stand. Lined caps and hats keep you warmer than thin cloth, although you may want to have one cap for warm weather and another for cold. Stocking-

This hunter's hard-finish shell jacket is bound to scrape against limbs, giving the hunter's presence away. Much better to wear soft fabrics while bowhunting.

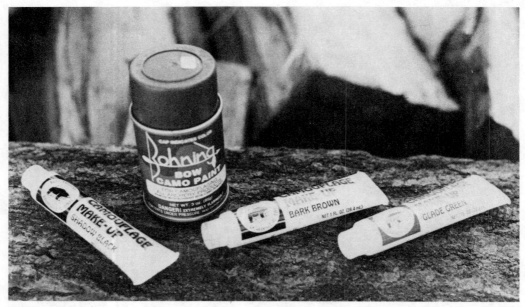

Camo bow spray paint (second from left) and tubes of face cream help the hunter blend into his surroundings.

type camo hats are nice, can be pulled down over your ears to keep them warm, and make no noise. They can also be wadded up into a jacket pocket when not needed.

Camo-finish hunting gloves are available on today's market, but I don't think you need go that far in camouflaging yourself when a simple pair of leather-palm knit gloves works just as well. The important thing for gloves is that they be supple enough to allow you to draw your bow silently and without straining to hold the string steady. Color isn't really important; any dark shade of green, blue or brown will do fine. Gloves for bow-hunting should be fairly tight fitting so you don't lose your dexterity at exactly the wrong moment.

A friend of mine, and a very successful bowhunter, doesn't wear camo on the top part of his body. He prefers to wear a soft cotton shirt that's several sizes larger than his normal shirt size. The extra roominess allows him to wear the shirt over whatever inner clothing is required by the weather, while the outer shirt's soft fabric lets him remain quiet in the woods. The shirt itself is colored a dull green-olive color with a small print pattern that helps my friend fade into the undergrowth much like a regular camo shirt might do. The shirt has been through so many wearings and washings that it has long since become faded and as soft as doeskin. The wearer believes it to be the ultimate outer wear for him, and he's killed enough white-tails at close range so that I believe him. The important factor about any garment used to camouflage the hunter is that it allows the hunter to blend into his surroundings quietly. Anything that accomplishes this will do just fine.

Footgear

If scent weren't a factor, you'd wear anything that kept your feet warm and dry and was capable of quiet foot travel in the woods. But most materials used in shoes and boots carry human scent; in fact, they become permeated with our scent after a while and all the added commercial scents in the world won't completely eliminate that smell.

Rubber-soled boots don't become permanently scented with human smell, so any boots you use for bowhunting should have rubber soles. That's simple enough. But warmth and comfort also are important, whether you still-hunt or remain on stand all day.

One good way to meet all of these requirements is to use what are known as waterman boots, all-rubber, soft boots that reach up just below the knee and that include shoe-type bottoms. These can be worn over several pairs of socks, depending upon air temperature, or with one pair of socks and felt inserts that serve to keep the foot warm while cushioning it. Rubber waterman's boots don't become scented with human smell, and they remain soft to the touch—and are therefore quiet in the woods. The relatively soft soles of these boots let you detect sharp stones and twigs underfoot, allowing for quieter movement as well.

L.L. Bean sells a boot model, in both high and low styles, featuring an all-rubber foot and leather top. These also work well, and provide additional support for the instep and ankles because of the way they lace up—important if you walk a lot or remain standing in a tree platform all morning and evening. You can find similar boots, with rubber soles, at discount stores and other sources. The important thing to remember in selecting boots is suitability to your needs, overall quality and lasting life, and price.

No matter how much or little you spend on boots, remember that your comfort, or lack of it, will directly affect your ability to remain in the woods, and to hunt longer and more effectively, than the hunter who isn't as well equipped. This isn't necessarily a pitch for the most expensive boots available, but don't cut your equipment budget in the shoe department. You and I and everybody else hunts to enjoy, and if your footgear isn't up to the job, it becomes, with apologies to ABC Sports, an agony of de feet.

Watch the Wind

It sounds elementary to say that you should keep your eye on wind direction while hunting, but you'd be surprised how many bowhunters are surprised when a cool autumn breeze tickles the back of their neck.

The autumn before last I was still-hunting along an old and brushy fencerow when I spotted a small but decently antlered forkhorn walking toward me, coming down the fencerow from the opposite direction I'd been walking. I checked my arrow nocking, test-drew the bow once, and waited for him to cross a small creekbed and come within range. I was so sure of success that I had my "you're-mine-you-big-dummy" look on my face.

Well, that deer kept walking until it was about to cross the creek. Then, all of a sudden, I felt the cool fingers of a little breeze on the back of my neck. The wind, once almost directly in my face, had done a 180-degree turnaround and was now blowing my scent ahead of me, along my path of travel. The buck stopped in his tracks as if he'd hit a glass wall, his tail came up and so did the hairs on his neck, and did as fast a swap-and-go as I've ever seen, all without me so much as drawing my bow or even moving where he could have seen me. That buck got a whiff of my scent on that #!¢(**!#!! turnaround breeze, the

One of the most useful accessories is a simple wooden match to tell you which way the breeze is blowing in the woods. Don't drop it until it's dead out, however.

same once-friendly breeze that had been keeping my scent a secret when I'd started still-hunting earlier that morning. The day didn't turn out all that bad, however, because an amazingly unwary 8-pointer came wandering by my ground stand late that afternoon and I nailed him through the spine at a paced 55 yards.

But the fact remains, had I been more alert to what the wind was doing, I'd perhaps have had a shot at that 4-pointer. At the very least I could have made a 90-degree change in the direction of my still-hunting, relying on the crosswind to keep my scent from deer up ahead. As it was, I didn't think about it until it was too late. Funny how we never have time to do it right, but we always have time to do it again . . .

Watching the wind can mean never putting your man-scented feet where a deer can detect the scent, and this goes triple when approaching or leaving your permanent stand. If your stand is located along the edge of a cropfield or food plot, for example, you wouldn't be smart to just walk diagonally across the field to your stand. Human scent can and will remain on soft, tilled soil far longer than on dry, sandy soil, and you'd chance Mr. Big feeding to a point just outside bow range, sniffing one of your smelly footprints, and leaving somewhat faster than he arrived. Much better to skirt all possible (or at least anticipated) approach routes you expect the deer to use, perhaps making a wide circle to come in downwind through heavy, leg-grabbing thickets in order to reach the stand. And keep it up. Once you've worked out a route to and from your stand that doesn't spook deer in the area, stick to it. Deer by and large are creatures of habit, and they aren't likely to run across your approach route if it's through heavy cover and doesn't intersect any active deer trails.

Regardless of how I'm hunting, I like to keep a six-inch length of white sewing thread tied to the tip of the upper limb of my bow. This little tag of lightweight thread acts as a constant wind vane, telling me not only wind direction, but its approximate strength as well. It's quick and easy to check the thread's direction and position every minute or so while hunting; and had I done this two seasons back, I wouldn't have spooked that forkhorn with my scent. If you're on stand, try tying a short length of thread to a nearby twig. This serves the same purposes as thread tied to your bow, but keeps your eyes at ground level, where they should be, instead of checking your bowlimb and perhaps missing the silent, stealthy approach of a buck.

And while we're still on the subject of wind-carried scent, it might not be a bad idea to postpone donning your hunting outerwear until you actually get into the woods, or perhaps even arrive at your stand. Casual outerwear can be stowed in a plastic sack carried for the purpose, while your hunting clothing, hung outdoors between hunts to keep human scent at a minimum, is put on when the actual hunting begins. It may be a bit foolish to step out of a pair of pants come late October, but if it can make the difference between seeing and not seeing deer, isn't it worth the momentary discomfort?

Floating for Deer

At the beginning of this chapter I mentioned the use of a small, light canoe for silent approaches on watercourses in deer country. This is a very pleasant and easy way to hunt, see lots of country, and most important, get right on top of the game without alerting them.

There are several things you can do to enhance a canoe's usefulness for this sort of stalk. One is to avoid the use of aluminum canoes if possible. Aluminum can be extremely loud, giving off audible clanks, scrapes and bangs whenever it touches your bow, a boot sole, snags in the river, gravel bars, and so on. Much better to go with fiberglass or with canvas over wood, both of which are much quieter than aluminum. Fiberglass is also much easier to repair should the canoe become punctured.

I like a 15-foot canoe for this type of hunting. This length is short enough so that you can maneuver on even the smallest streams and rivers, yet large enough to float out your deer, your hunting buddy and yourself. And believe me, being able to paddle your deer out to the car is a lot easier than carrying or dragging it out. You can often park your vehicle at a bridge and float your deer practically into the car trunk.

A dark, dull finish on the canoe will also help. I use a 15-footer finished in a dull green. To a deer still half-asleep in its bed along the river, I suspect it looks no more threatening than just another log drifting down with the current. My canoe is a fiberglass model with hickory gunwales that I've customized somewhat. The wood itself is pretty quiet compared to aluminum, of course, but I've added some pieces of plastic foam glued to the gunwales for extra padding. Now I can rest my bow against the foam, or maybe bump my bow against the foam by accident, without alerting every deer within half a mile. I've also added a piece of indoor-outdoor carpeting the length of the canoe. The carpeting isn't fastened down because a freshly-dressed deer carcass has a way of messing up the bottom of my canoe, but the carpeted floor does keep boot scuffs and equipment quiet.

A canoe used for bowhunting also has to include a pretty decent keel in order to keep the canoe from wiggling side to side at just the wrong moment. My canoe has a three-inch keel along its bottom,

and the steadiness it provides more than makes up for the little extra effort it takes me to make sharp turns or to drag the craft over the shallows now and then.

It's possible, of course, for a single archer to take his canoe downstream, spot a deer, ease into position and arrow his game, but it's much easier—and more fun, too—if you share the day with a buddy. Only the hunter in the front is actually prepared to shoot, but both hunters hone eyes and ears in search of game and the rear hunter handles the

Nothing succeeds like success. This heavy-beamed buck came from the Lexington-Bluegrass Army Depot in Kentucky.

paddling and maneuvering for the guy up front. Trade off every hour or so, so each hunter gets an equal chance to score.

I can't overemphasize how unwary deer can be when they're bedded along a river. They usually choose the river-bottom for bedding because the air next to the water is slightly warmer than elsewhere, and will often lie down within three feet of the water, especially if the riverbank includes some tall grasses or weeds for padding and cover. Deer just don't seem to recognize the canoe and its contents as a threat. In fact, they usually just lie there and stare at you without even getting to their feet. You'll have to snake that arrow between the grass stems to put it into the vitals, but at a range of 15 feet, most of us can handle that.

There is no such thing as getting *too close.*

16

Doing It Right, Every Time

The secret of hitting with the bow and arrow is to do everything right, and then to do it that way every time.

That's simple enough. It's also difficult if you don't know enough about yourself and your tackle to let the two blend into a one-piece machine.

Last fall I'd just had my buck checked in at a state deer check station, set up in an indoor archery range, when I took a few minutes to watch a local bowhunter shoot a few dozen shafts at a six-inch target 20 yards away. Time after time and arrow after arrow, the shooter drew his bow, came to full draw and paused, released the shaft and watched it thud into the black circle at the far end of the room. He did everything exactly the same way every time; so much so, in fact, that I could have photographed him at any point in his regi-

men, and all of my photos would have been identical. That's precision. That's what you have to do to be accurate when it counts.

I asked that shooter about his accuracy and he smiled a little and replied, "Oh, I'm shooting fairly well, I guess. But I gotta stay on top of it or the edge just slips away on me."

Just like that shooter punching hole after hole in the 20-yard ring, you have to stay on top of it or it'll slip away on you, sure as white spots on a fawn. And the only way to do that is to practice and get a professional archery instructor to help correct any bad habits you may have developed.

Larrel Dick, owner of the Primitive Weapons Arena near Cincinnati, Ohio, helped me iron out a flinching problem I had, but only after I'd unsuccessfully tried for weeks to develop a smooth release while keeping both eyes on my target. We went over to Larrel's indoor range and he had me shoot a dozen arrows at the 20-yard ring before saying anything. But when he did speak, it was like snapping on a light in a dark room: "You're not anchoring where you should," he said. "You're bringing your draw fingers low on your cheekbone when you should be anchoring at the left corner of your mouth. Here," he said, "try this." He had me assume a full-draw position without the bow and, taking my draw hand in his while standing behind me, placed it so that the top of my left thumb (I'm a leftie) rested snugly under and against my jawbone. With this position, my three draw fingers naturally stopped just at the left corner of my mouth, and, wonder of wonders, I found my eyes properly positioned to look *past* the bowstring so that the sight pin on my bowsight rested smack in the middle of my target.

After I'd practiced coming to this position without the bow a few times, Larrel had me take bow in hand and draw to the corner of my mouth without releasing an arrow. Then came actual shooting, and I was pleased at how easily I was able to do it all together, once I had the mechanics down. The pin found the center of the target, and when I released I was able to keep both eyes open and watch the arrow in flight. More often than not, the shaft went exactly where I aimed it. Since then, I've had no problem with flinches or anchoring.

But, just like that shooter I observed last fall, I have to stay on top of it in order to shoot well all the time. I've heard tennis players, pros who make their living at the game, say the same thing: Practice a lot, and often, or lose the edge, the perfected mechanics.

Once overall form is correct, you can add this and that to make yourself comfortable. Extending the forefinger is one way to gain balance.

Drawing a bow and making an unhurried, smooth release involves rather unnatural mechanics, I think, so it's no wonder you and I and every other bowhunter has to learn it and then fight to keep it. First comes intellectual understanding of what needs to be accomplished, and then you have to teach your muscles to put the mechanics into reality. It's similar to driving a rental truck when all you're used to driving is the family car. Driving that truck involves a whole new set of skills, and until you've

Practice doesn't have to be a pain. Using the right equipment and making accuracy a challenge help make it fun.

driven the truck enough to become familiar with it, the new skills are going to make you a tentative trucker at best. But get behind the truck's steering wheel day after day, and the skills soon become second nature. You eventually become as good with a truck as you are with the Chevy four-door.

I saw a lot of white in my neighbors' eyes last summer when my wife, Arlene, and I set up a backyard target range for bow practice. They wondered what the bales of hay were doing stacked up against the side of my wooden shed, and they *really* got apprehensive when I tacked a colorful bull's-eye target to the bales. They envisioned stray arrows zinging all over the neighborhood, impaling house pets and small children, but after a couple of shooting sessions they decided we could at least hit the bales, and they relaxed a little.

You'd be surprised how shooting a few arrows into a side yard target will draw curious neighbors. The first to show up, predictably, were the kids. They stood around and watched, talking among themselves, and then they began to ask questions. Pretty soon the adults began coming over to look, and soon we had half the neighborhood out back. From the adults' point of view, kids play with bows and arrows, and it was satisfying to see real interest spark the adults into asking questions, test-drawing one of our bows, and a few even asked to take a shot or two. Two of my neighbors have taken up bowhunting since our practice target first went up.

Not every community allows archery practice within city limits. Dayton, Ohio, for example, recently banned the shooting of bows and arrows within city limits, so a good friend of mine, ironically enough Dayton's former city manager, had to dismantle his backyard practice range and move it outside the city. He managed to duplicate it in a nearby woodlot, which was fortunate because the range included both ground-level and treestand-level practice positions. He used half a dozen hay bales stacked atop each other, and pinned a deer silhouette to the front as a target. A large old tree 25 yards from the target had a crotch where he was able to build a plywood platform, which allowed him to practice shooting at a downward angle from up in the tree, or from ground level from several points and distances near the base of the tree. Like me, he found himself getting strange looks from his neighbors, but the wild looks changed to interest quickly.

I once asked a tournament archer with Olympic experience how good he felt he had to be to be competitive, and he replied simply, "As good as I can be." I took it to mean that the archer honed and re-honed his shooting mechanics over and over and over until the edge was as sharp as his abilities could make it. "I never really know how good I can be, so I stay on the practice field four hours a day," he said.

How good can *you* be with your bow? Unless you're a pretty experienced archer, you probably can't answer that question with assurance. Most of us put the tackle aside during the offseason, picking it up again a few weeks before the season starts, and as a result we never really know if we've practiced enough to bring our ability to its maximum potential. There is only one way to reach the peak of performance, too, and that is to shoot the bow enough so that your shooting reaches a plateau and stays there.

Consistency is everything, in my opinion. Let's say you practice all summer and by late August you're able to put half a dozen arrows into a pie-plate-sized bull's-eye at 10 yards, 15 yards, 25 yards and 35 yards—every time. You're shooting a nice, tight group at all those ranges, and maybe you can call your shots, such as "This one's going into the upper right corner of the bull." You draw, aim and release, and the arrow goes into the upper right corner every time you call it. This kind of consistency comes only with practice, becoming entirely familiar with the peculiarities of your tackle, how smooth or hesitant your release is and so on. Allow, of course, for temporary conditions that might alter your strength, such as a head cold, sore muscles and the like. But aim for total consistency, and settle for nothing less.

All this may sound like work, I know, and unless you truly enjoy bow*shooting*, and not just bowhunting, it can seem like work. But for any bowhunter to settle for going afield underequipped with too little practice time, is akin to going without your arrows or your camo shirt. You wouldn't leave essential equipment at home, so why do without the

One way to make practice fun is to expand your archery horizons. Here a couple of hunters use the summer warmth to bowfish for carp.

dependable accuracy needed to arrow your buck under any condition you're likely to meet?

All this doesn't mean that practice time can't be made into fun, of course. You might, for example, consider visiting the local archery shop and inquiring about competitive shoots scheduled for the offseason months.

A local shop near my home holds indoor and outdoor matches all summer and early autumn. Shooting distances vary from 15 to 40 yards, with the longer ranges located in safe locations outdoors. The outdoor range, in particular, offers challenges approaching those encountered under normal hunting conditions. Shots vary greatly in distance, and shooters must shoot from actual treestands of various heights, uphill and downhill from ground stands, and at game-shaped targets over broken terrain that trains the eye to accurately judge distance from bow to target. Each archer shoots an entire round, with points added or subtracted depending on how each shoots at bull's-eyes appearing on each game-shaped target butt. Target shapes vary from full-sized deer to fox, bobcats, wild turkeys and even groundhogs, all normal targets for bowhunters.

Some of the targets require that you shoot from seated or bent positions, others require that you snake a shaft between tree trunks to reach the bull. This sort of shooting can be just plain fun, with a bit of competition thrown in for spice. The companionship you gain in competitive shooting goes a long way to making new friends with similar interests, and it's also a great way to learn more about your sport and your personal shooting form.

Archery clubs are also good outlets for offseason shooting on a regular basis. Members set up their own ranges, both straight targeting and woodland hunt-simulation routes, and many such clubs hold competitions every weekend, with the public invited to come along and observe.

Clubs and archery shops will often offer the services of a pro or semi-pro archer, someone who, upon request, can take a close look at your tackle and your form, and suggest improvements in release techniques, foot position, tackle tuning and so on. This is a real shortcut to reaching the fuzzy goal of your *best* shooting peak, too. Just as shop owner Larrel Dick helped me with a release problem, so can your local pro do the same for you. All you have to do is ask. It won't cost you an arm and a leg, either. I paid exactly $2 per hour for shooting instructions, inexpensive enough so I can go back for a refresher lesson when I feel the need.

Make use of those few free hours on weekends and evenings by taking a leisurely hike through nearby fields and woods, plinking away with field tips at so-called targets of opportunity. These might be rotten tree stumps, fallen pine cones, maybe bits of disturbed soil on a sod hillside. Use the same tackle you'll carry when deer season opens, cranking the compound bow's draw weight down a bit if you haven't shot in a while and your arm and back muscles need some toning. The important thing is to use your normal hunting materials, and shoot *regularly*. Shoot consistently, and your shooting will be consistent.

A hunting buddy of mine and I used the pheasant hunting season to get in some extra bowshooting. We carried our normal deer tackle and added the ser-

Outfitting a few of your arrows with flu-flu fletching will allow you to do some wingshooting. This hunter collected a rooster pheasant on the wing with his bow.

vices of a dandy little Brittany spaniel pointing dog to wind and point the roosters for us. When the little Britt went down on point, we walked up on the scene, bows up and arrows nocked, and when the big ringneck flushed, whichever of us had the best angle drew quickly, took a fast aim and released the special flu-flu arrows used for bird hunting. Truth to tell, we didn't hit every pheasant we flushed, nor even most of them. But we got in lots of shooting time, and did manage to connect with enough roosters to put some weight in the game-bag by afternoon.

I wish you better luck than my buddy had on our last hunt, however. He was using shafts tipped with .32 caliber pistol hulls, figuring the blunt surface of the hull would stun the birds so much that they'd roll over and fall immediately. Well, he didn't figure on the power of this compound impaling, instead of stunning, the pheasant, and one fat rooster took a shaft in the body and kept right on flying away, disappearing into some distant trees with the shaft in tow. The Britt found the bird later, of course, but I can't describe the utterly helpless look on the hunter's face as the bird flew away with his surefire quick-kill contraption.

Most backyard shooting ranges, and ranges provided by tackleshops, are located on smooth terrain with nothing between the archer and his target except flat ground and open air. Such a setup is fine for tuning your initial shooting form and accuracy, but I think you'll agree that this hardly imitates the conditions you're likely to encounter while afield.

All too often that buck shows up along the spine of a low ridge while you're stalking along its base, and you must shoot upwards to get a shot at all. The same type of situation occurs if the deer appears downhill from you. And while deer may certainly appear across level ground from you, there are usually little hummocks, brush, trees and other objects between you and deer—not enough to prevent a shot, but more than enough to make your distance estimation a problem.

For all of these reasons, I strongly suggest tailoring your practice to match actual hunting conditions, as much as possible. Try taking some shots from the other side of a backyard evergreen tree, or from the far corner of a paling fence, or maybe while kneeling to see under the low branches of a tree. The trick here is to tune your shooting eye so that you can immediately lock onto the target regardless of where it's liable to appear.

I was bowhunting in New England some seasons back and had positioned myself in a makeshift treestand about 18 feet off the ground. I heard or saw nothing for more than an hour, and then a tiny sound behind and below me made a sneak glance worthwhile. Somehow, a 7-point buck had pussyfooted directly *under* my platform and was even then nosing around for acorns. I could have killed him by dropping a bowling ball on him, if I'd had one along. I had to turn around, lean far out over the edge of the platform, draw my bow and try to put my arrow between his shoulder blades. That's what I *tried* to do, anyway. What actually happened was that I leaned out too far while aiming, lost my balance and almost landed on the back of one very startled whitetail. Fortunately, I was able to pitch my bow and

If you normally hunt from a raised platform, your practice should use the same angle to be effective. Here, Jim Kunde practices hitting from above.

nocked arrow to one side as I fell, or I might have gotten a broadhead in me instead of the deer.

Sure, I agree this was a most unusual predicament, one you're not likely to encounter very often. But if I'd practiced shooting straight down out of a tree I might have had the skill to arrow that buck without alerting him. Maybe not. But I'd certainly have made a better show of it than I did.

The point is, you just cannot *know* ahead of time where the buck is going to show up. You might be still-hunting when a deer suddenly rises from its bed 10 feet away and you have to take what the situation gives you. This happened to me on a Kentucky hunt some time ago. A fellow hunter had just mentioned that a nearby honeysuckle patch often contained bedded deer when a big doe stood up and stared at me; we were both belly-deep in honeysuckle at the moment, and it wasn't until the doe turned to leave that I woke up, drew and fired. The arrow went a little high because the thick cover made me overestimate the distance from me to the deer, but the arrow hit the spine and put the doe down where she stood.

Quick shots are common if you hunt white-tailed deer. This is no news to you. But it stands to reason that practicing those quick shots puts you where you want to be when the big moment comes around this fall. Even if you use a compound bow with a considerable let-off on the bow's weight at full draw, holding for long periods makes any of us begin to wiggle and perhaps ruin a firm aim, so shooting quickly in practice can really pay off.

I do this by sort of stalking around my backyard. This gets odd, I-told-you-so looks from my neighbors, but suddenly having a clear shot at that target butt leaning against the shed, and taking that shot the moment it's presented, helps me develop a quick shooting eye. If you are a trophy-only hunter, you may want a few more seconds to judge the deer's rack, but even in this case a quick draw, aim and release regimen can help.

An old hunting chum of mine has shot a recurve bow all of his adult life. The bow is clean (without sights), and he is one of the fastest and most accurate hunting archers I've ever seen. His shaft is released the moment it reaches full draw, and he hits far more often than he misses. I once asked him about his method and this is how he explained it.

"I'm taking aim while I'm drawing the bow, so when I get to full draw I'm ready to shoot," he said. "I think this really helps my hunting because so often I've had to shoot right now, or miss it altogether."

This chap is an instinctive shooter who's used the same equipment for so long that it's become an extension of his body. And since his bow is a rather heavy one—it pulls 68 pounds at full draw—the ability to release quickly helps him avoid the muscle twitch and arrow creep suffered by hunters who must hold at full draw for several seconds while a tight aim is achieved.

Practice time is also when you should be tuning your bow and other tackle, making sure it's in the best possible condition. If your arrows go pretty consistently to the right and you're a right-handed shooter, you might want to look closely at your arrow rest, especially if it's a model that has the little spring-

This target is designed to accommodate broadheads and should be your final stop enroute to complete accuracy. You must know how your broadheads fly on the practice range.

loaded button used for horizontal shooting adjustments. If the problem is vertical, then check the nocking point on your bowstring. If the bow seems loud when you release, see if you can quiet it with the addition of cable servings, extra padding on the bumper stops, thicker padding on the arrow rest assembly, or a changeover to more efficient sound absorbers on the bowstring. Take a look at the bowstring and see if it's showing wear; simply going over it with a stick of string wax might put it in new condition, or maybe the end servings where strings on recurves and longbows meet the limb tips are so worn

and frazzled that it's time to change to a new string.

And what about that bow camouflage? Does it still seem to absorb light instead of reflecting it, or is it time to put a new coat of camo spray paint on the limbs and riser? Practice time is the time to carefully inspect all of your gear and repair anything that isn't right. It's too late if you're in a treestand and the first light of dawn reveals a worn string or a noisy bumper.

Persistent practice can sometimes do truly amazing things. A woman I once knew shot right-handed and became so good with the bow and arrow that she was named international women's target champion. Then something happened to her health and she found she could no longer shoot right-handed; it just wouldn't work for her on that side anymore. So she began to practice using all left-handed equipment. She practiced for months, at a variety of short- and long-range distances. And that woman became international women's champion archer again, shooting from the port side. When mixed with a liberal amount of determination, practice can do amazing things.

Imagine what it would take for you to switch from right to left, or vice versa. It would be nearly impossible for me,

considering that the left eye is my master eye, and that all of my shooting muscles, everything, is on the left side. Yet I'll bet it can be done, even for the likes of you and me, casual bowhunters and not honed-to-the-fletching field archers, and practice makes it happen.

And if practice can accomplish championship form after switching sides, just think what it can accomplish when all you're doing is trying to put that arrow into a small group *from the shooting side you're used to?* Comparatively speaking, it's a snap.

Everyone in my family shoots, all five of us. Only my wife and I are serious bowhunters, mind you, but we all just

There's nothing like firsthand instruction from the master. Here Fred Bear goes over the elements of a smooth hold and release with students at Alabama's Westervelt Lodge.

plain enjoy punching target points into bales of hay covered with a three-ringed bull's-eye. We have a side yard that's long and wide enough to safely accommodate an archery range of up to about 25 yards, plenty long enough to practice within the distances most bowhunters encounter. So practice for us isn't really practice, not in the usual pain-in-the-neck way that practicing anything is usually thought of. As this is written, my 15-year-old daughter Kelly's interest in every-evening target shooting has just recently caught fire, and she totes her tackle out to our little range every day it doesn't rain. She may only shoot a total of perhaps 40 arrows or so per day, but in doing so she is developing a shooting eye, the muscles needed to pull and hold the bow, and a good deal of pride in being able to put a five-arrow group into the red or yellow inner bull almost every time.

I've also made sure that every member of my family with even minimal interest in shooting has his or her own tackle. I believe owning your own stuff encourages pride and therefore use of the tackle. Target shooting is something that encourages family participation, and like most anything else, getting friends and family interested encourages you, too, to pull your bow all year long and not just during deer season.

It must be said that I tried to get all my family members interested and equipped, not for practice alone, but as a way to get us all involved in a family activity. With three teenagers in the family, finding something that we all like to do at the same time isn't easy, but a backyard archery range and tackle all around have proved their worth.

For me, someone with the usual array of responsibilities, plus the usual range of interests such as brown trout, black bass and cottontails, the range offers the chance to practice a lot without thinking of it as practice. Sure, I'm out there putting perhaps 75 arrows through my bow on an average shoot, but somehow it doesn't seem like practice (read *work*) when there are other interested people around. I think you can do the same thing, either with your own backyard range, club membership or maybe just a casual day of plinking in the woods once or twice a week. With extended daylight hours in the evening, thanks to Daylight Savings Time, it's gotten easier to find the time once you've discovered the inclination.

One offseason element of conditioning I've found helpful is the use of a soft rubber ball about three inches in diameter. I squeeze the ball with my bow hand so much that my son asked if I was taking up pitching a baseball. The squeezing strengthens my fingers, hand and forearm, giving me greater ability to properly and steadily anchor a nocked arrow without the arrow creep I used to suffer. Arrow creep, by the way, is the slow slackening of the anchoring hold on the string at full draw, causing the arrow to inch forward along the arrow rest. Part of this is caused by insufficient upper arm and back muscle development, of course, but you can prevent a lot of it by strengthening your hand and lower arm muscles. This is why I squeeze the rubber ball while I'm watching football or baseball on television. It simply keeps the important parts of your anatomy in tune, and this can only help your shooting.

If you're a relative newcomer to bow-hunting, by all means don't overbow yourself by starting out with a bow that's too powerful to be comfortably pulled by muscles not used to the task. If you shoot a compound, make sure it's capable of being cranked down to a minimal pull that you can handle. In this way you can slowly increase the draw weight of your bow as your muscles permit, sort of like the farm lad who lifted his prize newborn calf off the barn floor every afternoon and was therefore able to tote the full-grown animal 18 months later. Your task increases as your abilities improve; this is the beauty of the compound bow, assuming its minimal weight isn't beyond your abilities in the first place. Nothing is worse or less fun than trying a too-powerful bow for the first time. If you watch someone in this type of situation, you'll first see the poor chap test the string with one limp finger and try to hide a grimace. Then he'll pull the string back, get halfway and stop, strain and still fail to reach the proper anchor point. He'll give his companion a weak smile, look over the bow once more as a courtesy, and announce that he'll find another pastime, thank you very much.

It shouldn't be like that. Bows for women and girls should be lighter than those for men and boys, simply because most males are stronger than most females of the same age. Boys who are 12 years old can't pull your hunting bow, so why straddle them with a starter bow that's too powerful for them? It's been said that the most important element of a kid's first fishing trip is that he or she catch fish; all else is secondary. The same idea applies to introducing youngsters, or any newcomer, to bowshooting. They must be able to pull the bow comfortably.

The same sort of theory applies to even experienced bowhunters. At the end of last year's season, you were pulling, holding and shooting your 65-pound bow with ease. No struggle on the draw, no wiggle in the hold, a smooth release and good, tight shooting. But that was last year, and your shooting muscles are shouting, *what have you done for me lately?* Use 'em or lose 'em, pure and simple. And the only way to strengthen and tune your shooting muscles, not to mention your shooting instincts, is to shoot a lot, shoot daily if you can, shoot and shoot and shoot. Over lawn furniture, under low limbs, at colored bulls and at target silhouettes shaped like various views of the white-tailed deer. Saturday mornings before the chores start, late Saturday afternoons when the chores are (nearly) done, maybe Sunday afternoons as an alternative to golf.

If you're having friends over for a summer cookout, suggest they give target archery a try, and get in some shooting yourself. If your time on the shooting range attracts a few neighborhood youngsters, so much the better. Answer all their questions, no matter how obvious, and then show them how to draw, hold and aim a bow and arrow. Who knows, maybe there's another Howard Hill living just around the corner. Invite your bowhunting buddies over for a short-range shoot, maybe combining it with a steak barbecue or a pizza bash.

Any old excuse will do. The important thing is to shoot as diligently and as consistently as you possibly can, and do it as often as you can sneak out.

Let me exhort you, however, *not* to

do what my older sister did when we were shooting simple stick bows in the backyard maybe 30 years ago.

Now it's important to know that my sister had never shot a bow and arrow before, and probably hasn't since, so she was totally ignorant of even how to hold the thing, much less get an arrow to fly. She started out by holding the string in one hand and trying to draw the bow back with the other, and darned if she could get the arrow to stay where she thought it belonged. The arrow kept dropping to the ground, and when she finally let the bow go, it promptly rapped her smartly in the forehead. But did Pat get angry? Did she swear or stomp off?

Nope. She threw the bow so hard that it went through the window of a neighbor's garage, and I had to admit the misdemeanor in order to get the bow back.

Bow practice shouldn't be like that, not even for older sisters on whom you wish every misfortune a 9-year-old can conjure. No, shooting a bow and arrow should be fun and pleasurable and it should have an element of competition, if the competition is only *I'm gonna learn this thing if it takes the whole damned weekend*. Practicing with the bow can be fun. Honestly, it can be. But like most anything else, it depends on how you think about it.

17

Going for a
Pope & Young Buck

If you have taken an adult white-tailed deer with bow and arrow and have done it under the rules of fair chase, you are eligible to belong to the Pope & Young Club (see address at end of this chapter).

If that comes as a surprise, don't feel alone. I'd bet that the majority of bowhunters aren't aware that the one or two or three whitetails they've arrowed in seasons past enabled them to belong to bowhunting's most prestigious awards fraternity.

You don't have to collect a record-class buck to become a member, either. An adult deer will do the trick. Of course, that is Associate Membership, and you'll be among about 1000 others holding the identical distinction. If that tempers your enthusiasm somewhat, it shouldn't. It still puts you in a pretty small minority, not to mention an elite

group, among all the bowhunters across this broad land.

Regular Membership is another matter. To become a regular member you must have taken three adult big-game animals with your bow, each of a different species. Not only that, but your reputation as a hunter, sportsman and all-round good guy must be spotless, and you have to wait until the chap with more seniority than you either passes away or resigns, because the club rules allow only 100 regular memberships to be in force at any one time. In other words, you could collect your third big-game animal, one of them maybe a big whitetail buck, with the bow, and still have to wait years until a slot on the club roster opened for you.

Heard enough? No? Then consider Senior Membership. There are no quo-

There is nothing in this world like a trophy buck on the meatpole to make a hunting trip complete.

tas for Senior Membership rolls, although the number is considerably fewer than 100 at present. The Senior Member must have taken an adult big-game animal of four different species with his bow under fair chase rules, and at least three of those animals must qualify as trophy-class by club measurements. You could, for example, collect record-class elk, black bear and whitetail buck. The buck must tally a minimum score of 125 by the Pope & Young method to be eligible. Each deer species is considered separately.

If you're an experienced whitetail bowhunter, you know how tough it can be to put a record-class buck on the ground. This book makes the point time and again how differently large bucks behave, especially during the fall hunting seasons. These busters simply don't do what does and lesser bucks do. They feed late in the evening or after full dark, use different travel routes, bed alone instead of in the company of other deer, and they seem to have a built-in sixth sense when it comes to the avoidance of being seen.

I hunt a 1000-acre plot of hardwoods every fall, and so far have managed to take my buck there annually, but it has yet to be the buck I'm after. Several other hunters who hunt this property report having seen a positively *huge* buck. A few of them have even seen the deer at close range and have been able to count the buck's points, and they all come up with the same total: 28 points on an extremely heavy rack of antler of typical formation. I have yet to see this deer, even though I hunt the place several times and for several days each trip, but I've seen his tracks. His hooves are nearly four inches long, not counting the marks

left by his dewclaws, and when he puts his foot down in soft earth, his weight is so great that the space between his toes is nearly an inch wide.

I've seen one of this buck's rubs, too. He destroyed a five-inch-thick cedar along an old forest road, completely stripping away the cedar's flaky bark and removing or shredding every branch he could reach.

This is *some* deer. He hangs around the edges of cornfields at night, coming into the open for waste grain only when darkness covers his movements, and the only time I've hunted near his rub he failed to make an appearance.

From others' descriptions of this buck's antlers, there is no question in my mind that he would easily make Pope & Young's record book, entitled *Bowhunting's Big Game Records of North America*, if I could put an arrow into his engine house, but to do this I have to find him—or let him find me. And when you're talking trophy whitetails, you're talking one tough task.

I once chatted with relief pitcher Tug McGraw just after he'd come into the ballgame late and helped the Philadelphia Phillies defeat the Cincinnati Reds by a close score. I asked him his philosophy of relief pitching, and his response has an application for trophy hunters:

"The batter is my problem, but he's also my solution," McGraw said. "He can hurt me if he gets a hit, but he's also my way out of the problem if I make good pitches and get him out. So he's really the problem and the solution all in one."

McGraw has a lot of moxie as a reliever, and he uses his screwball to best advantage to preserve close leads late in the game, and what he said applies to your decision to hunt one buck and one buck only.

Going after just one deer eliminates all the peripheral problems you might encounter if you hunt just any buck. All you must deal with, once you've begun, are the peculiarities of just one animal, just one set of habits, just one local territory. The buck is your problem, but he's also your solution. Solve his riddle and he's yours.

Of course, Tug McGraw's second theory might apply if you try hard for the trophy but still come up empty. He calls it his Iceball Theory: When, millennia from now, the sun has gone out and the earth has turned into a big ball of ice, who will really care one way or the other whether you got that big buck or not? Seen in this light, failure shrinks into near unimportance.

But let's not even consider failure. Let's think positively and *know* that when this autumn's season is done, you will have put your broadhead into that big son-of-a-gun's boiler room and then shouted hallelujah loud enough to be heard in New York City. Know it, believe it with everything you've got, because the harder you believe it *will* happen, the more willing you'll be to stay on stand during lunchtime and when the weather is frigid. You'll scout harder and longer and not be hesitant to change your stand location if the situation calls for doing so. Any hunter, no matter what his quarry or his hunting tools, must first believe in himself and his eventual success or we'd all be hunting within 50 yards of the highway and quitting at 11 a.m. to go home and sulk. This goes many times over for trophy whitetail hunters.

Isn't it strange that a creature as common as the white-tailed deer buck should be so tough to hunt successfully? You'd think that with so many of them out there, getting a good buck every fall shouldn't be all that tough. This doesn't consider the fact that the male of this species, once he passes his third birthday, can be as hard to find as that nymphomaniac who owns a liquor store we all promised ourselves when I was in the U.S. Air Force. Nobody I ever knew in the service ever ended up with a woman like that, although a couple of them came pretty close. But that's another story.

Once you've found proof that, (a) the one big buck you want does in fact exist by reading the sign he leaves or maybe even getting a glimpse of him, and (b) his home bailiwick is in a certain area, which you've discovered by intensive scouting, never vary from the task you've set for yourself and settle for a lesser animal. This happened to a close friend of mine, and he has yet to forgive himself.

This fellow is a hard hunter. He scouts all year for a set of very large tracks and then, once he's found them, sticks with them until he can distinguish the tracks among all others. He scouts intelligently, and, over a period of several months, gets to know where the buck hangs out, his daily habits, and where he's likely to be found at most times of the year, especially during the fall bow season.

He did all of this a few years ago and found himself a real buster of a 10-point buck. He had the deer all to himself because the land he was hunting was on the western edge of one of the largest metropolitan areas in the Midwest. Who would believe such an area, remote and

Careful measurements will tell an official deer measurer how your deer stacks up, but the official taping must wait until at least 60 days after the kill.

hilly though it might be, would contain such a big deer? Not many, a fact that allowed my friend to keep hunting by himself—a must for the serious trophy hunter. So I won't divulge his name and location.

So, this chap decided where to place his treestand and was in place before first light on opening morning in a spot where the buck had passed every morning for the past three weeks. He'd been careful to keep his human scent away from the spot, chosen his camouflage carefully, and honed his shooting until he could almost shoot through a rolling doughnut without marring the powdered sugar.

He waited a good two hours and then heard a sound off to his right. He picked up his bow and nocked an arrow, waiting and ready on the string. Out of the brush to his right ambled the 10-point buck; its antlers were heavy and wide and he estimated it would weigh well over 250 pounds on the hoof. The buck he'd been after for the past 12 months was finally at hand! I'll let him tell the rest of the story.

"It was still a little dim under the trees and when I drew and released at about 25 yards, the buck snorted and ran off and I wasn't really sure whether I'd hit him or not," he said. "I stayed in the tree and searched every inch of the ground, looking for my arrow, but I couldn't spot it anywhere. Then I got down out of the tree and found the shaft. It had no blood or body fluid on it at all, so I climbed back up into the stand and stayed there.

"About 20 minutes later a nice little 8-pointer came along and I decided I couldn't pass him up. My arrow hit him high in the shoulder, and I could see the fletching as he ran off."

The end of the story came when he was climbing down half an hour later to start tracking his 8-pointer. Just as he reached the ground, the big 10-pointer he'd scouted so long and then missed came back, saw him and ran away again. "I could have shot him easily, he was so close," the poor chap later told me. "Here I'd settled for a mediocre 8-pointer and could have taken the buck I wanted all along if I'd just waited a little longer. I kick myself every time I think about it."

Persevere. The payoff is worth it.

People sometimes luck into trophy bucks—I've done it myself a time or two—but success for the trophy hunter usually comes only after all efforts have been directed toward just one animal. The how of all this is covered somewhat throughout this book, but let's consider what the average archer has to do to bring home the trophy bacon.

All-Year Scouting

If you enjoy pre-season scouting about as much as visits from your mother-in-law, getting yourself to scout all year might be a task. Yet it may take this long to run across the type of sign you're looking for. Nearly every good deer area has a so-called legend buck in local folklore; sometimes these bucks are figments of imagination, and sometimes they really do exist. Personally, in running down these big-buck rumors, I like to stick to the experts, those who have no ax to grind one way or the other. These include rural mail carriers, taxidermists, game wardens, school bus

Tabulate on the chart while the hunter waits. This can take what seems to be a lifetime.

drivers and the like. These people are out in the deer country every day and they may well have spotted a deer large enough to get their attention, even if they themselves are not deer hunters. If enough of these people tell me they've seen an unusually large deer, and their descriptions of the animal parallel one another, then the stories bear more research.

It's probable that the deer will have been reported in one general area, and this narrows the landowners you must contact for permission to look over their land. If the deer happens to live on public land, such as a state or national forest or huntable parkland, so much the better. More likely, however, the big buck tucks himself away on a square mile or less of private land where human interference in his daily routine is minimal. Once you start inquiring for hunting permission, however, be prepared to run up against resistance, especially if the landowner is himself a deer hunter or if he just enjoys seeing the big deer now and then. I once heard of a really big buck that hung out in the hills surrounding Winchester, Ohio. Locals called him Big Red because of his reddish coat, and wildlife officials way over in the state capital had heard of this deer, his fame had spread so much. Yet when I began asking for permission to bowhunt the animal around Winchester, I found quite a bit of resistance to hunting this particular animal. He'd become a local legend in recent years and people just didn't want him removed. Most of the answers I received were vague at best, and no landowner in the three-farm area where he hung out would grant me hunting access. I had to be content with knowing he was there and

with the fact that this buck would pass on his superior genes through normal reproduction, and just maybe one of his offspring would show up in a few years with a rack like his daddy's and I'd get the chance to try for him.

Not all landowners are that protective, of course, and you can probably gain permission to do some looking around. If you get that far with the owner of the land, you're just about guaranteed he'll let you back on his place come bow season.

Now comes the hard stuff, the work of familiarizing yourself with this particular buck's tracks. Look for them in midsummer around creekbeds and maybe the edges of small, remote ponds or sloughs. His water supply gets more important during dry summer months, and the soft earth around such places hold tracks better than the rock-hard soils where the sun strikes the ground. Get so you can recognize that track anytime you see it, then center your efforts on only that area where the buck lives.

If the deer lives on one farm or straddles the boundary between two farms, there is a reason why he lives there and not someplace else. That reason is that his territory meets his needs in terms of food, water, minerals in the soil which he gets by eating the plants (carbon and phosphorus are believed to develop large-racked bucks, and salt is also important—though more so in summer than in winter), and because the home ground contains dense patches of cover, enough does to satiate him in the rut, and little or no human intrusion.

If you look around the farm enough, you'll soon discover some important things about this buck's habits. You'll find his tracks along the edges of corn, soybean or wheat fields, in orchards and in the small, overgrown fields that used to be tilled and now lie wild and brushy. You'll see his sign in the narrow necks of cover, usually paralleling creekbeds or fencelines, connecting one woodlot to another. These are the routes the buck uses to move about his area without leaving cover. And you'll see his day bed, solitary except just before and during the rut, just inside wood-lines on the edges of remote fields, on high benches overlooking broad valleys and sometimes even farmhouses, and in evergreen plantations where the dense tree growth shelters him from wind and rain.

Look around enough and his move-ment patterns will start to form in your head. Look for the routes he uses to and from water, food and his bedding spots. If the rut is near, you get a real break because he'll start finding trees and rubbing the velvet off those glorious antlers, then making serious scrapes, usually a single, long line of them using some natural land feature such as the spine of a wooded ridge, an unused tim-ber road through the woods or a remote fenceline. One big buck I hunted but never got used a barbed-wire fenceline with dense brush on both sides of it; all of his scrapes were on the south side of the fence, and I never found one of his scrapes anywhere else.

There may be a dozen or more scrapes in that long line, but you'll soon dis-cover that the buck doesn't visit all of them daily, nor will he keep all of them fresh with hoof gouges and splatters of urine. This daily effort is limited to the scrapes in his core area, and this is where you should concentrate your efforts.

If the rut is on—and hunting during the rut when you're after a particular big, old buck gives you a tremendous advantage—you can help yourself by learning the right way to rattle antlers. Fighting bucks don't actually rattle their antlers together. They are big, heavy an-imals and prefer to try to shove each other off the fighting spot, with the loser abandoning the territory to the victor. Your rattling should consequently be more grinding than anything else, be-cause a true deer fight makes a sound like grinding. Add to this an occasional rattle and maybe rake the brush or a nearby tree limb with the antlers to im-itate the sounds of two large bucks in combat. The best time to rattle is just *before* the peak of the rut, when the dominant bucks are still arguing with other mature bucks over just who is going to kick butt around here and who is going to tuck tail and find someplace else to hang out.

If your chosen trophy animal hears the sounds you make by grinding two large-sized antlers together and is con-vinced that what he's hearing is genu-ine, he's going to come looking for the interlopers. You can help this along by saving the urine from the next buck you get, then putting a few drops around your stand location. The buck smells the buck urine and figures another buck has moved into his bailiwick, so when he comes to your rattling his neck and back hairs will be standing on end, his ears will be back and he'll actually stomp his feet in anger. He is ready to fight for his territory, and you can sometimes hear him coming before you see him because he'll make a grunting noise and not be particularly stealthy about his ap-proach. He's big, his antlers are huge, and he is king of the woods. He's like the husband who comes home early to discover his wife with the guy from down the street: deeply steamed.

So you hear him coming. Now is the time to make sure your arrow is nocked properly, that you have a backup arrow close at hand, and that you can maybe get your hands to stop shaking long enough to get a decent shot. A friend of mine stalked a huge old mosshorns one fall, and when the buck finally showed up all the poor guy could do was look at him. "I would have taken a Valium," he said, "if I could have gotten my teeth unclenched."

So here he comes, back hair all standing up, those honey-colored antlers bobbing their way through a sun-dappled hardwoods. Maybe he's grunting as he comes, maybe he's approaching quietly and pausing to look left and right as befits a creature so handsome and dominant. He passes on the other side of a few trees and you take the opportunity to sneak a breath or two, and then he's *right there* and it's now or never.

You will not remember drawing the bow. So much practice has made the movement second nature now. But you do notice where the anchor is made and you frantically wonder for a half-second whether you're anchoring where you should, but then the motion begins to feel like something you're used to and you're not about to take your eyes off that buck, anyway. You put your point of aim on the buck's shoulder and suddenly remember about the angle from treestand to ground level, and you force yourself to drop the point of aim to the buck's belly line. Later it will occur that at no time during all of this activity, compressed into just moments of time, did your sights waver or your hand shake at all. Funny, you think to yourself.

Funny because I shook a lot while practice shooting. Funny it didn't happen when the deer showed himself.

The sight pin settles where it belongs, a bit above midway between withers and belly line, and just before you release the buck raises his head, perks those big ears forward and concentrates on something you can neither hear nor see, but it's too late now and the fingers on your shooting hand slowly relax and the string slaps forward and the arrow is in that little space between you and the buck.

You will remember what that arrow looked like in flight for a long time, even if it lasted only a mini-second. The way it glinted briefly in the shaded woods, the way the twist of the feathers slowly turned it over, spinning in the air, and how it seemed to disappear for a moment before wondrously showing up imbedded deeply in the shoulder of your buck. Because he *is* your buck now. No animal ever survived a hunting shaft and a broadhead punched that deeply into lungs and liver and maybe the upper corner of the heart, and as he snorts and runs away you are numb, not daring to begin believing that you have, in *fact*, put an arrow into the trophy buck you've been studying and dreaming of and hoping for lo these many months.

You've been advised to wait awhile before beginning to track, so you do just that, perhaps hauling out a smoke and noticing just how hard it is to put match to tobacco with your hands shaking like this. Wait a while, a long while, and check your watch. Three minutes since the shot. Better wait a little longer. Stub out the smoke and loop your rope around the bow and lower it and the quiver to the ground and check the watch again. Four minutes gone and you'd better wait some more. Climb out of the stand, collect your bow and nock another arrow. You try to hit that stump across the clearing just 15 yards away and miss it by six feet, the arrow skipping away into the woods.

The actual follow-up is anticlimactic. Less than 40 yards through the woods, you find the deer. You tried to do the right thing, tried to track him very slowly and carefully, but the blood is everywhere along his path and you could have tracked him at midnight during a snowstorm if you had to.

And there he is. The shape of him slides into your vision, but it is the one exposed antler that grabs your attention. He's lying on his left side in the leafy carpet and that one blond antler is stuck up in the air, the main beam nearly as big as your wrist and gnarled like an old tree. The brow tine is as thick as Christmas candles, and straight and pointed and the color of coffee stains on a white tablecloth.

You know he is quite dead, but you remember all the stuff about caution and approach from the rear and in the direction of his back. No movement as you approach, but just to be sure you reach out with a dead branch and tap the glossy brown globe of his right eye. It doesn't blink. You won't need the follow-up arrow on the string, so you quiver it and you put the bow down.

How many times in the past autumns have you just settled yourself on stand when some other hunter, oblivious to your presence, came crunching through the woods just when you began to hope a deer would come along? You glared at him without speaking and thought angry thoughts even after he'd wound his way off through the trees. But now you have a trophy buck down and dead and tagged and damn you if you're not

completely alone out there. How satisfying it would be to have someone, *anyone*, come along just now, someone to walk up and say hello and then spot the deer. You could stand there like the cat that ate the canary and watch the guy's eyebrows jump right off his forehead. You couldn't help acting a little smug at a time like that, proud of your accomplishment and not afraid to show it just a little. But nobody comes along and it occurs to you that you can't even roll this big sucker onto his back for field-dressing, much less drag him by yourself out to the car. Not all by yourself, you can't. He's just too heavy for one man.

Once help arrives and you get the deer onto his back, field-dressing is easy. Start at the brisket (the bony structure just to the rear of the front legs near the belly) and insert your knife point to begin the long cut down the belly. Insert a finger on each side of the blade to make sure you hold the skin and the hide up and away from the viscera inside the belly cavity. Continue the cut down the center of the belly and just to one side of the genitals, which should be left intact for positive sex identification at the check station.

Once the belly cavity is open, reach inside and carefully sever the thin membrane that holds the large organs and intestines in place. Carefully trim the diaphragm (the thin membrane that separates belly cavity from chest cavity) free, and cut the membranes anchoring the lungs. Reach as far up inside the neck as possible, severing the esophagus. The deer can then be rolled onto his side and the viscera rolled onto the ground.

Again roll the deer onto his back. Use a small hatchet or meat saw to cut down

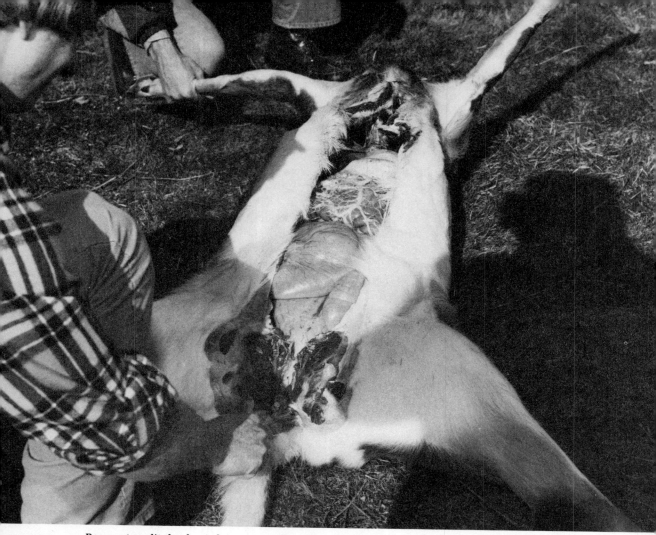

Be sure to split the deer's loins apart, using heavy knife or hatchet, so the anal canal can be removed. *Ohio DNR*

into his loins; be sure not to cut into the anus. Use a knife to "core the apple," cutting the tissues holding the anus so it can be pulled out of the body a few inches. Use a bit of twine to tie off the anus securely, then pull it back into the body cavity and remove, along with the organs attached to it. Be extremely careful not to let any urine or feces touch the meat.

Next step is to roll the animal onto his belly, all four legs askew, allowing the loose blood and body fluids to drain. The heart and liver should be placed in a plastic bag for later meals.

That's what the Big Moment is like. At least, that's what it was like for me. I felt like shooting a celebration arrow up through the trees and into the blue October sky but held off because I didn't

Once all viscera have been removed and the body has drained, prop the body cavity open for quick cooling. *Ohio DNR*

know just where my hunting buddy was. I felt like smiling ear to ear, and I did it until my face hurt. And that evening I felt like talking (and talking and talking) about it, over and over and over, and I did that, too, until the rest of our hunting party threatened to throw me out if I didn't change the subject. "OK," I said. "Enough about my killing the biggest buck any of us ever saw any-

where. You guys want to hear what kind of arrow I used?"

This day and this moment and this euphoria will come for you, too. Work at it, learn your craft well, and love the sport and the equipment and the crisp autumn woods and the pride of being a dedicated bowhunter, because only if you love it, truly love, will you give it the effort needed to go all the way to

The taxidermist relies on the hunter to provide what he needs for a complete and attractive mount. He'll give you welcome tips if you visit him before the season opens.

the top. Pope & Young requires that a candidate buck score a total of at least 125 points by the Pope & Young method (borrowed, incidentally from the Boone & Crockett scoring method) to enter their record books. You develop your own record book and determine what is exceptional and what is success for yourself, because when you get right down to it, who needs another opinion when you already have your own? Don't be afraid to criticize your performance, nor be afraid to compliment the results.

You've checked out the available taxidermists well ahead of the season and stop on the way home to alert the one you've chosen of your trophy's arrival. If he doesn't know of an accredited scorer affiliated with either Pope & Young or Boone & Crockett, give your local game warden or state wildlife office a call. They can then put you in touch with the right person. My home state of Ohio offers the Buckeye Big Bucks Club, whose members have killed by bow or firearm bucks of unusually large size, and this club has several official scorers among its ranks. Perhaps your home state offers something similar. A minimum of 60 days must elapse between the date you killed the buck and the day it is scored for the record, to allow for possible shrinkage.

If, or rather *when*, you take a buck you believe may qualify for the roles of this prestigious organization, drop a note to Jim Dougherty, President, Pope & Young Club, 4304 E. Pine Place, Tulsa, OK 74115, phone 918/836-9161.

Good hunting!

Index